CHEROKEE ODYSSEY

New Studies in Southern History

Series Editor: John David Smith,
The University of North Carolina at Charlotte

George Galphin and the Transformation of the Georgia–South Carolina Backcountry
By Michael P. Morris

Race, Gender, and Film Censorship in Virginia, 1922–1965
By Melissa Ooten

Leisure, Plantations, and the Making of a New South: The Sporting Plantations of the South Carolina Lowcountry and Red Hills Region, 1900–1940
Edited by Julia Brock and Daniel Vivian

The Federal Theatre Project in the American South: The Carolina Playmakers and the Quest for American Drama
By Cecelia Moore

The Development of Southern Public Libraries and the African American Quest for Library Access, 1898–1963
By Dallas Hanbury

Backcountry Slave Trader: William James Smith's Enterprise, 1844–54
Edited by Philip Noel Racine and Frances Melton Racine

Setting Slavery's Limits: Physical Confrontations in Antebellum Virginia, 1801–1860
By Christopher H. Bouton

The Development of Southern Public Libraries and the African American Quest for Library Access, 1898–1963
By Dallas Hanbury

Mixed-Race Identity in the American South: Roots, Memory, and Family Secrets
By Julia Sattler

African Americans, Death, and the New Birth of Freedom: Dying Free during the Civil War and Reconstruction
By Ashley Towle

Cherokee Odyssey: The Journey from Sovereign to "Civilized"
By Michael P. Morris

CHEROKEE ODYSSEY

The Journey from Sovereign to "Civilized"

MICHAEL P. MORRIS

LEXINGTON BOOKS
Lanham • Boulder • New York • London

Published by Lexington Books
An imprint of The Rowman & Littlefield Publishing Group, Inc.
4501 Forbes Boulevard, Suite 200, Lanham, Maryland 20706
www.rowman.com

86-90 Paul Street, London EC2A 4NE

Copyright © 2023 by The Rowman & Littlefield Publishing Group, Inc.

All rights reserved. No part of this book may be reproduced in any form or by any electronic or mechanical means, including information storage and retrieval systems, without written permission from the publisher, except by a reviewer who may quote passages in a review.

British Library Cataloguing in Publication Information Available

Library of Congress Cataloging-in-Publication Data
Names: Morris, Michael P., 1959– author.
Title: Cherokee odyssey : the journey from sovereign to "civilized" / Michael P. Morris.
Other titles: New studies in Southern history.
Description: Lanham : Lexington Books, [2023] | Series: New studies in Southern history | Includes bibliographical references and index. | Summary: "This study examines how, during the eighteenth century, the Cherokee transitioned from a sovereign people allied with the British to a nation subjugated to the US government"— Provided by publisher.
Identifiers: LCCN 2022038707 (print) | LCCN 2022038708 (ebook) | ISBN 9781666914085 (cloth) | ISBN 9781666914092 (epub)
Subjects: LCSH: Cherokee Indians—History—18th century. | Cherokee Indians—Government relations—History—18th century. | Cherokee Indians—Politics and government—18th century.
Classification: LCC E99.C5 M87 2023 (print) | LCC E99.C5 (ebook) | DDC 973.0497557—dc23/eng/20220915
LC record available at https://lccn.loc.gov/2022038707
LC ebook record available at https://lccn.loc.gov/2022038708

∞™ The paper used in this publication meets the minimum requirements of American National Standard for Information Sciences—Permanence of Paper for Printed Library Materials, ANSI/NISO Z39.48-1992.

This work is dedicated to the memory of my friend, Gene Griner, who made all my trips to the Great Smoky Mountains a magical experience.

Contents

Acknowledgments   ix

Introduction: Rivers of History   1

CHAPTER 1
The Anglo-Cherokee War of 1760–1761: The Past Is Prologue   21

CHAPTER 2
Cherokee Diplomacy after Easton: A Coming Storm   61

CHAPTER 3
Diplomacy after Fort Loudoun: "Till the Bloody Hatchet Is Buried"   93

CHAPTER 4
Snowball in the Sun: Dragging Canoe and the Spirit of 1776   123

CHAPTER 5
"The Great God of Nature . . . Has Not Created Us to Be Your Slaves"   167

Selected Bibliography   181

Index   187

About the Author   195

Acknowledgments

THIS WORK WOULD NOT have been possible without the tireless efforts of Karen L. Haven, MLS, Access Services, and research librarian of the Clara Wood Gould Library, College of Coastal Georgia.

Introduction
Rivers of History

I<small>N THE RECENT PAST</small>, the Eastern Band Cherokee Nation (EBCI) built a small monument to a tragic segment of their history in Chattanooga, Tennessee, on the river front. Near the popular aquarium, the monument at first was small and unobtrusive, more likely to found by playful children than by adults. They built a small stream running the length of the building down to the Tennessee River. Now an expanded version of the monument called "the Passage" is found there, with the Cherokees having added artwork and information disks along the wall that tell the Cherokee story. Originally the monument was simply a stream that started out calmly and then gradually switched to a series of small rapids before resuming a calm flow near the end of the stream. The changing flow of the stream was meant to remind visitors of the calmness of Cherokee life later disrupted by turbulent events such as wars, epidemics, and ultimately removal to reservations. However, the stream ended with a return to calm flow, an artistic way to echo the sentiment of many tribal peoples that "we are still here."

Cherokee history and culture are uniquely tied to rivers and bodies of water. Even today, summer tourists take their children out to the shallows of the Oconaluftee River on the Qualla Boundary on a hot summer day to wade and play in one of the few free activities available to cash-strapped parents on vacation. Older adults may tube down the river toward the shallows, and the EBCI even replenish the river with fish in the summer for tourists. When most visitors wade or fish in the river, they remain unaware of just how much Cherokee history has flowed down this river or others much like it. Traditionally, rivers were a part of Cherokee life both in the physical sense, in which their very presence made life easier with respect to fresh water and travel, and in the economic sense, with access to food in the form of fish and shellfish. The Cherokees favored such fish as trout, bass, pike, sunfish, catfish, drum fish, and crappies. They also consumed crawfish, eels, garfish, and minnows.[1] If the rivers nourished the body, they also nourished the soul as a part of Cherokee spiritual renewal and social life.

Cherokee culture struggled with English attempts at political and economic domination as well as excessive military violence between 1760 and 1770. Cherokee society successfully adapted to these stresses by producing a triumvirate of leadership in the 1760s rising to the political occasion, with a particular leader assuming charge of the situation based on the particular threat at the moment. Between 1768 and 1774, the twin pressures of increased demands for land and the threat of military reprisal from the English in Carolina reached epic levels. Cherokee society, in response, produced the Dragging Canoe rebellion, a phenomenon of singular leadership disobeying the rule of its own, older generation. The rebellion leader, Tsyu-gun-sini (Dragging Canoe), was uniquely connected to British Indian Superintendent John Stuart in a familial way. Both Dragging Canoe and his adopted brother tried to stop Cherokee land dispossession at the hands of colonial settlers.

Ultimately most Cherokee political leaders in the eighteenth century helped negotiate a series of treaties between the Cherokees and the English named for those rivers—Keowee, Sycamore Shoals, Hopewell, and Holston. These river treaties sequentially signed away most of the traditional lands of the Cherokees. A unique set of Cherokee rulers tried to negotiate these turbulent years between 1760 and 1774. Like the rivers, these leaders rose and fell with the challenges of the times—various conflicts with the English colonies of Virginia and South Carolina. The Overhills leader Attakulla and his son, Dragging Canoe, rose to differing versions of these general problems in different decades. The father answered the challenge of leadership in the 1760s, and the son answered the challenge of the 1770s. Both men responded to problems caused by an intruding British-American culture. The father constantly searched for ways to keep the peace, even by giving up land, while his son threw down the gauntlet to challenge colonial land dispossession with a rebellion. Like a divide in the river, father and son took the Cherokees down two very different paths.

Historically, the Cherokees may have migrated into their territory from Virginia by way of the New River and the upper Holston River. Due to continuing migration pressures, they moved southward to the Little Tennessee River, eventually establishing the Middle Town settlements.[2]

Experts conclude that the ancestors of the modern Cherokees assumed their place in the Southeast between 1000 and 1500 AD, with a frequently cited date of 1300 AD.[3] Their settlements clustered around the rivers for the obvious benefits of freshwater, fishing, and travel.

Archaeological remains appear along the headwaters of the Savannah River, where the Lower Town settlements existed. They are found in the Appalachian Summit, where the Valley Towns, Middle Settlements, and Out Towns were found. Archaeological remains confirm a Cherokee presence at the Overhills sites as well. The remains document Cherokee occupation to between 1000 AD and 1450 AD.[4]

Once established, the Cherokees began to build the circular buildings of their yi (towns) beside rivers, probably at the end of the Mississippian Period. The eighteenth-century naturalist William Bartram recorded that some of their structures were built atop mounds.[5] In all these communities, nearby rivers provided dependable supplies of fish, eels, crawfish, and mussels that helped add variety to diets that otherwise consisted of hunted wild game and corns, beans, and squash.[6] Fishing weirs, square or rectangular wooden traps lowered into the river, provided their share of food to Cherokee families. The Cherokees enshrined these rivers in their spirituality early on. They called the river Long Man or Yunwi Gunahita. According to early anthropologist James Mooney, who spent time among the Cherokees in the nineteenth century, they believed that Yunwi Gunahita's head was in the foothills of the mountains running all the way down to his feet at the coast.[7] Their settlements followed Long Man for much of that territory.

The modern-day seven clans of the Cherokees—Wolf, Bird, Wild-Potato, Deer, Blue, Paint, and Long Hair—are based on seven original mother towns spread out over their territory.[8] The towns that surrounded the mother towns were deemed brother towns, a term used frequently by Cherokee political figures who interacted with the British.[9] Cherokee society was matrilineal, with a child deriving his/her clan identity from the mother's clan. Tribal people often proudly boast there could never be a bastard in such a society. Brother, therefore, was the biological uncle of the child but fulfilled the father role, and the real biological father became the favorite uncle figure. The mother and brother were the same clan affiliation as the child, but the biological father was always a different clan. British officials may have misunderstood the term of "father" when they used it with tribal people. It did not carry the same meaning to tribal peoples as the authority figure that it meant to people of British extraction.

The rivers and soil composition also made it possible for the Cherokees to develop pottery as a tool to hold surplus goods. Along with fresh water, fish, and travel, Cherokee potters needed both the rivers and their clay in order to make pottery such as the Pisgah and Qualla ceramics.[10] Even today, the Qualla Boundary's Mauney family potters pass their art down to younger members of the family, and they provide pottery demonstrations to the public in the "Education" wing of the Museum of the Cherokee Indian.

English records about the tribes continue to be the imperfect lens through which we view groups such as the Cherokees. While those records give great detail about political events, trade prices, and rough population estimates, they omit much about Cherokee daily and spiritual life, which often involved rivers. In fact, water runs consistently through Cherokee traditional beliefs, binding the people to rivers and streams that keep pace with the Cherokees' journey through history. Cherokee creation explanations speak of the humble water beetle who left the overcrowded sky arch of the world above and descended into a middle world covered by water. Burrowing into the bottom, the beetle carried the wet earth toward the surface of the water, where it expanded to form the land so that other animals from the sky arch would have a place to go. Once fully expanded, the land was tethered to the sky in the four cardinal directions, according to ethnohistorian James Mooney.[11]

The Cherokees further believed in a lower world beneath that which the water beetle made. In many ways, the lower world mirrored the middle world, except its seasons were reversed. The Cherokees believed the only way to enter such a world was to follow the rivers and streams of their lands to pass through a special doorway to be found at the headwaters of these rivers. According to Mooney, a Cherokee would need to undergo fasting before an attempt to pass into the lower world but would require one of the spirit people as their guide to make it.[12]

Cherokee creation stories speak of the first Cherokee man and woman, Kanati and Selu. Cherokee creation stories link fish with both fertility and the underworld because rivers were the way to reach these alternate realities. According to the creation stories, Kanati struck Selu with a fish from the river and told her to multiply. She began to produce a child every seven days until the world had enough people in it. When there was a danger of overpopulation, Selu began to have only one child per year, and so it was fixed for all other women to have only one child per year.[13] Thus rivers and the creatures from them were responsible for the origin of the Cherokee people according to Cherokee creation stories.

Such stories further detail the lives of the first couple and their son, linking them again back to the river. This son had a mysterious friend who came from the nearby river. The two parents contrived to capture their son's playmate. They captured this other child and named him Wild Boy because he retained a mischievous and disruptive nature despite the family's attempts to civilize him. This child from the water helped convince the son of Kanati to follow him into the woods to discover Kanati's secret concerning the hunt and why he was always able to return with game animals. They learned that Kanati had been going to a secret cave and rolling away a stone so that one game animal would come forth for him to take down. Later the boys returned to the cave and accidentally released all the animals from their captivity, forcing humans to have to hunt for their game, rather than obtain them from a secured magical cave.[14]

The Wild Boy from the water continued his mischief, convincing Kanati and Selu's son to spy on his mother next. When they saw her rub her belly to magically fill baskets with corn and beans, they determined that she was a witch who must be killed. Before her death, Selu instructed her son and the Wild Boy what to do to ensure the continued production of corn and bean crops in the future.[15] Thus, at least in Cherokee creation stories, the original Cherokee family did not fare too well once they let this Wild Boy from the water into their lives.

Similarly, Cherokee lore contains stories of darker beings who resided below the waters. These water cannibals resided at the bottoms of rivers and come forth driven by a craving for human flesh, especially that of small children. They arose from the rivers at dawn and traveled unseen as they looked into Cherokee homes for an unlucky soul still sleeping. The Cherokees believed they shot the sleeping person with invisible arrows and carried his/her dead body back to the rivers for a feast. Strangely, the water cannibals left behind a doppelganger of the victim that acted as the deceased person had for seven days before it withered and died. Parents told children to get out of their beds early lest these cannibal hunters catch them at their most vulnerable.[16]

In terms of daily life, the river also played an integral part in people's lives. New mothers went to the river on the thirteenth day after delivery to wash themselves and the clothes worn during delivery. Emerging from the river, they put on clean clothes, having used the river to wash away the contamination associated with birth and blood loss. Traditional Cherokees were supposed to go to the river and immerse themselves after sexual relations, again allowing the river to wash away their uncleanness.[17]

Historian Theda Perdue reminds us that the river was also important in the lives of pregnant Cherokee women. These women rose before sunup and took an herbal potion designed to ensure an easy and quick delivery as well as to ensure the long life of the child. Traveling to the nearby river, she met a shaman and either her mother or the baby's father. The shaman and woman entered the river as the healer sought to divine answers about the child's sex, its personality, and any clues about the child's future. Once concluded, the couple paid the shaman in goods for his services.[18]

Cherokee newborns began their relationship with the rivers at a young age. A few days after birth, a shaman first waved the child over a fire. Then, four or seven days later, the same priest took the child to a creek and submerged it underwater, covering its mouth and nose. This was the child's naming ceremony, with a prominent older woman from the community presiding and offering up the child's new name. The relationship with water continued, as the child received a daily bath from its mother at the river, no matter the temperature, for at least the next two years.[19]

New mothers had clear-cut guidelines to follow concerning first foods of newborn children. New mothers frequently gave their infants a potion made with water from a particularly loud stream or waterfall. The potion contained cockleburs, and mothers believed it gave the newborn a strong intelligence and quick memory for learning.[20]

Cherokee boys undergoing training as shamans returned to the river as a part of a series of rituals that included immersion themselves in the river seven times with their faces turned, alternating between the east and west. While there were steps following this ritual, it was an integral part of the ceremony.[21]

During ceremonies such as the Physic Dance, shamans ordered the whole population of a village to the rivers in the two hours before sunset, where they immersed themselves for purification. This mid-October event coincided with the first full moon of the month, when shamans believed that falling leaves infused the river with special medicinal qualities and especially strong healing powers. Men waded in and remained as a group upstream while the women and children waded downstream and waited as a group. Both groups ducked under water seven times. Ten days later, the village returned to the river for a Reconciliation Ceremony that probably marked the start of a Cherokee new year. Some members wore old clothing, which they removed, letting the river wash it downstream.[22] These ceremonies carried away both their troubles and their impurities, as the participants put on new, clean garments as they emerged.[23] Similarly, the

New Moon of Autumn Festival included a communal trip to the river by the village for immersion.

Cherokee healers ultimately took family members who had lost a loved one to the river, where they both prayed for them and washed their living members in the river to cleanse the contamination of death. Family members in the process shed the clothes they had worn and let the river carry them, their contamination, and possibly their sorrow with the current.[24]

During war time, the Cherokees even took their captives to the river to undergo ritual washing. Shamans let the river carry away whatever physical and spiritual contaminations these strangers brought into the town. Such purification made them fit to reside among their captors.[25] During darker periods in Cherokee history, the rivers of Cherokee country still played a major part in tribal life. According to medical historian Paul Kelton, Cherokee shamans often treated Kosvki Askini (the Cherokee name for smallpox) by having their patient lie outdoors to fight their fevers. The shaman also poured cold water on their chests and then had them take a sweat bath. Following this step, the shaman ordered the patients to cool off in nearby streams or rivers. The eighteenth-century trader James Adair believed these treatments of cold water condemned the patients to certain death. However, smallpox causes high fevers that could lead to coma, brain damage, or death. Cooling the patient by applying cold water or cold baths probably kept fevers down. Of course, such shamans hoped the river would carry away the disease from the patient in an appeal to the spirit world to help restore balance.[26]

To the Europeans who would eventually come among the Cherokees, the river was just a mode of travel and of trade, a source of fish and fresh water, and little more. Its centrality to Cherokee life and to Cherokee spirituality was unintelligible to them. However, they entered Cherokee country along these rivers as well.

Members of the Hernando de Soto expedition of 1539–1541 entered the land of Chalaque at the end of the Mississippian period by reaching the Keowee River where the Lower Town settlements began. De Soto's expedition recorded the people of the province as poor, although their land abounded in wild turkeys. The Lower Town settlements apparently did not have food to share or were unwilling to do so, and thus the Spanish travelers moved on to another settlement called Guaquili. An expedition member recorded that the Indians here generously shared their food with the Spaniards, feeding them a small, peculiar species of cooked dog. Ranjel, the reporter, may have overestimated the generosity of the Lower

Town Cherokees because he was unaware that they were feeding him cooked possum, something the Cherokees would not eat themselves.[27]

In terms of English records, other Southern Indian groups showed up in colonial history before the Cherokees. The Powhatans of Virginia were first in 1607, but, several decades later, colony records mentioned the arrival of a tribe, called by the Powhatans as Rechaherians or Rickahockan, known to others by the more well-known name of Westos. Some older materials confuse the Rechaherians with the Cherokees. These Rechaherians or Westos showed up in Virginia colony records in 1654 when a large number, six hundred to seven hundred, arrived at the falls of the James River. Virginia colony leaders determined that there was no place for these new arrivals after recently completing a devastating war with the Powhatans. Colony leaders activated about one hundred militia men and obtained an auxiliary force from the Pamunkey tribe, who added another hundred warriors. The Anglo-Indian forces engaged the Rechaherians to the defeat of these Westos with much bloodshed, and Virginia records do not indicate prolonged or follow-up conflicts.[28]

Nearer the end of the seventeenth century, the English came into contact with the Cherokees. At that time, Cherokee land claims included all or parts of the modern states of Virginia, West Virginia, North Carolina, South Carolina, Georgia, Alabama, Tennessee, and Kentucky.[29] In 1673, a Euroamerican traveler named Gabriel Arthur visited the Cherokees. Arthur visited the Overhills Cherokee town of Chota, which he said was built along a river on one side of the town while the other three sides had palisaded log walls of twelve feet in height.[30] According to James Mooney, a delegation of Cherokee chiefs went to Charles Town in 1693 with presents for the colonial governor in a show of the friendship they desired with the colony. Apparently they also asked for the colony's protection against their enemies, the Catawbas (Ye Iswa), the Shawanos, and the Congarees. In addition, they requested the South Carolina government's help in recovering Cherokees kidnapped by these other Indians but were told that such repatriation was no longer possible.[31] Tennessee records date the first introduction of the English gun among the Cherokees as taking place around 1700.[32]

The dawn of the eighteenth century places the Cherokees well within the historic period, with population estimates provided by resident fur traders. Eleazar Wiggan set up the first permanent trade outpost among the Cherokees in 1711.[33] According to demographers Ted Gragson and Paul Bolstad, the Cherokees occupied or claimed some 125,000 square miles of the Southern Appalachian region.[34] The authors further defined some sixty-two Cherokee towns as "autonomous decision-making units" composed of residential homes and a central council house. The government was decentralized in the extreme without an all-powerful ruler whose power was binding on all individuals. Governance derived from decisions made by a consensus of the central council.[35]

Perhaps the most influential non-Cherokees in proximity to these settlements at the beginning of the eighteenth century were fur traders like Wiggan who provided snapshots of these cultures. These merchant/diplomats set the Lower Towns in 1715 at eleven towns with a population of 2,100 people. Middle Settlements contained thirty towns and 6,350 people, and nineteen towns among the Overhills Cherokees with some 2,760 men and women, for a total of 11,210 people.[36] In their 2007 study, Gragson and Bolstad concluded that these towns contained some 16,487 men and women by 1721, considerably more than Wiggan's 1715 estimate.[37]

The Scots-Irish fur traders, like Wiggan, were often the vanguard representatives of mercantile firms that helped impose a "nascent capitalist economy over tribes through the creation of the fur trade in deer skins and the practice of warfare for the purpose of taking Indian slaves."[38] Though driven by economic motives and not cultural ones, the fur traders helped undermine the stability of native societies as they "cycled" through their own rise and fall sequences. The fur trade helped created what ethnohistorian Robbie Ethridge has termed a "shatter zone" of native communities made dependent by the trade in European goods that came with the fur trade. Once shattered, these communities fell into the orbits of influence created by the fur traders and the Indian agents and colonial governors who followed them.[39] Wiggan, along with Alexander Long, induced the Cherokees to raid the Yuchis (Creeks) in 1714.[40] Finally, trade based on credit—that is, purchases made by tribal members in the current year to be paid in skins the following year—created a growing tension between Indian communities and the fur traders, who ultimately sought redress from colony governments when those payments in skins were not forthcoming.[41]

English records continue to fill in the gaps in the Cherokee story. Alexander Cuming's assignment to make contact with the Cherokees both signaled the beginning of long-term relations between the English and the Cherokees and provided a record of his impressions of their society. He described them in 1730 as the Cherokee nation and wrote that seven Mother Towns governed the whole of their nation. Cuming mentioned the towns of Tannassie, Kituwah, Ustenary, Tellico, Estatoe, Keowee, and Noyohee. Of these, Cuming mentioned ruling leaders from Tannassie as being in charge of the Overhills settlements. Cuming believed leaders from Kituwah ruled over the Middle Towns and rulers from Ustenary ruled over the Lower Towns.[42] However, he misunderstood the rank of the mother towns, believing they directly governed surrounding towns. While the mother towns were places where leaders resided, they did not rule surrounding towns.[43]

Cherokee towns by the eighteenth century had both a peace chief (or uku) and a war chief, symbolized by the colors of white and red, respectively. The white (peace) chief held ascendancy over local town life for most of the time. The war chief, or red chief, was frequently younger than his peace counterpart and assumed command during a military conflict.[44]

Besides these leaders, Cuming noted that each town had a head warrior, called a Raven by the Cherokees. Cuming speculated that the Cherokees esteemed these warriors over their civil chiefs unless that magistrate was a Raven also. Further, Cuming noted the power that Cherokee conjurors held in their villages over all matters. He went on to identify the conjurors of Tellico, Tapelchee, Iwassie, and Noyohee as the most important of these men.[45]

Officially, the Cherokee people began their long and winding relationship with the colony of South Carolina in 1721. Governor Francis Nicholson concluded a treaty with their chiefs drawn up in Charles Town that year. Ostenaco, who carried the title of Outacite (or Mankiller), led the delegation that transferred land between the Santee, Saluda, and Edisto Rivers to South Carolina. There were no towns in this region of fifty square miles, but it was their first land transfer. It would not be their last land transfer, however, nor the last treaty made by a river.[46]

Alexander Cuming was present at Nikwasi (present-day Franklin, North Carolina) on April 3, 1730, for the next transformative step in the Cherokee-Anglo relationship. The English on that day bestowed the title of emperor on Moytoy, the ruler of Great Tellico, in the presence of several Indian traders, including Ludovic Grant and Eleazar Wiggan, themselves aristocracy among the early fur traders to the Cherokees. Surrounded by Cherokee leaders of varying levels, Sir Alexander wrote that Cherokee warriors stroked him with eagle feathers as singers performed from morning until night. When it was Cuming's turn to perform, he rose and gave a speech telling the assembled leaders that he was there among representing King George II. He required them to acknowledge that they were now subjects of the great king and must do what he asked of them in the king's name.[47]

The Cherokees were giving their English neighbors on the coast a single leader who could speak for all Cherokees, or so the English thought. Cherokee leadership style was more varied, however, with different leaders speaking out based on need and proximity to the problem at hand.

Alexander Cuming was the author of a plan to take a group of Cherokee men with him to England to pay homage directly to King George II.[48] The trip would mark another significant milestone in Cherokee history and produce a diplomatic alliance. When Europeans took tribal peoples back with them to England or the Continent, they most assuredly hoped the visit would overawe tribal people and make them compliant with colonial or imperial wishes.

One month and one day later, a group of Cherokee leaders boarded the British man-of-war *Fox* on May 4, 1730, and were taken across the biggest body of water the Cherokees knew—the Atlantic Ocean. The group included Oukah-Ulah, Oukanekah (or Attakullakulla), Kittagusta, Tathtiowie, Clogittah, Collanah, and Ounakannowie. Eleazar Wiggan, trader and translator, came along as interpreter. In early June 1730, the group arrived in England through the port of Dover, from which point they traveled to London. Alexander Cuming obtained some rather inauspicious lodgings for them—in the basement of an undertaker's home.

When they visited Whitehall Palace, the Cherokee leaders reaffirmed their allegiance to Great Britain, pledging not to trade with other Europeans in North America. In early September, the group received a lavish display of presents. In the treaty that followed, the Board of Trade formalized the Articles of Friendship Treaty from April of that year. The document asserted that the Cherokees were dependent on the Crown of Great Britain and that the Crown could now assert a British title to the lands of the Cherokee. Their translator deliberately misinterpreted that part of the speech, downplaying British hegemony over the tribe. The agreements further bound the Cherokees to protect their fur traders, to fight for the British in Carolina, and to return escaped slaves.[49] In the two days before the last reading and final signing, the Cherokees visited and questioned Alexander Cuming about the treaty one more time; he assured them it was in their best interests to sign. South Carolina governor Robert Johnson looked on as the Cherokees made their mark on the September 29, 1730, treaty.[50]

After the treaty signings, the Cherokee delegates again questioned their hosts and translators about the true meaning of the Board of Trade's words when it came to British claims of Cherokee lands. As historian Daniel Tortora pointed out, these delegates represented no nation and had no authority to sign away land for the nation they did not represent. Cherokee delegates like Kittagusta ultimately chose to interpret the Crown's words figuratively, as ceremonial rather than a literal subjugation.[51]

The group departed London shortly afterward when they boarded the transport ship loaded with presents that brought them back to the South Carolina coast, with debarkation in Charles Town on May 11, 1731. They eventually made it back home to Cherokee country after a year's absence. In much of Cherokee spirituality, people believed that rivers and bodies of water were doorways to an alternate place or existence. For leaders like Attakullakulla, who would later dominate Cherokee politics in the decade of the 1760s, the visit changed him just as surely as if he had gone to the alternate reality of the lower world. The visit later gave him a political currency among the Cherokees as someone who had crossed over the water to visit the English in their home country, something most other Cherokee had not done and could not do. The visit elevated Attakullakulla to a position of prominence, which he would enjoy throughout the 1760s as he began to supplant the British-chosen emperor, Moytoy, as a leader. It also fixed him firmly in British service as a pro-British Cherokee leader.[52] On their return, Cherokee leaders questioned the seven men on the subject of whether they had given away any lands and were satisfied the delegates had not.

Sometimes Cherokee political leaders who made bad decisions or had bad policy outcomes had to use the river to temporarily escape the town when politics found the leader on the wrong side of either the people or the council (or both). Historian Tom Hatley notes that the Overhills leader Old Hop (or Connecorte) once found himself in such a predicament and left the village by river for a few days.[53] None of the Cherokee delegates who visited London in 1730 to sign the Articles of Friendship had to make such a hasty exit. If anything, the document drew the Cherokees ever more tightly into the British sphere of influence.

The 1750s was the decade in which the British of South Carolina built forts, at the invitation of the Cherokees, among the Overhills Cherokee settlements and among the Lower Town settlements on Carolina's doorstep. Of course these forts were built on or near the rivers running through Cherokee country. The British built Fort Prince George in 1753 on the Keowee River right across from the largest of the Lower Towns, also named Keowee. A few years later, the British built Fort Loudoun in 1756 on the south side of the Little Tennessee River, about five miles south of Chota, an Overhills Town.[54] The colony of Virginia also promised to build and maintain a fort in Cherokee country during this time period.

They, too, built their fort across the Little Tennessee River from Chota among the Overhills settlements. Although the Virginians built the fort, they never named or manned it.[55]

The Keowee River, which was the scene of the diplomatic conclusion of the Anglo-Cherokee War in 1761, is just under twenty-six miles long. It runs through western South Carolina and is formed by the confluence of the Whitewater River and Toxaway River in present-day Oconee County in South Carolina. It originally flowed through the heart of the Lower Town settlements, particularly close to the principal town of Keowee, as well as the villages of Estatoe and Sugartown.

Sycamore Shoals is part of the Watauga River, running from modern Eastern Tennessee into Western North Carolina. Its headwaters form from the slopes of Grandfather Mountain in Hickory Nut Gorge and from Peak Mountain at Linville Gap in Avery County, North Carolina. Watauga was also the name of a later and illegal colonial settlement on leased Cherokee lands. Some experts say the name is a derivation of the Cherokee word *Watagi*. White colonists from the Nashville area claimed the area during the American Revolution when they realized Britain could not enforce the Proclamation Line of 1763, nor could the Cherokees hold the region.

The Holston River was the scene of a final diplomatic agreement between the Cherokees and the United States government in 1791. The river runs some 136 miles from present-day Kingsport to Knoxville, Tennessee. French explorers originally named the river the Cherokee River, a name that remained in common usage until around 1796. Settlers renamed it at that time to honor an early Euroamerican settler, Stephen Holstein, who built a cabin on the upper river in 1746.[56]

Traditional Cherokee land usage and claims spread out over nine modern U.S. states. It ran almost 350 miles from east to west and then 300 miles from north to south. Much of the western territory they claimed was strictly for hunting usage, including modern Kentucky, which would have been their upper hunting grounds. Lower hunting grounds including the area along the Cumberland River running south to its confluence with the Tennessee River. Their habitation areas covered some 15,000 square miles of territory, with core settlement in the mountains between modern North Carolina and Tennessee.[57]

Cherokee settlements numbered at least sixty villages, possibly more, divided into what the English and South Carolinians called the Lower Towns, Middle Settlements, Valley Settlements, and Overhills Settlements. Most towns covered up to about 400 acres and contained about 350 people. Towns usually contained a round council house, a ceremonial ground, and up to 200 wattle-and-daub construction homes. Frequently situated near rivers, the towns usually were surrounded by palisaded walls.[58] Towns can be defined further as having a ceremonial-political center, often called council house, in addition to an open court square ground surrounded by benches or poles. The Cherokees frequently built homes close enough to these central places to be bounded by defensive walls.[59]

Although definitely separated by geographic location, the matrilineal clan system of seven clans made sure that members of one's clan could be found in towns other than one's own. The clan system thus meant that one could find support in other towns as well as revenge in the form of retributive justice, called the law of blood by historian John Phillip Reid. The death of a clan member as a result of foul play in one town often initiated a retaliatory act from the members of the wronged clan in other towns. Simply put, the unwarranted death of a clan member allowed his clan to take their revenge in measured portion (that is, the killing of someone in the perpetrator's clan).[60] Thus, the call for revenge could easily come from another town or settlement area entirely. Cherokee towns were linked by clan ties in a way that Euroamerican towns were not.

Historians of the Cherokees such as Theda Perdue and Tyler Boulware remind us that, while the British and the French only analyzed the Cherokees based on their geographic location and their allegiance to leaders like Attakullakulla or Cunneshote, there was a third element involved: clan membership, which outsiders often ignored or failed to fully appreciate. For these two historians, kinship was the only factor that created a unity among the Cherokees, who otherwise lacked a central government.[61]

By 1750, there were four powerful Cherokee communities based on river groupings that spanned the distance from what later became Eastern Tennessee down to Western South Carolina and Northern Georgia. By the end of the century, some, like the Lower Towns that were closest to the Scots-Irish communities of Belfast and Hillsborough, had ceased to exist.[62] All of the others were radically changed by war, by disease, and by displacement by new interlopers like the Ulster-Scots. The importance of towns could change and diminish over time. Conversely, towns could grow in importance, with brother towns rivaling mother towns in status. Because the Cherokee political leaders made certain towns temporary or permanent bases of operation, and because the Carolinians and Virginians built forts adjacent to them, some discussion of the Cherokee settlements is warranted.

The Lower Towns were closest to the English in South Carolina and later Georgia. The rivers that bounded these communities—the

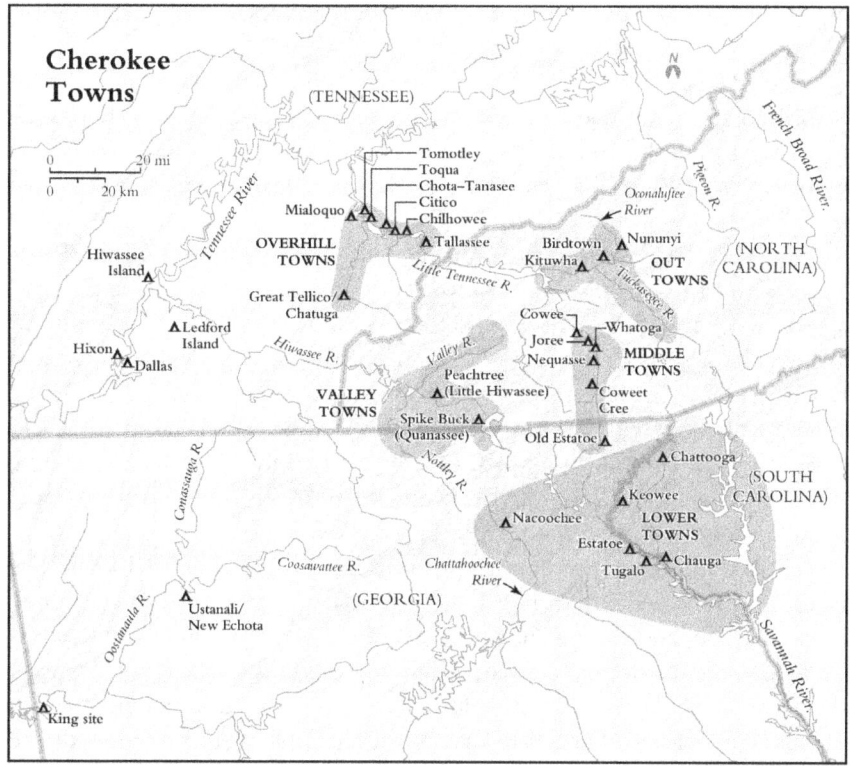

Figure I.1. Cherokee towns map (courtesy of Robert Cronan, Lucidity Information Design, LLC)

Chattooga, the Tugaloo, and the Keowee—are the headwaters of the Savannah River. These were rich environments for settlements, and some of these Cherokee towns were built on the former sites of Mississippian chiefdoms, demonstrating the long continuity of human occupation. Their neighbors to the east—the Ye Iswa, the Catawbas, and the Lower Villages—were the first to be changed by close contact with the British in Charles Town.[63] Cherokees of this region spoke an eastern dialect of Cherokee, Elati, which became extinct when these communities suffered under attacks in 1760 and 1776. Their survivors frequently relocated to the Middle and Overhills towns.[64]

Some of the more well-known Lower Settlement towns were the principal towns of Keowee, Toxaway, Sugar Town, Estatoe, Echy, Oconnne, Chauga, Tomassee, and Tugalo. Of these, Tugalo was the mother town with the remainder being brother towns.[65] Cherokee settlement experts Gragson and Bolsted concluded that Tugaloo was an important crossroads point for the Cherokee people.⁶⁶ These Cherokees also spoke the Elati dialect of the Cherokee language.⁶⁷

The British Indian interpreters, often called linguisters in the old records, had to be well versed in the settlement dialects. While such translators could be Indian fur traders, they could just as easily be native women. South Carolina governors used James Beamer as a translator for the Lower Towns, those with the Elati (Eastern) dialect, and a linguister named Robert Bunning for the Valley Settlements, which used the Kituwha (Western) dialect.⁶⁸ The Cherokees built Estatoe, Chauga, and Tugaloo on the sites of the Mississippian era sites of Ocute and Cothiquithi.⁶⁹ During the Creek-Cherokee War, some of the Lower Towns, including Keowee, Echy, Tugalo, Oconne, and Tomassee, were destroyed in 1752.⁷⁰ The British built Fort Prince George near Keowee in 1753 and, due to poor original construction, had to effectively rebuild it in 1756. The Cherokees were at war with the British in the early 1760s, and Colonel Montgomery destroyed the Lower Towns in 1760.⁷¹

The Middle Town settlements were bounded by the Little Tennessee River and included towns like Echoe, Nikwasi, Cowee, Watauga, Joree, Ellijay, Sticoe, and Kittowah. Other Middle Town settlements with similar names included Tuckaretchi, Tuckorechee, and Taskeegee.⁷² Among these towns, Nikwasi was the mother town, with the remaining settlements being the brothers.⁷³ All of these settlements were poised to utilize Cherokee hunting grounds to the north in what is present-day Kentucky and the Ohio River Valley.⁷⁴ These towns spoke the Kituhwa dialect still spoken by the majority of native speakers on the Qualla Boundary today.⁷⁵

The Out Towns were located to the northeast of the Middle Towns and included Kituwah, Stecoee, Oconaluftee, Tuckaleetchee, and Tuckasegee. Kituwah was the mother town of this cluster, with the remainder being brother towns.⁷⁶ Their Cherokees also spoke the Kituwha dialect. The Valley Settlements included the upper Hiwassee, the Valley, and the Notley Rivers. These river valleys contained towns like Little Hiwassee, Little Tellico, Tomotly, and Noyowee. The Overhills settlements included the Little Tennessee, the Tellico, and the lower Hiwassee Rivers. The towns here included Chota (the mother town) and Chestuee, Tallassee, Tanasi, Great Tellico, Chilhowie, Settico, Tuskegee, Toqua, and Tamotley as the brother towns.⁷⁷ These Cherokees, both Valley and Overhills, spoke the Atuli dialect. It is part of the Western dialect frequently spoken by traditional speakers among the Western Band Cherokees of Oklahoma today.⁷⁸ Chota was one of the mother towns whose influence spread beyond its river grouping over the eighteenth century. Some fur traders called it the "mother town of the nation." Its influence extended at least as far as the Middle Settlements, whose people regarded it with respect. British authorities even deemed it the "Metropolis of the Country."[79]

During the turbulent period of the 1750s, the British military and government of South Carolina began to treat Chota in the Overhills as a national capital of the Cherokee people. Both British officials like the influential John Stuart and other Indian peoples like the Muskogee Creeks of Georgia began to rendezvous in Chota for matters important to the whole of the Cherokee people.[80] Such actions on the part of the British restructured Cherokee society in ways both big and small. Elevating one town over another, or favoring one leader over another, had consequences. Even when fur traders undersupplied certain Cherokee towns, the Cherokees perceived it politically as a slight. The Articles of Friendship treaty also changed their society.

In September 1730, Alexander Cuming brokered a treaty for the Cherokees, the one that Attakullakulla had travelled across the Atlantic to sign, that bound them more closely to the British than the Cherokees understood at the time. It bound towns more closely together than they had been before. It required the response of a nation-state, which the Cherokees were surely not at the time. They were a collection of towns clustered along rivers and organized by clans based on the seven original mother towns. Their treaty and growing trade interaction brought changes to the towns along the river valleys, and frequently those changes came by river themselves. The rivers brought changes that often destabilized Cherokee society by challenging the continuity of traditional life. Scots-Irish fur traders who took Indian wives had biracial children with those women. The children had clan status, but their fathers often demanded patriarchal rights over those children. These new Cherokees were profoundly changed in many ways. While the towns of the Cherokee people either adapted willingly or were forced to change, the river flowed along beside them, companion to their journey like some silent observer of their history, and perhaps that was the true function all along of Yunwi Gunahita, the Long Man.

It was in this new decade that an Overhills Cherokee man, Attakullakulla, came to power. He entered political life at a time of crisis caused by Cherokee participation in the French and Indian War. He was buoyed in his efforts by his status as one of the Cherokees who had visited London in 1730. Attakullakulla was further helped by the fact that the British had elevated the Overhills Towns where he resided in importance over the other settlement clusters. To some Cherokees and to many British leaders in Carolina, he seemed to be a more effective leader in dealing with the latest problems between the two cultures. In stepping into this new role, he walked a fine line between the needs of the Cherokee people and the irresistible power of Britain and its colonies in South Carolina and Virginia.

Notes

1. Raymond D. Fogelson, "Cherokees in the East," in *Handbook of North American Indians*, edited by William C. Sturtevant (Washington, DC: Smithsonian Institution, 2004), 343.
2. James Mooney, *Myths of the Cherokee* (New York: Dover, 1995), 21.
3. Thomas E. Mails, *The Cherokee People: The Story of the Cherokees from Earliest Origins to Contemporary Times* (New York: Marlowe & Company, 1996), 25.
4. Fogelson, "Cherokees in the East," 337–338.
5. Roy S. Dickens Jr., "The Origins and Development of Cherokee Culture," in *The Cherokee Indian Nation: A Troubled History*, edited by Duane King (Knoxville: University of Tennessee Press, 1979), 4.
6. William L. McLoughlin, *Cherokee Renascence in the New Republic* (Princeton, NJ: Princeton University Press, 1986), 9.
7. Tom Hatley, *The Dividing Paths: Cherokees and South Carolinians through the Revolutionary Era* (New York: Oxford University Press, 1995), 13.
8. Daniel J. Tortora, *Carolina in Crisis: Cherokees, Colonists, and Slaves in the American Southeast, 1756–1763* (Chapel Hill: University of North Carolina Press, 2015), 11.
9. Tyler Boulware, *Deconstructing the Cherokee Nation: Town, Region and Nation among Eighteenth-Century Cherokees* (Gainesville: University Press of Florida, 2011), 24.
10. Dickens, "The Origins and Development," 28.
11. James Mooney, *Myths of Cherokee* (New York: Dover, 1995), 239.
12. Mooney, *Myths of the Cherokee*, 240.
13. Theda Perdue, *Cherokee Women: Gender and Culture Change, 1700–1835* (Lincoln: University of Nebraska Press, 1998), 14.
14. Perdue, *Cherokee Women*, 13–14.
15. Perdue, *Cherokee Women*, 14.
16. Mooney, *Myths of the Cherokee*, 349.
17. Mails, *The Cherokee People*, 136.
18. Perdue, *Cherokee Women*, 32–33.
19. Mails, *The Cherokee People*, 72.
20. Perdue, *Cherokee Women*, 33.
21. Mails, *The Cherokee People*, 151.
22. Fogelson, "Cherokees in the East," 349.
23. Mails, *The Cherokee People*, 180.
24. Mails, *The Cherokee People*, 77.

25. Hatley, *The Dividing Paths*, 13.

26. Paul Kelton, *Cherokee Medicine, Colonial Germs: An Indigenous Nation's Fight Against Smallpox, 1518–1824* (Norman: University of Oklahoma Press, 2015), 88–89.

27. Mooney, *Myths of the Cherokee*, 24–25.

28. Mooney, *Myths of the Cherokee*, 29–30.

29. Robert J. Conley, *The Cherokee Nation: A History* (Albuquerque: University of New Mexico Press, 2005), 25.

30. Conley, *The Cherokee Nation*, 26.

31. Mooney, *Myths of the Cherokee*, 31–32.

32. Mooney, *Myths of the Cherokee*, 32.

33. Tortora, *Carolina in Crisis*, 15.

34. Ted L. Gragson and Paul V. Bolstad, "A Local Analysis of Early-Eighteenth-Century Cherokee Settlement," *Social Science History* 31, no. 3 (Fall 2007), 436.

35. Gragson and Bolstad, "A Local Analysis," 439–440.

36. Mails, *The Cherokee People*, 25.

37. Gragson and Bolstad, "A Local Analysis," 446.

38. Kristofer Ray, *Before the Volunteer State: New Thoughts on Early Tennessee, 1540–1800* (Knoxville: University of Tennessee Press, 2015), 38.

39. Ray, *Before the Volunteer State*, 38.

40. Michael P. Morris, *The Bringing of Wonder: Trade and Indians of the Southeast, 1700–1783* (Wesport, CT: Greenwood Press, 1999), 78.

41. Ray, *Before the Volunteer State*, 38.

42. Sir Alexander Cuming, "Journal of Sir Alexander Cuming," in *Early Travels in the Tennessee Country 1540–1800: With Introductions, Annotations, and Index*, edited by Samuel Cole Williams (Johnson City, TN: Watauga Press, 1928), 122–123.

43. Boulware, *Deconstructing the Cherokee Nation*, 25.

44. Fogelson, "Cherokees in the East," 346.

45. Cuming, "Journal," 122–123.

46. John P. Brown, *Old Frontiers: The Story of the Cherokee Indians from Earliest Times to the Date of Their Removal to the West, 1838* (Kingsport, TN: Southern Publishers, 1938), 41.

47. Cuming, "Journal," 125–126.

48. Brown, *Old Frontiers*, 43.

49. Tortora, *Carolina in Crisis*, 19.

50. Tortora, *Carolina in Crisis*, 19–20.

51. Tortora, *Carolina in Crisis*, 19–20.

52. Conley, *The Cherokee Nation*, 33–35.

53. Hatley, *The Dividing Paths*, 13.

54. Kelton, *Cherokee Medicine*, 109.

55. Ludovic Grant, "Historical Relation of the Facts," *Journal of Cherokee Studies* XXVI (2008): 21–22, endnote 25.

56. George R. Stewart, *Names on the Land: A Historical Account of Place-Naming in the United States* (New York: Houghton Mifflin, 1967), 146.
57. McLoughlin, *Cherokee Renascence*, 7.
58. McLoughlin, *Cherokee Renascence*, 8–9.
59. Fogelson, "Cherokees in the East," 341.
60. Boulware, *Deconstructing the Cherokee Nation*, 2.
61. Boulware, *Deconstructing the Cherokee Nation*, 4–5.
62. Boulware, *Deconstructing the Cherokee Nation*, 18–19.
63. Fogelson, "Cherokee in the East," 338.
64. McLoughlin, *Cherokee Renascence*, 16–17.
65. Boulware, *Deconstructing the Cherokee Nation*, 24.
66. Gragson and Bolsted, *A Local Analysis*, 444.
67. Tortora, *Carolina in Crisis*, 11.
68. Boulware, *Deconstructing the Cherokee Nation*, 22–23.
69. Hatley, *The Dividing Paths*, 16.
70. Betty Anderson Smith, "Distribution of Eighteenth-Century Cherokee Settlements," in *The Cherokee Indian Nation: A Troubled History*, edited by Duane King (Knoxville: University of Tennessee Press, 1979), 48.
71. Smith, "Distribution of Eighteenth-Century Cherokee Settlements," 49.
72. Smith, "Distribution of Eighteenth-Century Cherokee Settlements," 53.
73. Boulware, *Deconstructing the Cherokee Nation*, 24.
74. Fogelson, "Cherokee in the East," 338–339.
75. McLoughlin, *Cherokee Renascence*, 17.
76. Boulware, *Deconstructing the Cherokee Nation*, 24.
77. Boulware, *Deconstructing the Cherokee Nation*, 24.
78. McLoughlin, *Cherokee Renascence*, 17.
79. Boulware, *Deconstructing the Cherokee Nation*, 27.
80. Boulware, *Deconstructing the Cherokee Nation*, 27.

The Anglo-Cherokee War of 1760–1761   1
The Past Is Prologue

CHEROKEE SOCIETY underwent tremendous political, economic, and epidemiological pressure and change in the early eighteenth century between 1730 and 1790, culminating with the Dragging Canoe rebellion of 1776. Epidemic disease played a role in the profound changes, and so did the Cherokees' new relationship with the British after 1730. The French played their own part in the destabilization of Cherokee society, and it was exactly that pressure which impelled the Cherokees into a closer relationship with the British. More specifically, it was dealing with the complex and new relationship with the British precisely at the time when the French sought to destabilize Cherokee society that increased social pressure on the tribe. Between 1755 and 1775, a triumvirate of Cherokee leaders emerged and attempted to deal with these issues, particularly with the governments of Virginia and South Carolina. These leaders—Ostenaco, Oconostota, and Attakullakulla—learned to deal with British civilian and military officials, perfecting a system of treaties that occasionally exhibited Cherokee sovereignty but almost always involved Cherokee land concessions. That strategy worked until the period of 1768–1774, when land cession requests and treaty readjustments became too numerous and the triumvirate leadership failed. In its void, the Dragging Canoe rebellion appeared in a desperate and ill-fated attempt to stem British colonial growth at the expense of the Ani-yun-wiya.

Outbreak of epidemic disease in the late 1730s and then again mid-century also brought a social pressure to bear on the Cherokees and changed those who survived the disease. The arrival of the Scots-Irish first along the borders of Cherokee lands in Virginia, and both North and South Carolina, ultimately ended with a series of illegal settlements on

Cherokee lands later validated by transfer treaties. These encroachments provided their own challenges to Cherokee society between the Anglo-Indian War and the Dragging Canoe rebellion. The colony governments of South Carolina and Virginia brought economic pressure to bear on the Cherokees as South Carolina sought to impose a trade monopoly on the Cherokees, edging out the Virginians—their first suppliers.

Both the Anglo-Indian War of 1760–1761 and the Dragging Canoe Rebellion of 1776 illustrate Cherokee society's response to these myriad pressures. The first crisis produced a triumvirate of leaders—Ostenaco, Oconostota (often called the Great Warrior), and Attakullakulla—to handle different issues. While Oconostota generally took the lead in military matters, Ostenaco sometimes took that role in Oconostota's absence. Attakullakulla generally took the lead in diplomatic matters such as the peace treaty ending a war. Members of the triumvirate leaned in different directions as they exercised power. Attakullakulla generally worked within the British sphere of influence while Oconostota reached out to the French many times. Ironically, Attakullakulla, the diplomat, was married to one of Oconostota's daughters. Ostenaco prided himself on an independent posture and yet wrangled a trip to Britain for himself at the conclusion of the Anglo-Cherokee War. Each crisis produced a rising leader, ironically from different clans.

Attakullakulla's son, Dragging Canoe, assumed leadership in the crisis of 1776, casting aside the leadership of his father's entire generation in a moment of reckoning. Each leader was an example of the Cherokees exerting agency over their generation's crisis caused by non-Indians in proximity to the Cherokee towns along the rivers. While both sets of leaders experienced crisis caused by a multiplicity of cultural pressures, Carolina government exerted the most pressure in its attempts to reign in the Cherokees in the imagined British Empire.

Some Cherokee leaders, like Attakullakulla, exercised agency when it came to dealing with governments of the two European superpowers and the two colonies. However, no human society can withstand critical social, economic, political, and epidemiological pressure over time without some reaction. Thus, our traditional view of the Dragging Canoe Rebellion of 1776 has been that of an aberration against Cherokee norms and traditions. Instead, it should be viewed as the culmination of a series of venting reactions to tremendous social, economic, military, and epidemiological pressures. If the Dragging Canoe Rebellion represented the venting of those pressures, the build-up began as the Cherokees found themselves by mid-century increasingly entangled in the imperial struggles between Britain, France, and Spain.

The relationship between the three European nation-states was a complex one, to be sure. Spain interpreted Britain's founding of Georgia in 1733 as an aggressive step into Spanish domain. It strained relations between the two countries, which had enjoyed limited trade at the conclusion of the War of Spanish Succession in 1713. At that time, Spain granted to Britain the *asiento*, allowing it to send one vessel into the Caribbean each year to trade in British-acquired slaves. British traders exceeded the limit, and smugglers abounded in a difficult-to-control situation. Historian Francois Furstenberg points out another geographic challenge as European nations vied to establish hegemony over significant parts of North America. The Appalachian Mountains stymied each of their efforts to claim an empire.[1]

The mountains strained the ability of these would-be empires to maintain what was, at best, a tenuous hold over these regions. These same nations claimed sovereign control over Native peoples even as those Native peoples saw themselves as allies and not as subjects. When the British claimed sovereignty over groups like the Overhills Cherokees (western-most), they fancied that it gave them control over the mountains because their subject people lived in those mountains. Thus, the colonizers had a theoretical empire with an imagined control over the Appalachians.[2] As British colonists in North America edged ever closer to the mountains, the British government looked to the Cherokees, particularly the Overhills Cherokees, as a way to exert control over this region.[3] Such control, the British government believed, gave them dominion over the lucrative Ohio River Valley and a way to challenge French control over that region.[4] For the French, control of that region meant connections between Canada and La Louisiane. Spain's plan for the Appalachian Mountains was to use them to protect the Spanish Gulf Coast possessions from both the British and the French expansion.[5]

In 1730, the British dispatched Scottish nobleman Sir Alexander Cuming to make contact with the Cherokees at a time when the Cherokees felt a distinct political grievance against the French. Cuming met with the Cherokee leaders at Nikwasi (modern-day Franklin, North Carolina), and the tribe entered into agreements aligning them with the British, probably to counterbalance the French encroachments into the western edges of Cherokee country.[6] The document illustrates that Britain was trying to exercise dominion over the Cherokees. The Articles of Friendship stated, "The said Moytoy and all the Cherokee people, has laid the Crown of your Nation . . . at H.M. [His Majesty's] feet, in token of your obedience."[7] The document gave the Cherokees permission to live on their hereditary lands, further illustrating British perception of dominion over the Cherokees.[8] The document also charged the Cherokees to reject traders of other nations and to prevent whites of other nations from building within their territory, again making the Cherokees an extension of British authority when the British government could not police those actions themselves.[9]

Cherokee leaders responded, trying to tell the British government that "the Crown of our Nation is different from that which the Great King George wears, and from that which we saw in the Tower; but to us it is all one, and the chain of friendship shall be carried to our people."[10] In telling the British that the Crown of the Cherokee Nation was different from that which King George wore, perhaps the Cherokees were telling the British that they were allies and not subjects, just as they were not subjects of their Cherokee leaders.

As the document continued, it stated that the chain of friendship between the two peoples was fastened to the breast of Moytoy of Tellico, the British-proclaimed emperor of the Cherokee people.[11] The British were trying to impose what did not exist naturally among the Cherokees: a central leader with authority over all sets of towns. To carry the point further, the British had a theoretical empire that included the Cherokee people and a theoretical emperor of those people. That empire, by the Articles of Friendship, made them subjects of the British Empire, but, as

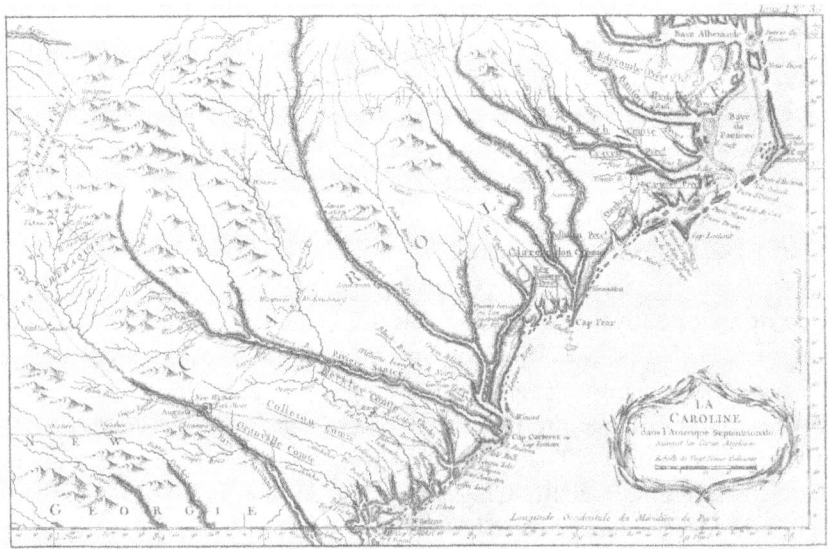

Figure 1.1. South Carolina coast labeled *La Caroline dans l'Amerique* (courtesy of the South Caroliniana Library, University of South Carolina, Columbia)

stated above, the Cherokees saw themselves more as allies. The British part of the Articles concluded by referencing geography, stating that the friendship would last "as long as the mountains and rivers shall last, or the sun shine."[12] Ironically, the ending touches on the aspect of geography that the British could never fully control—the mountains and the rivers that brought such overwhelming change to the Cherokees, started originally by the fur trade.

The tone of the Cherokee response is plainly stated as that of allies pledging a mutual support more than a people surrendering to British government. One passage to that point states, "in war, we shall always be as one with you; the Great King George's enemies shall be our enemies; his people and ours shall always be one, and dye together."[13] A further passage welcomes settler communities near the Cherokees, but as equals, stating, "your white people may very safely build houses near us, we shall hurt nothing that belongs to them, for we are children of one Father, the Great King, and shall live and dye together."[14] Other historians have pointed out before that a child's maternal uncle carried out the duties of a father figure in the matrilineal Cherokee culture. The two cultures most likely had different ideas when speaking of the authority of a father figure.

As a further cementing of loyalties, seven Cherokee chiefs visited England, where they renewed the treaty, pledging their loyalty to the British Crown, which included promises to restrict their trade only to Britain as well as forbidding any alliances with a rival power. The London treaty also required them to forbid white settlers among them and included a commitment on their part to repatriate runaway enslaved men and women. When both sides concluded the treaty in September 1730, the Cherokee delegates returned by way of Charles Town, South Carolina.[15] Interestingly, Dragging Canoe's father, Attakullakulla (Cherokee name Ada gal' kala), was part of this delegation. Their visit probably overawed the Cherokees, as such trips were often designed to do. The willingness of the chiefs like Attakullakulla to bend to British positions in the future may have originated with this visit. Dragging Canoe and his followers rebelled, in part, because their fathers' generation caved to British desires on most political and economic matters.

It is clear that in the years following the Articles of Friendship Treaty, the Cherokees saw themselves as privileged allies, to be sure, but not as subject peoples. The British desired that the Cherokees make peace with the northern Haudenosaunee (Iroquois) peoples, something in which the Cherokees were not particularly interested. However, much to the

Figure 1.2. Seven Cherokees who visited London in 1730 (courtesy of the South Caroliniana Library, University of South Carolina, Columbia)

pleasure of the British government, the Western or Overhills Cherokees did began to provide intelligence reports about the Ohio River Valley incidents in the years after the treaty. Further Cherokee parties seized French cargo vessels traveling the Tennessee River and turned those crews over to British authorities. Such efforts, on the part of the Western or Overhills Cherokees, caused the British to elevate the importance of the Western Cherokees over those of the Middle or Lower Towns.[16]

Unfortunately, as the British and the Cherokees aligned themselves politically with the Great Chain of Friendship, smallpox outbreaks began to ravage both South Carolina and various Cherokee polities alike. This disease brought its own critical pressures to bear on Cherokee society. The disease first appeared in the southeast in 1696 in the Virginia colony before spreading to the Carolina coast and then the Piedmont region. The Cherokees traded with the Virginians, who had supplied them first and continued to do so long after the Carolina colony was established. By 1698, the pestilence showed up among the Catawbas, the closest tribe to the east of the Cherokees.[17] To make matters worse, the disease appeared in both the 1730s and the 1760s, affecting at least two generations of Cherokee society.

The variola pathogen seems to have spread to the Cherokee communities closest to Charles Town, which had an outbreak from 1711 until 1712.[18] If this dating is correct, then members of the Cherokees who faced the documented epidemic of 1738 and 1739 were the survivors of an earlier plague. Cherokee shamans dubbed the disease Kosvkv Askini and conceptualized it as a devil predisposed to do evil in the world.[19] Once named, Cherokee medical practitioners created a treatment protocol that included isolation of the patient, which probably slowed the spread of the pathogen. Treatment also included cooling the patient down by pouring cold water on the chest or a dip in a nearby river itself.[20] Shamans created a seven-day ceremony to combat the disease based on their conceptualization of it as a demon.[21]

The first recorded outbreak occurred in either 1738 or 1739, and it was brought to South Carolina by fur traders, like James Adair, who served the Cherokees.[22] Some estimates say the initial outbreak took out half the population at that time. Historian Paul Kelton believes the Cherokees named the disease and created a treatment protocol for it sometime between 1739 and 1752.[23] According to James Adair, many Cherokee shamans discarded sacred tools and relics when confronted by the disease because they found that the tools lacked efficacy. Most curiously, Adair further reported that many proud warriors who survived the disease could no longer bear their own appearance, which was now marked with smallpox scars.[24]

Before the trade era, native peoples had to content themselves with an imperfect reflection of their faces as seen from pools of still water. At the time of the fur trade, Indian traders had long provided the Cherokees and others with small hand mirrors, with which they could now see their imperfect faces with far greater clarity. Adair wrote that some men shot themselves and others cut their own throats, while still others threw themselves into fires and burned alive.[25] More recent scholarship challenges the reasons for such suicide. Instead of human vanity or despair over beauty lost, more generalized fears of the future for their people, compounded by fears of witchcraft as the cause of the epidemics, appear more likely reasons for suicide. Shamans may also have taken their own lives because they feared possession by spirits of the dead for failure to perform funeral rituals in a proper way.[26]

The decade of the 1740s opened with a smaller Cherokee population as well as the establishment of a new trade path between the lower Cherokee towns down to the frontier town of Augusta, Georgia. The Georgia colony was busy fighting the War of Jenkins' Ear as James Edward Oglethorpe led attacks between Savannah and St. Augustine, further complicating the relationship between Great Britain and Spain.[27] At the same time, in 1744, the War of Austrian Succession brought Britain's slow, simmering rivalry with France in North America to the boil. Now the question of Indian alliances in North America became critical, involving much more than mere profit margins. The French used groups like the Choctaws to harass those, like the Cherokees, who were aligned with the British. In so doing, the French could effectively drain British resources as they struggled to minimize British influence in the backcountry, particularly the Ohio River Valley. The potential effects of the escalating competition for Indian alliances were sobering. If British settlements lost an Indian ally to the French, they would lose profits from trade with that ally as well. The loss of too many former allies could have potentially ignited the tribes of the backcountry in a war against the British, and the British would lose the theoretical control they held over Cherokee country. In that case, the fur traders and Indian agents would have become hostages with which the tribes could have bargained with the British. As the various tribes of the backcountry gained experience with Europeans, they learned to use the language of trade to manipulate these fears to their own advantage.

In October 1744, a Cherokee headman wrote to the newly installed governor of South Carolina, James Glen. Normally, Indian groups made ceremonial trips to greet new British officials, and there was little that officials could do to prevent tribes from doing so when they expected gifts and lavish treatment at such events. Having learned that the British were at war with both the Spanish and the French, the headman chose to avoid a trip until the following spring, believing that Glen and his "beloved men and warriors [sic] would be very busy about ordering and preparing for the warr [sic] and that we might be troublesome at such a time."[28] The headman also told Glen that since his people owed great debts to the traders, they needed to hunt that fall in order to pay those debts.[29]

One of the first tasks undertaken by Governor Glen in his new position was to thwart French efforts in the backcountry. When Cherokee headmen finally paid him a visit in the fall of 1746, they pledged their loyalty to the British. Despite such public assurances of Cherokee fealty, the Cherokees were, in fact, divided in their loyalty. Cherokee leaders told Glen that those members of their tribe living near the Mississippi River, the Overhills tribes, were visited frequently by the French and French-aligned Indians. Their proximity to French forces left them somewhat vulnerable, and these Cherokees cooperated with the French out of fear. Glen told the Board of Trade that, at that juncture, he proposed building a fort in their homelands to counteract French influence. As Glen noted in his own style, a fort would "bar the door against the French, & be such a bridle in the mouths of the Indians themselves, & that would forever keep them ours."[30] However unflattering the horse metaphor of the Cherokees was, it gives a stunning example of the Carolina perception of their Cherokee allies. Equals do not wear bridles, nor do they carry riders, and the Cherokees had emerged from the Articles of Friendship seeing themselves as equal partners with their British allies. As forts are tools of war, the Cherokee response in the Articles of Friendship stated, "in war we shall always be as one with you."[31]

In the matter of construction costs, the building, garrisoning, and supplying of such a fort would be expensive. Perhaps mindful of that cost, Glen reminded the board why he thought such an outlay necessary. The Indian trade had made Carolina prosperous because it involved the exchange of low-cost items produced by British manufacturers for deerskins. At that time, he noted that Charles Town was exporting six hundred to seven hundred hogsheads of skins annually, with one hogshead bringing 50 guineas in Charles Town.[32]

Some tribes of the southern backcountry resisted the notion of Euroamericans building forts in their homelands. Yet others quickly realized that such forts had many advantages. First, they provided ready shelter for the Indians should their own enemies' attack. Second, such fortifications would serve as a deterrent to enemies of the tribe on whose land it was built. Third, forts often served as repositories for larger amounts of trade goods than traders could carry—an appealing situation to Indian trade partners. In April 1747, Glen wrote to the board with an update on South Carolina's status with its Indian neighbors. He noted that while the French still tried to alienate the Cherokees from the British, the Cherokees themselves had petitioned him for the construction of just such a fort. In fact, they had promised to cede land as its site, to provide labor for its construction, and to help provision it for the first two years.[33] The implied French threat to the Cherokees was forcing Britain to consider building forts among its aligned Indian tribes, thus increasing costs in Indian management. If the British chose to refuse the request, they risked alienating the Cherokees and sending them into the arms of the French. Thus, the actual cost of maintaining Indian alliances and the Indian trade rose during the tension between the two intruding European powers.

In July 1748, Governor Glen regretfully informed the board that French Indians had attacked British settlements and carried off people as slaves. The threat was so great that the Indian traders were afraid to leave Cherokee lands without armed escort. He used the opportunity to press his idea about fort building, which he had expanded in light of continuing trouble in the backcountry. In addition to recommending the fort among the Cherokees, he called for building one in the Choctaw lands. He also believed that the British should construct one between the Catawbas and the Cherokees and still another between the Chickasaws and the Creeks.[34]

In December 1749, Glen wrote to the board with further proof of French machinations. When he recently invited Creek and Cherokee headmen to Charles Town for peace talks, the French in Mobile and the Alabama Fort started rumors that the Cherokees had been called there to be put to death.[35] The Cherokees and the Creeks responded to Glen with a request that the meeting be held at Fort Moore across the river from Augusta, Georgia, at a distance of some 150 miles from Charles Town, but Glen refused to meet that far inland and continued to pressure both groups to meet at Charles Town. When the Cherokees refused Glen's offer to come to the coast, they cited Charles Town's propensity for sickness as a reason not to send more leaders who might lose their lives as result of the visit.[36] Ironically, when they arrived, many of the Indian leaders fell prey to disease and died in great numbers, especially the Cherokees. Cherokee survivors started back home only to learn that French Indians had attacked several of their Overhills towns.[37] Thus disease and French actions had made the rumors appear to be true.

Prior to the outbreak of hostilities in the Great War for Empire, the Cherokees entered the Ohio River Valley in 1752 to enlist the aid of the Shawnees, Delawares, and Mingos. The Cherokees wanted these tribes to induce the British to build trade outposts in Cherokee territory. Strategically placed British forts would not be built until 1753 and 1756 among the Lower and Overhills towns. Desperately in need of ammunition for their ongoing war with the Muskogee Creeks, the Cherokees noted that they might be forced to move toward the Ohio River Valley if they could not be supplied in their own lands.[38] Those northern tribes, as well as the Cherokees, would be pivotal in the dynamics of the French and Indian War.

In the spring of 1754, Virginia governor Robert Dinwiddie wrote to Oconostota inviting him and other prominent chiefs to Winchester, Virginia, to begin talks of enlisting Cherokee military aid in exchange for presents and weapons. It would take three invitations from the governor and a gracious supply of guns and ammunition to elicit the desired visit from the Cherokees, who dutifully reported to Williamsburg, Virginia. Oconostota and others leveraged the desired military support in exchange for the construction of the desired second fort. Dinwiddie agreed to this request and was already in talks with South Carolina's Governor Glen about it.[39]

That same year, representatives of the British and French began unofficial hostilities when Dinwiddie sent a young George Washington and 160-odd men to the Pennsylvania backcountry to eject the French and their new Fort Duquesne. As is well known, the French began fort construction to link the two halves of French America, Canada and Louisiana, as a countermeasure against westward expansion of the British colonies. Much to his dismay, Washington found the fort fully operational and well manned. When he exchanged gunfire with his French counterparts, he fired the salvos that started the French and Indian War. As historian Paul Kelton has observed, France's Indian allies, the Shawnees, Delawares, and Mingos, were not at all enthusiastic about going to war on behalf of France. Indian representatives refused to take the wampum belt a French officer had offered; instead, the Ohio Indian leaders kicked it back and forth among themselves.[40] As historian Greg Dowd has observed, the war involved Indians from the St. Lawrence River to the Mississippi Delta and demanded "deep changes in the diplomatic relations among and the social relations within Indian peoples, changes that would shape history for a generation."[41] The French entreated Ohio River Valley tribes like the Mingos, Shawnees, and Delawares with talks and wampum belts well before General Braddock's defeat, and many of those tribes responded favorably.[42]

By contrast, the British had groomed the Cherokees and Haudenosaunee for this situation for a long time. First, military service on demand was written into the 1730 Articles of Friendship, as "the Cherokees must . . . be always ready, at the Governor's command, to fight against any nation, whether they be white men or Indians, who shall dare or hurt the English."[43] The Cherokees reaffirmed the requirement in their response, stating, "the Great King's enemies shall be our enemies."[44] Part of the preparation process included trying to promote peace between the Cherokees and Haudenosaunee (Iroquois), making these great tribes available for other duties, rather than bogged down with wars of retributive justice.

Part of the French threat, though not always fully considered as a real threat, was the propaganda introduced among British allies like the Cherokees. In December 1754, Governor Glen of South Carolina wrote to three Cherokee headmen: Tacite of Hiawassie, Colane of Eurphorsee, and the King of the Valley. He told them of his desire to hold a conference with both their people and the Creeks. Glen wanted this conference to confirm the peace between the two peoples, a peace he warned that the French wanted to destroy. He also warned the Cherokees that the French were attempting to enlist the Tawasaws and other northern Indians against the Cherokees while bringing in the Choctaws and Creeks against them from the south.[45]

The French threat was palpable, as was the threat of their Indian allies, the Ohio River Valley Indians. After helping the French defeat General Edward Braddock, commander of British Forces in North America, in June 1755, the Shawnees, Delawares, and Mingos went on to attack the settlers of Pennsylvania, Maryland, and Virginia, killing some two thousand people and taking one thousand settlers as captives.[46]

The ulterior motive of Governor Glen's warning should be considered carefully. The French were seeking to attract as many Indian allies as possible, just as the British hoped to do. The French had more than proved what their native allies were capable of achieving both under direct control and unleashed on unsupervised raids. When it came to the task of recruiting Indian allies, both the British and the French needed to be on their best behavior among the tribes they hoped to entice. Yet, as longtime Scot trader Ludovic Grant noted, the British effort was being jeopardized by an enemy within: the fur traders themselves. He wrote to warn Glen in March 1755 of trader irregularities that he believed would hurt Britain's attempt to maintain good relations with the Indians at this critical time. He noted that the Carolina traders extended too much credit to the Cherokees, more than they could ever hope to repay. This economic pressure remained a constant on Cherokee society, as interest charges only increased the amount owed. Offering his own psychological opinion of the effect, Grant believed that the Indians developed a dislike of the traders because they owed them so much money. The close presence of the traders among the Indians exacerbated native disdain for their creditors. Thus, Grant believed the Cherokees were tempted by distant traders, probably alluding to the French. He believed the problem of excessive credit was a critical one, given the French threat; if it were not corrected, Grant believed the Indians might take drastic steps to extinguish their debts—by extinguishing the traders.[47] Again, such move would relieve a growing economic threat to Cherokee stability. At the same time, the Cherokees British allies began to pressure them for military service on demands, as specified in the 1730 treaty.

The Cherokees responded to their English allies' call for aid. In 1755, chiefs Old Hop, Oconostota, Attakullakulla, and the Raven led a delegation of five hundred Cherokees for a seven-day diplomatic meeting with Governor Glen of Carolina. Attakullakulla, peace chief and a great orator, began by referencing his position as one of the seven Cherokees who had gone to England. He then took a Cherokee child by the hand and presented the boy to Governor Glen, saying the Cherokees were all "children of the great King George."[48] English ears probably missed a critical component in the speech telling just how different the Cherokees were from their English allies. The great peace chief mentioned that the Cherokees and their wives were all the children of the king. He opened a bag of earth and placed it at the governor's feet, indicating Cherokee cooperation in another land transfer. Attakullakulla pledged that the Cherokees would fight for the British if they would only supply the arms and ammunition.[49]

Governor Glen tried to leverage the Cherokee desire for the next fort by persuading the Cherokees to surrender all their lands to the British and declare themselves British subjects.[50]

Just as matrilineal tribes viewed the maternal uncle as the father figure, the tribes typically viewed the earth as eternal and mortal beings as temporary residents, unable to own it individually or transfer it all away. That said, the Cherokees concluded the Treaty of Saluda in 1755 with their ally, Governor Glen.[51]

Away from diplomatic circles, routine trade irregularities and low-level espionage always had the ability to erode the relationship between the Cherokees and their colonial neighbors. Now an international war far to the north that began in backcountry Pennsylvania had made its way south. France's Indian allies, the Shawnees, Delawares, and other Ohio Valley tribes, had attacked the Virginia frontier in the summers of 1755 and 1756. Colonials, like George Washington, believed that the only way to fight Indians was with other Indians.[52] To that end, colonial governors and military officials from Virginia began reaching out to the Cherokees for their services as mercenaries in the French and Indian War. When the original request for aid went out, the Cherokee leaders were in conference with Governor Glen drafting the Treaty of Saluda.[53]

In 1756, only thirteen warriors responded to Virginia governor Robert Dinwiddie's call, prompting the governor to label them as naturally lazy. Some earlier groups of Lower Town Cherokees had gone to battle for the British but were dissatisfied with the presents given as payment by the Virginians and quit the mission. At Washington's request, Nathaniel Gist went to the Cherokees to again request their help. He was successful partly because Shawnee had committed acts of war in Cherokee country that begged for retaliatory justice.[54] The Overhills town of Chota responded to this request, however, and agreed to send one hundred warriors under Ostenaco or Judd's Friend, in exchange for a British promise to build forts

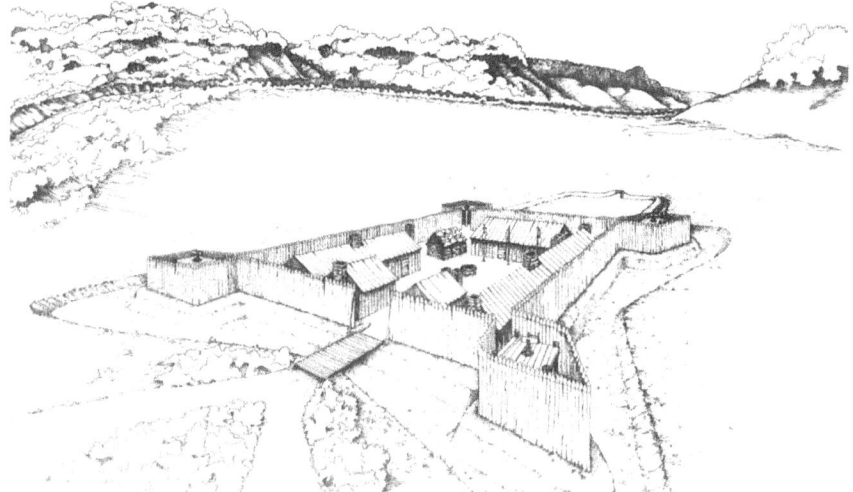

Figure 1.3. Fort Prince George (aka Fort Keowee) (courtesy of the South Carolina Institute on Archaeology and Anthropology, University of South Carolina)

in Cherokee country as a counteragent to French intrigues among the Cherokees of their region.[55]

Former South Carolina governor James Glen had Fort Prince George constructed in western South Carolina in 1753 near the Cherokee Lower Town of Keowee and the present-day town of Pickens, South Carolina. The British also built the much-requested Fort Loudoun in 1756 in eastern Tennessee near the Overhills town of Chota to fulfill promises for earlier service. Interestingly, the Virginians felt compelled to maintain a presence among the Cherokees and finally built yet a third fort, called the Virginia Fort, promised to leaders like the Swallow Warrior, across from Chota, but it remained unmanned.[56] Yet it was the construction of British Fort Loudoun and their own need for retaliatory justice that prompted some of the Overhills Cherokees to respond to the battle call given by their British allies.

Then and only then did a Cherokee war party leave Chota in February 1756 to engage the Shawnee Indians, who were their frequent enemies. Cherokee historian Robert Conley rightly notes that this was not the usual time of year for the Cherokees to fight. This was normally the end time of white-tailed deer hunting. The Cherokees lost their food supplies in a rain-swollen river, ultimately having to butcher their own horses for food.[57] Once this latest group arrived, they, too, asked for presents—more presents than the British commander, Colonel George Washington, could give. Major Andrew Lewis was in charge of supplying the Cherokees, and his own supply boats overturned in the crossing of an ice-filled river.[58] Unfortunately, Native American styles of combat differed greatly from European ones. Some of the Cherokees made good on a threat to quit the battle and returned home to Cherokee country through the Virginia backcountry and looted some of its newly settled inhabitants for new horses and supplies to replace the presents they never received and their own horses sacrificed for food.[59]

Peace chief Attakullakulla teamed up with war chief Oconostota to lead Cherokee troops against an attack on Fort Toulouse, also known as the Alabama Fort at the confluence of the Coosa and Tallapoosa Rivers in Alabama. Another wave of Cherokees left Cherokee country in September 1756, headed for Virginia now that Fort Loudoun had been constructed and garrisoned. Ostenaco led these men, along with Wauhatchie, Tiftowe, Saloue, Willenawah, the Raven, Moytoy, Ucahala, Round O, Scolacutta and Oskuah.[60]

The French were trying very hard to alienate the Cherokees from the British in the marketplace if they could not defeat them on the battlefield. Of the two major British-aligned tribes, the Cherokees were the weak link. However, the French did not focus all their attention on them. In May 1755, Lachlan McGillivray, a Scot fur trader licensed to trade among the Upper Creeks through his organization of Brown, Rea and Company, wrote to Governor Glen that a French captain met both Upper and Lower Creeks in April of that year. Bearing gifts, the captain wanted to mediate a peace between the Creeks and France's Choctaw allies. In order to tempt the Creeks, McGillivray noted that he also showed them an impressive array of trade goods with prices matching those offered by the British. Further, the Frenchman told the Cherokees that French fur traders would continue to undercut British prices on trade items. The French felt they could afford to do this, since they shipped their goods by water, instead of by land.[61] The French had clearly thrown down the gauntlet. The resulting competition to obtain Indian loyalty would create a price war, lowering profits for everyone involved, from British merchants to backcountry traders. The southeastern Indians enjoyed a buyer's market as two superpower nations sought to buy their political loyalty through the fur trade.

To the benefit of the British, the Cherokees did not easily run to the French when they had problems with the British or with the colonials.

However, the Cherokees always checked with the British about rumors told to them by the French. During a visit to the Overhills town of Great Tellico (modern Monroe County, Tennessee), British Commander Raymond Demeré was quickly asked by the Cherokee leader what he thought of the disaffection of one Cherokee town to French influence. When Demeré replied that such a move saddened him, the Cherokee emperor asked Demeré whether French people lived among the British at Charles Town. Demeré tried to explain that those Frenchmen were Huguenots, coreligionists, and were now loyal British subjects.[62] The French used half-truths and lies to weaken the British link to the Cherokees even further. In October 1756, Demeré addressed Connecorte (aka Old Hop) and Attakullakulla (aka Little Carpenter) at the Overhills town of Tomatley in response to questions they had about the building material being sent there for construction of the fort. The French had told them that metal was being sent to clap their women and children in irons, after the British first had killed all the Cherokee men. In reality, the Cherokees themselves had insisted the British build a fort among the Overhills people, who were more exposed to the French-aligned Indians, before the Cherokees would commit to sending forces into the Ohio River Valley to help the British in the French and Indian War.[63]

Lack of a Cherokee central government with clear communication lines made rumors like the one mentioned to Demeré an occupational hazard. As he responded, Demeré reassured the Cherokees that the metal was for the fort that their own government had requested, which would hold some 180 men. Demeré fully expounded on the usefulness of the fort, stating it would provide the Cherokee people protection from their enemies, and yet he chastised them for allowing some of their people to request a French fort in Cherokee lands. Using trade as a threat, Demeré told them that no other nation could supply them as well as the British and no Indians were poorer than those who aligned themselves with the French. If the French could not adequately take care of their closest Indian neighbors, then the more distant Cherokees could expect even less from them.[64] Finally, Demeré resorted to an old trick, albeit with a new twist. He told the Cherokees that, should they allow a French fort in their lands, such close proximity between the two hostile European powers would result in severed supply lines for both, ending all trade.

Demeré blamed the war on French ambition to dominate North America, as if the British did not aspire to the very same goal. Knowing that the Indians liked to side with the winner, he told them that the French had already lost thousands of men in the conflict, though in fact Britain was losing the war in 1756.⁶⁵ While he clarified the purpose of the building materials sent to Tomatley, Demeré cleverly threatened the cessation of trade as a means to induce the Cherokees to reject the overtures of the French.

The Cherokees' response to Demeré's talk likewise hinged on trade and was, in its own way, just as clever. Connecorte told Demeré that, in addition to the forts among the Overhills people at Chota and Tomatley, he wanted yet another built within such a distance that a gun fired at one would be heard by the other two. The Cherokee leader observed that while the British had come to give them a talk, they had done so empty-handed and at a time when the Cherokee warriors were out fighting enemies or hunting. The Cherokee headman warned that his towns were dangerously low on gunpowder and bullets, strongly hinting that the British should resupply them. In an example of how Euroamerican values had changed Indian perceptions, Connecorte told Demeré that while the British men had fine red uniforms, he was naked and could not sit with Demeré without "disgracing" him. The headman expressed the wish that when the British fort was completed, it would be well stocked so his warriors and headmen might obtain clothes, so "that they might look like men, and not be ashamed to show themselves, for an empty house looks but poorly."⁶⁶ Obviously, the Cherokees had assimilated European values about nakedness and now equated clothes with prosperity.

Again, the main message to the British was clear. The Cherokees expected them to supply guns and ammunition if the British wished them to continue opposing the French. At the same time, any British fort erected in their homelands would be expected to provide a plentiful supply of desired goods with the occasional outlay of gifts.

The French continued to make inroads among the Cherokee people. The Old Warrior of Tomatley wrote to Raymond Demeré in November 1756 with more news about Cherokee disaffection. He reported that not only were the Tellico people firmly under French influence, but the people of Chatuga had also joined them. Both Great Tellico and Chatuga were clustered together and at a distance from the main body of Overhills towns. The Old Warrior noted the two towns were planning to relocate to Hiwassie Old Town. In addition, Old Warrior noted that when the Tellico people went to the Alabama Fort for presents, they had been beaten there by a group of Creeks, who took all the gifts. The commanding officer of the French fort had received the Cherokees from Tellico warmly and told them to expect his visit in their homelands both to study the British trade and to observe abusive British Indian traders. He promised to supply the Cherokees with everything they needed and to wage a price war with the British, as he was determined to undercut them. Finally, the French official told them to expect soon a great quantity of gifts for their wives and children as a prelude to their new relationship.[67] Demeré's work was cut out for him. As British forts arose in Cherokee country, Cherokee resistance to the military obligations outlined in the Articles of Friendship treaty receded. By the end of 1756, a few hundred Cherokee warriors traveled north to fight the French and their allies.[68]

Just as the Europeans learned that the Indians aligned themselves with the strongest military power, they also learned that the Indians aligned themselves with the best trade provider. Price wars and an upsurge in gifts were the natural outcome of such European competition from which the Indians benefited. In November 1756, a very concerned Raymond Demeré wrote to South Carolina's Governor Lyttelton that if the British lost the Overhills people at Tellico, they ultimately would lose all of the Cherokee people. He believed that the fates of both South Carolina and Georgia were inexorably tied to the fates of the Creek and Cherokee tribes. If Britain lost either tribe, the other would surely soon follow. Should the Creeks and Cherokees join forces with the French-aligned Choctaws, Demeré believed the resulting coalition eventually would absorb every other Indian group of consequence in North America. The British captain noted that attracting the Cherokees was of such import that the French would spare no cost: "Indians are a comodity [sic] that are to be bought and sold and the French will bid very high for them. And on this particular occasion if we don't bid as high we shall [absolutely] lose them."[69] Demeré did not know his tribes well enough to know that such a merger of Creek and Cherokee forces was highly unlikely. However, his early fear of a pan-Indian movement in the 1750s among the southeastern tribes would reappear later in the American Revolution during the 1770s. Such fears were perennial, though unlikely, and over time became as powerful as any fact.

From all available indicators, the British were well on their way to losing the Cherokees in the mid-1750s. Intelligence reports from a Cherokee leader named Ostenaco (called Judge's or Judd's Friend by the British) in December 1756 confirmed a meeting between the French at the Alabama Fort (Toulouse) and the Cherokee Mankiller of Tellico.[70] Ostenaco earned the title Mankiller (Outacite) early in life, and his town affiliation seems to have been the Valley Town of Hiwasssie. In the 1740s, he was one of the guardians of the thirteen-year-old Ammonscossittee of Tellico, the second of the British-selected emperors, son of the first emperor, Moytoy.

His initial experience with the British came from contact with the Indian traders from Charles Town.[71] As it turns out, Ostenaco was one of the earliest Cherokees to respond to British calls for Cherokee participation in the French and Indian War. In November 1755, he led 130 Cherokees to Virginia to stop the Shawnees from attacking settlers in southwestern Virginia. Early in the new year, he fought with Major Andrew Lewis in a joint Cherokee-British mission against the Shawnees called the Sandy Creek Expedition. For much of his military and later diplomatic career, he managed to avoid the label of British servant or lackey.[72] Now, late in the year, he provided information.

Ostenaco's intelligence indicated that the French fort official told the Mankiller figuratively that the "French house" had been darkened for a long time because of the Cherokees' ties to the British. Every time the French had reached out to the Cherokees, the British called them to Charles Town. Once there, the British wined and dined them and gave them a "fine red coat." Perhaps alluding to the recent ill-fated visit of the Cherokees to Charles Town to see the former governor James Glen, the French official noted that British gifts, like clothes, were tainted with death. He told the Mankiller that "the Carolina people had conjourors [*sic*] . . . that could send up bundles of sickness to their Nation . . . from which proceeds the decrease of their people."[73] Ironically, this propaganda preceded the 1758–1759 outbreak of smallpox among the Cherokees. The Frenchman accused the British of beating Cherokee warriors and molesting Cherokee women. He also brought up the issue of materials being shipped to Tomatley and repeated the claim that those materials would ultimately be used to make shackles to enslave the Cherokee people. The French official ended his meeting with the Mankiller by stating that the Tellico people should go to New Orleans and guide a boatload of free goods back to the Cherokee homelands.[74]

Once more, the French were playing on Indian insecurities. North American Indians had long viewed Europeans as conjurors, since they mildly experienced European illnesses which often proved fatal to native peoples. Indians, like the Overhills leaders, often refused to go into heavy population centers, like Charles Town, until after the summer's heat, for fear of illness. Some British traders did cheat and misuse the Cherokees. Thus, the French overemphasized the unscrupulous behavior of some traders to represent the actions of all of them. They continued to misrepresent the purpose of British building materials shipped into the backcountry to the detriment of British interests. Other intelligence reports in December 1756 noted that the Mankiller of Tellico expected French John to give him thirty horse loads of ammunition. Meanwhile, the Tellico people were reported to be in the process of building houses in anticipation of the arrival of the French.[75]

Subsequent intelligence from Cherokee territory revealed that the only reason for the Mankiller's visit to the construction site of Fort Loudoun had been to reconnoiter its progress. He had been instructed by the French to scalp some of the colonials there and return with their scalps as tokens of Cherokee fidelity. Then the French would attack and kill the British in the Cherokee homelands.[76] To cement this new alliance, the French offered that one item more tantalizing than all others—commerce. They increased the quantity of free gifts promised to the Cherokees to unbelievable proportions. Their subsequent offer promised a caravan of one hundred horses sent to them four times. After this massive bounty of gifts, the French planned to send one hundred horse loads of trade items for sale. As if this were not enough, the French stated they would accept as payment all manner of skins, not just deerskins.[77]

The British traders among the Cherokees in January 1756 noted the continued defection of the Tellico people. British merchants Thomas Leaper and James Kelley abandoned their trading house in Tellico fearfully and transferred their wares from Tellico to the nearby town of Chatuga. They reported that a group of Indians under the direction of the Mankiller had staked out the route into Tellico from Chota and now patrolled it in search of the British scalps needed to cement their deal with the French at the Alabama Fort.[78] Demeré quickly sent out warnings to travelers to avoid the usual route into Tellico.[79]

While this group of Cherokees continued to drift into the French orbit, other members of that tribe sought to strengthen their British ties. Demeré wrote to Governor Lyttelton that Connecorte (Old Hop) had summoned him to a meeting at Chota, where the elderly Cherokee strove to convince the British captain of the loyalty of seven towns among the Overhills Cherokee. On returning to his fort, Demeré found the Mankiller of Tellico waiting for him. In the meeting, Demeré learned that the main source of much of the disaffection of the Tellico people was trade problems. The Mankiller wanted better trade for his town—specifically, a permanent, resident trader. Further, he wanted a steady supply of goods at cheaper prices than previously supplied. On investigating the matter, Demeré had found that a trader, Robert Gowdy, had been licensed to operate in Chatuga and Tellico. Yet Gowdy had abandoned his tradepost in order to sell goods at Ninety-Six, South Carolina, to men described by Demeré as disreputable. These merchants had paid higher prices for their goods from Gowdy, and so Gowdy took fewer articles to sell at Tellico and Chatuga. Once there, he charged the Indians even higher prices for the few goods he offered and would advance little or no credit.[80] Thus, one reason that the Tellico and Chatuga Indians were leaning toward the French was the lure of better trade agreements promised by the French. Because the trade items had been incorporated thoroughly into tribal life, poor supplies and high prices were creating the frustration associated with the British alliance. Tribes perceived that shoddy or scarce trade items were a sign that whatever European power was behind that particular trader held them in low esteem or was punishing them for some reason. Although traders were often rank opportunists as best and scoundrels at worst, the tribes perceived them as ambassadors of that culture. Rogue traders like Gowdy were a definite threat to Anglo-Cherokee relationships. To put it another way, the marketplace was causing problems that were affecting the Cherokees and their battlefield obligations.

Captain Demeré dispatched Lieutenant Robert Wall to Tellico in January 1757 to address the issue of trade in connection with recent Indian behavior. The Mankiller met with Wall, telling the British lieutenant that the Tellico Cherokees had considered themselves "children of King George" but had wondered lately whether he looked on them as his children. The reason for their doubt rested on the issue of trade. The Tellico people felt slighted because they never received free gifts as surrounding towns did, and they believed they had been abandoned by the British.[81]

Other trade irregularities began to surface with direct connection to the disaffection of some Overhills Cherokees during this time of war. Connecorte summoned Demeré for a meeting, at which the elderly Cherokee leader produced a price schedule with the signature of the former South Carolina governor, James Glen. The Overhills leader stated that the traders, like Gowdy, stationed among the Cherokees had no regard for the price schedule; they charged what they wanted despite government guidelines. Glen also had promised Hop that another trader would be sent to Chota, but the government had not made good on this promise. As a result, Hop told Demeré his people looked on the schedule as "nothing but lies as they did on all the rest of the papers that came from Carolina, and that Charles Town was a place where nothing but lies came from."[82] Questioning the local trader, John Elliott, Demeré found his prices for trade goods exorbitant, especially on the most commonly requested items such as clothing.[83] Demeré, like others before him, such as Ludovic Grant, warned Governor Lyttelton that if colonial government continued to ignore such irregularities, there always would be factionalism in the Indian country. Demeré stated that "the traders are for the most part a sett [*sic*] of villains who studdy [*sic*] nothing but their own narrow views . . . without having the least regard to justice."[84] Old Hop produced a sample of red paint used by them in body adornment, long a traditional practice. Sold by the trader John Elliott, it was found to contain lead.[85]

When men of low character operated among them in such a manner, they all but negated any diplomatic effort made by colonial government. Despite the intent of colonial policy formulated in London, Savannah, and Charles Town, it was the day-to-day behavior of traders like Gowdy and Elliott, actors on the periphery of empire, whose actions caused consequences that had to be dealt with in the imperial capitals like London and Paris. Historian Francois Furstenberg has dubbed this the "tail wagging the dog" effect of empire.[86]

During Demeré's meeting, Old Hop told him that his people had expected a supply of guns, powder, and bullets for a long time and that shipment had never arrived. Using the leverage of trade, he told Demeré that the French sent their Indians to war fully supplied with all war necessities and rewarded them handsomely for scalps once the Indians returned.[87] Thus, southeastern Indians learned to play competing European powers off each other to correct trade irregularities imposed either intentionally or unintentionally. The meaning of the message was clear: disaffection among the Cherokees was due, at least in part, to a failure of the British to live up to mutually agreed-on trade guidelines. If the British wished to maintain the Cherokees' loyalty, they would have to perform as well as the French. Obviously, playing off one power against the other could be done too often and for frivolous reasons. Until each side reached its financial limit, however, both would experience an upsurge in Indian expenditures, with Native Americans often gaining from the contest.

On the battlefield in 1757, 140 Cherokee warriors led by Wauhatchee traveled to Virginia to fight for Britain but found no presents awaiting them to formalize their service. In Cherokee culture, gifts from the giver to the recipient made the giver temporary family, entitled to ask things of the recipient, such as fighting on demand. British policymakers, especially Jeffery Amherst, came to see this gifting practice as a drain and a bribe and tried to discontinue the payment, especially because it did not guarantee full participation by a tribe or a successful ending to the mission. Cherokee leaders expected clothes and presents with which they could return to share with their wives and children. The Cherokees explained that the war party duty interfered with the hunting season that would provide deerskins to buy the needed items, and so the war party gifts were a necessary substitute.

Once larger numbers of Cherokees began to arrive in the North for battle duty, the British began their efforts at peacemaking between the Ani-yun-wiya (Cherokees) and the Haudenosaunee (Iroquois). These British-inspired attempts at intertribal peacemaking opened a dialogue among the tribes with the possibility of pan-Indian movements.[88] The northern superintendent of Indian Affairs, Sir William Johnson, had a deputy named George Croghan who took a Cherokee war party to meet a Mohawk sachem at Carlisle, Pennsylvania, in 1757. The Mohawk leader gave the Cherokees a large wampum belt and suggested the two tribes were together against the French. The Cherokees liked the words they heard and sent a small party of their own back to Six Nations Territory for extended talks. The Cherokees tried to gauge how the Haudenosaunee really felt about large numbers of Cherokees entering their territory. Out of respect and a sense of honor, the Cherokees told the Haudenosaunee leaders at Fort Johnson that they considered it only proper to discuss Cherokee plans with the Haudenosaunee rather than just sending a talk.[89] The diplomatic gesture was honorable and tactically sound by any standards.

As the Cherokees began diplomatic talks with another Indian nation, some British officials surely questioned whether the Cherokees were worth the payments in goods and gifts they demanded when arriving in the North. George Washington answered that question in letters to Virginia governor Robert Dinwiddie when he wrote in praise of the Cherokee allies. Washington spoke eloquently in November 1757 of the Cherokees going immediately from their long journey north to Virginia into battle for the benefit of the British war effort. He noted in his letter the arrival of a second group of Cherokees who did the same, this time stopping enemy forces from advancing into the territory that Washington's forces were holding. Washington told the governor that the new Cherokees all met with him after the battle requesting supplies and gifts, and he had none to give. He spoke of a Captain Gist on the scene, to whom Washington appealed for supplies and gifts for the Cherokees. Gist had none to give them as well and lacked even a translator through which to speak to the Cherokees.[90] If we may take Washington as a creditable source for estimating the value of the Cherokees, then failure to pay them was both a cultural and a tactical mistake.

Cherokee raiding parties also struck against the Ohio River Valley villages of France's native allies as well as attacks on Fort Duquesne itself. The Cherokees attacked the Shawnees and Delawares at least three times during the spring of 1757. A combined force of Cherokees and Virginians attacked and destroyed a Shawnee village while taking prisoners. In all of this, the Cherokees, like the British took their losses. The Lower Town leader Swallow Warrior was killed, and the Cherokees, in retaliation, killed their French prisoners, though they turned over a French officer to colonial authorities.[91]

With Cherokees deployed in the backcountry, Shawnee and Delaware raiding parties could not conduct raids without fear of a Cherokee reprisal. When the Cherokees captured a set of Delaware prisoners of war, those captives divulged the fact that the Delawares wanted peace with the British side. The Delawares also shared their belief that the French could not hold onto Duquesne without their Indian allies.

Diplomatic talks progressed between the Cherokees and the Haudenosaunee with a follow-up meeting in September 1757. Cherokee representatives told their northern counterparts they intended to make war against the French and their Indian allies. Northern superintendent Sir William Johnson urged the Haudenosaunee leaders to come up with a response to the Cherokee plan. After a few days of deliberation, an Oneida sachem invited the Cherokees to present their plan to the Haudenosaunee people at a spring assembly in 1758. Conochqueisa also asked the northern superintendent to add his name to the invitation to the Cherokees, wanting its added diplomatic weight to his message. Johnson authorized the Cherokees, who typically fell under the authority of Southern Superintendent Edmond Akin (served 1756–1761), to seek revenge for those Cherokees killed in battle while in the North.[92]

Back in Cherokee country as the year 1757 wore on, more evidence appeared linking British problems with the Tellico Cherokees to trader irregularities. In April, Demeré wrote to South Carolina's Governor Lyttelton with a new tale of trader intrigue: The Great Warrior of Chota had told him that John Elliott, the trader who had ill used the Tellico people, had incurred a debt to him and his people for horses and supplies. Elliott had promised them rum as payment, stating that he had a supply at the Lower Town of Keowee, and the Great Warrior had ordered eight kegs as payment. In truth, there was rum at Keowee. Lyttelton had ordered that it be confiscated there and not shipped into Cherokee lands. The treaty of Saludy that the Cherokees had signed with the former governor Glen had prohibited the shipment of rum into the backcountry. Though Demeré labored to explain this rule and the illegality of Elliott's behavior, the Great Warrior could not understand Demeré's failure to repay them. The Cherokee told Demeré that if the British refused to pay their debts, his people would do likewise. Demeré's refusal to comply seemed to lend credence to French talk of British duplicity in their dealings with Indians. Further, the Great Warrior intended to seize goods passing through Cherokee lands from Charles Town to recoup their losses.[93]

Demeré continued to receive intelligence reports linking problems with the southern Indians to trader activity. In April 1757, he also learned that some of the traders among the Creeks were selling trade items to French officers, who then supplied their Indian allies with the goods.[94] The French continued their recruiting activities among the Cherokees. During a meeting between the governor of New Orleans and a delegation of Cherokees and Shawnees, the governor told them again to initiate a war against the British, starting with one of their forts. He advised them to kill five hundred or six hundred British and clear them out of the backcountry so that the French might enter the Indian towns and properly supply them.[95]

By the summer of 1757, more disturbing intelligence reports from Cherokee country seemed to confirm that the Cherokees intended to comply with French requests. Daniel Pepper wrote to Demeré stating that two headmen from the Lower Creeks had warned him that the Cherokees intended to attack the newly built Fort Loudoun; the Cherokees had requested the aid of the Creeks in the plan, according to the report.[96] Rather than attack the British outposts, however, that same year some 230 warriors from the Lower Towns of Keowee and Estatoe answered Virginia colony's call once more and fought some thirty-five miles north of Fort Duquesne in the Pennsylvania backcountry. This time, the Cherokees fought the French and both killed and took prisoners, although it cost them the life of their leader, the Swallow.[97] To compound these difficulties, this military service was supposed to result in a gift of trade goods. However, these Cherokees did not find the goods they had been promised. They mentioned that they had been promised a trade fort in their country by Virginia as well as a trade alliance with Virginia strong enough to break the South Carolina monopoly. The Cherokee leaders spent part of their time visiting a series of Virginia forts in search of the promised trade goods but found none.[98] It is worth noting that Virginia's attempt to insert itself into the Carolina trade monopoly was creating an economic pressure for the Cherokees. From a British management standpoint, multiple actors involved in the Indian trade usually did not end well for British goals. From the Cherokee standpoint, this act indicates agency on the part of the Cherokees in their desire to leverage the trade system to their advantage by getting some healthy economic competition from Virginia.

Describing the Western Cherokees as pawns in a greater struggle between Britain and France over empire does not do justice to the Cherokees as a political entity with agency. They clearly made choices based on evidence presented and actions observed by their European allies and trade partners. However, the diplomatic tensions created by the trade war in the South are undeniable. The Cherokee-British alliance was based on two differing interpretations to begin with. If you were British, the Cherokees were subjects. If you were a Cherokee, the British were your allies and not your masters. Decentralized Cherokee leadership further compounded the problem, with each of the five regions (Lower, Middle, Out, Valley, and Overhills) having headmen. The British thought they had solved that problem by originally elevating Moytoy to the status of emperor, later followed by his son, but other voices also led the Cherokees. Finally, inserting the propaganda practiced by both the British and the French into the mix helped make the backcountry politically unstable. In August 1757, the British seemed to score a decisive victory, however, when the Overhills town of Chota raised a British flag during the annual Green Corn Ceremony. A small Catawba delegation was admitted to speak and gave a powerful talk pledging their support along with that of several other southern tribes, plus the Haudenosaunee. A British-inspired pan-Indian alliance had formed, it seemed, linking Onondaga with Chota and several points in between.[99]

Ostenaco returned home in August 1757 and continued his role as one of the more independent-minded leaders who avoided too close an alliance with any European power. That August, he was returning home from battle in service to the British in the Ohio River valley. Though he returned home with captured horses as prize and, apparently, a white indentured servant, he also brought complaints against the British allies who had not supplied him well in the battlefield. Despite his misgivings, he pledged to return to the battlefield soon. Several Cherokees did leave the Overhills heading north for battle, including Attakullakulla, a rising star among Overhills leaders who would soon supplant the second British-supported emperor, Ammonscossittee, son of Moytoy. The second British Cherokee emperor served until 1753, and the third, Moytoy of of the Overhills Town of Settico, did not begin until 1759. Around fifty Cherokees headed north, and the group returned in January 1758 with captives and scalps.[100]

In February 1758, the Lower Towns, like Keowee, near the South Carolina border, committed to the fight and entered dialogue with the Haudenosaunee on how they would recognize each other in battle avoiding confusion with French Indian allies. The Middle and Overhills settlements soon committed to fight. Warriors from these two towns originally intended to head directly to Fort Johnson but diverted to follow the command of a British army planning an attack. By late April 1758, just under six hundred Cherokees from some sixteen towns were in the field and others continued to travel northward. British Brigadier General John Forbes estimated that he had eight hundred Cherokees fighting in the war, and the Haudenosaunee Confederacy used that same number to account for Cherokee allies in the field.[101]

British military leaders and colonial officials continued to draw the Cherokees into their orbit and their war, and British efforts resulted in a new wave of Cherokees heading into the Ohio country. The colony of Virginia wanted Cherokee help once more to drive off the Shawnees, Indian allies of the French. Specifically, in April 1758, a delegation of Cherokees bound for Charles Town was intercepted by Virginian William Byrd II, assistant to the newly appointed superintendent of Indian Affairs for the Southern District, Edmond Atkin. The purpose of this action was revealed in a talk translated to the Cherokees by John Watts. Watts gave an explanation for Byrd's presence and what Lyttelton wanted them to do in his talk. The translated talk informed them that the Great King and his Great Warrior had resolved to make war against the French king. To that end, George II had ordered a large body of troops to march to the Ohio. Lyttelton stated that the great king wanted to have alongside these men "the brave and faithfull Cherokeees, who have always declared like good Friends and Brothers that our Enemies should be your Enemies."[102]

Governor Lyttelton stated that the king had sent William Byrd of Virginia to meet with them at Keowee and transport as many as would go to the Virginia frontier as possible. Lyttelton enticed Cunneshote (Standing Turkey) and the other leaders by stating, "I have authorized Lieutenant Colonel Howarth to promise that every warrior that shall march from Keowee with Colonel Byrd shall have from this Government before he goes from thence an handsome present in goods to fit you out for war."[103] Lyttelton closed by telling the Cherokee leadership, "Nothing you can do that will be more pleasing to your father, the Great King George, to me your elder brother and to all the good people of this province than that you should go in as great numbers as soon as possible to take up the hatchet upon this important service."[104]

This time some 180 Cherokees from the Overhills towns went to war in response to the combined request from Virginia and South Carolina officials. By the end of May 1758, around eight hundred Cherokees had traveled to Virginia and Pennsylvania colonies in seventeen separate groups. As the Cherokees reached staging grounds such as Virginia's Fort Loudoun, they saw few colonials ready to fight by comparison. The Cherokees fought other French-aligned Indians as well as the French. The Cherokees also tried to train colonial troops in Indian combat techniques. Yet the endless delays and waiting inherent in European-style warfare weighed heavy on native troops who were accustomed to direct strikes and quick conclusions. Such warriors hoped to return not only to see family but also to participate in the Green Corn ceremony of August and September as well as to hunt for their families in the fall.[105] In addition, such hunters were hunting to make payments on their previous year's debt to their local trader as well as feeding their families. Such debts had a way of magically increasing due to interest, which added to the strain of Cherokee-British relations and to mistrust. After all, collected skins did not increase in number as they waited to be traded. Yet debts owed the trader last year always increased if left unpaid.

Because Native American warfare often consisted of short, sudden attacks, scheduled after planting and before hunting season, the Cherokees began to become impatient. In their opinion, the British were slow in building outposts and supply houses along the route to attack the French fort. The job of supplying the Cherokees fell to Colonel William Byrd III, who was also slow to supply his Cherokee troops. Between Byrd and Brigadier General Forbes, the British failed in their obligation to feed and supply the Cherokees and did not use their military skill in a timely manner. From Forbes's perspective, he was failed by his own logistics chain and burdened with the task of supplying various groups of Cherokees scattered across the colonies. Forbes did not share George Washington's opinion on the value in native troops. In a letter to Virginia's Governor Dinwiddie, Washington wrote, "they are more serviceable than twice their number of white men. Their cunning and craft cannot be equaled. Indians are the only match for Indians." By contrast, Forbes had little but contempt for tribal soldiers, an attitude shared by his closest assistants.[106]

In addition to attitude, Forbes was hampered by his own failing health. He was ill with a serious stomach ailment whereby he was not eating or going to the bathroom. In late August 1758, he wrote a correspondent that he was in dire need of prunes for their laxative effect, or raisins, if prunes were not available.[107] His condition would soon prove fatal.

In May 1758, the current Moytoy of Settico led a band of warriors back out of the warzone headed home for Cherokee country. They were aggravated with their British allies over the loss of their horses and the failure of Forbes to replace them. On their return trip to Cherokee country, they stole about twenty horses from settlers in Halifax County, Virginia, including Henry Snow, John Hall, William Verdiman and his son William Junior, as well as Robert Jones and Richard Thomson. The Virginia residents obtained others to join them on a ride after the Cherokees hoping to recover their animals.[108]

The Virginians caught up to the Cherokees and entered their camps, making known their desire to recover their stolen animals. The settlers reported that the Cherokees became hostile and both sides exchanged gunfire, which killed John Hall and three Cherokees before the Verdiman party retreated and raised the alarm to others. A Virginia militia did follow, and the Cherokees in turn attacked and looted settlers' cabins near the Staunton River. Moytoy sent a runner to Chota to warn Old Hop of what had transpired and then led his troops into the Yadkin River settlements of North Carolina. On his return to Setticoe, he carried some nineteen scalps liberated from German immigrants living on the Yadkin River. The Cherokee need for justice in a balance of destruction and violence had been settled for Moytoy. Virginia militias who engaged other Cherokee troops took scalps in victory as well.[109] Even as these tragedies unfolded, new groups of Cherokee leaders and troops were waiting to come into the fray as promised.

Governor Dinwiddie had dispatched his assistant, George Turner, to wait on the Cherokees who would accompany Attakullakulla. The peace chief summoned Turner to a meeting at Fort Loudoun, though Turner was already impatient to lead them back north. When Turner acquiesced to the meeting, Attakullakulla informed him that their shaman had warned the group that it was a bad time for them to enter the war. He warned that only fatigue, sickness, and death awaited them. When Turner questioned the message, Attakullakulla asserted that the Cherokees were intent on following the will "of the Great Man above."[110] When Governor Dinwiddie learned of this latest setback, he sent word back to Attakullakulla that Cherokee war parties would not be bothered in Virginia and he would reimburse them for their property losses. He encouraged Cherokee headmen to visit him so that all differences could be resolved.[111] With those assurances, the next group of Cherokees under Attakullakulla departed.

In a September 1758 letter to Richard Peters, General Forbes noted the arrival of Attakullakulla with some sixty warriors. His next comments are a good gauge of what Forbes thought about his Native American allies. He judged the Overhills Cherokee leader to be "as consummate a dog as any of them; only seeing our distress has made him exceed all others in his most avaricious demands."[112] Begrudgingly, Forbes told his correspondent that, though he had foolishly spent thousands of pounds on the Cherokees, it was essentially too late to change policy with Attakullakulla now, and so he spent a few hundred pounds more.[113] General Forbes did not appear to be pleased with the Chain of Friendship at that juncture, but his displeasure indicates that Attakullakulla was exerting agency in asking for payment for military services that the British general would have preferred to receive for free. His correspondence speaks of injuries and death among his officers, and even of losses of horses and cattle, but is strangely silent on the condition of his Indian allies.

Forbes's army was not ready to move out until November 1758, and the delay moved the event into a time well within the hunting season for Cherokee men. In their own conflicts, the Cherokees would have concluded and been home by Green Corn ceremony to be set for hunting. The Cherokees abandoned the war effort, not because they wanted to harm the war effort but because extended delays were harming their own lives—no food for their families and no deerskins to pay their trader's credit bill from last year. The Cherokees began to return to Cherokee country early, after seeing the Tuscaroras go home first.[114] Ultimately, the British had exhausted the patience of the Cherokees, who waited for Forbes to assemble his army and for Byrd to provide supplies.[115] Forbes wrote of this situation in mid-November 1758 to Colonel Byrd, mincing no words in how he felt about the Cherokee departure. He spoke disparagingly of Attakullakulla and the Cherokees, who, in Forbes's view, had deserted the war effort after Forbes had given in to "every extravagant, avaricious demand that they made."[116] In fact, it was Forbes's rough treatment of Attakullakulla that made the Cherokees under him decide to leave. General Forbes could not stop the Cherokees from leaving the Pennsylvania backcountry before the final assault on Fort Duquesne, but, to his credit, Forbes supplied the departing warriors with their goods, though he called them scoundrels and blamed their greed for their disaffection from the war effort.[117] Though disgusted with the Cherokees, Forbes's army successfully attacked Fort Duquesne with greater numbers. French troops set fire to the fort before abandoning it. British troops found grim human remains of some of the Scottish troops captured by the French.[118]

Forbes ordered his subordinate to alert most of the outposts in Virginia and North Carolina along the probable Cherokee return route, particularly the commanders at Fort Cumberland and Fort Loudoun. He wanted them warned about the returning Cherokees entering the area armed, and he wanted the commander at Fort Cumberland to strip the Cherokees of their British guns, ammunition, and horses supplied to them for their missions.

He further conjectured that "they would commit all sort of outrage, so that it will be necessary to send a sufficient escort along with them."[119] Despite the orders, Attakullakulla and his party reached Cherokee country unmolested and without being detained. Though the joint mission with Britain was not ending well, it begs the question of what the Cherokee participation accomplished.

That contribution, as it turns out, was significant. Historian Paul Kelton believes that it was the Cherokee participation which drove the Shawnees, Delawares, and Mingos to the negotiating table at Easton, Pennsylvania, more so than French failures to outfit these tribes properly. Even General Forbes, who held low opinions of the Cherokees, spoke much about the power and fury of the Cherokees as leverage to get France's Indian allies to drop out of the war.[120] Before the departures began, some fifty-four Cherokees traveled to talk with the French-allied Indians to try to establish a peace, and they threatened their Indian counterparts that they would attack the towns of those who did not want peace. Some of these Cherokee peace delegates from the Lower Towns made a formal presentation to Pennsylvania governor William Denny that spoke of their recent peace treaty with the Haudenosaunee. The Cherokees also encouraged the Delawares to become their new brothers in peace.[121] When the northern Indian superintendent, Sir William Johnson, gave his final peace talk to France's Indian allies, he told them that their uncles the Cherokees wanted them to come away from the French at that time so they would not be harmed in Britain's war against France. Johnson told the Delawares that Britain held great affection and regard for their people.[122] In maternal societies, the uncle carried out a parental role for a child, and so Johnson's use of the term would have been meaningful. It also positioned the Cherokees as key figures in the negotiations.

Johnson sent a Moravian missionary, Christian Frederick Post, among the eastern Delawares to carry his talks to them. The Ohio River Valley tribes held a meeting with Post on September 1, 1758, in which they told him they had great reason to consider peace since the British sent so many soldiers and warriors into their lands. Ironically, this delegation also mentioned to him, "it is told us, that you [the British] and the French contrived this war, to waste the Indians between you; and that you and the French intended to divide the land between you."[123] The delegation's prophetic summation of the fate of Indian lands between the Appalachian Mountains and the Mississippi River would factor greatly in the coming British Proclamation Line. Ultimately, these French-allied Indians signed the Treaty of Easton, effectively dropping out of France's war with Britain.

Diplomatic gestures took place at the same time as the Cherokee warriors departed the battlefield. Cherokee troops engaged in livestock theft and home break-ins en route back to Cherokee country from summer to fall 1758 in Virginia's Halifax and Bedford counties. Estimates for the theft of horses ranged from a low of fourteen to a high of sixty horses. To the Cherokees, this was just compensation for both the lack of payment in trade goods by Forbes and wasting their time during hunting season.[124] To the Cherokee mind, these thefts restored the balance of unpaid war service and wasted time.[125] Backcountry settlers attacked and killed some of these Cherokees.[126]

In general, the Cherokees felt ill used by the Virginians before the raids, which may have prompted their actions coming home. The Virginia counties in which the Cherokees struck were settled by the Scots-Irish, who practiced their own form of retributive justice. When the remaining Cherokees in the field learned that the departing Cherokees had been killed by these settlers, they abandoned their mission in increasing numbers. George Washington observed their departure as a catastrophic event in writing to Major Francis Halkett in May 1758.[127] When Major Halkett responded to Washington, he wrote about the need for someone to go to the Cherokee homelands to repair the diplomatic damage done and hopefully to persuade the Cherokees to return to battle.[128]

From the colonial point of view, the Cherokees had not only not fulfilled their obligations as allies but also stolen livestock like common horse thieves. A group of Virginians had killed twenty-four of the Cherokee warriors and mutilated their bodies, which was an unthinkable act of their new British allies. The Raven of the Overhills town of Settico led one of these raiding parties of thirty men. Frontiersmen killed five of his warriors in retaliation and left their scalped bodies in the road to be seen by all. Those particular warriors had just finished a scouting mission with seven scalps and five prisoners; some of the Cherokees had been wounded in the mission for their colonial allies.[129] To many of the Cherokees who had waited for months to begin and complete hostilities, the slaughter of part of the Raven's group in the Halifax and Bedford counties of Virginia sealed the deal.

When he became aware of the killing, Virginia governor Robert Dinwiddie sent both apologies and presents to the Overhills town of Chota to resolve the diplomatic breach with the Cherokee war allies.[130] Soon after, South Carolina's Governor Lyttelton reached out to the Cherokees as well when he told that of his sorrow that some of their own had been killed. He charged them to remember that "the Chain of Friendship which the great King George has fixed, is unsullied and free from stain, but that it may always remain so."[131] The governor further reminded the leaders that when a white man killed a red man, it should not result in war between the two peoples. Rather, they were to appeal to the king's governor for satisfaction.[132]

Lyttelton told the Cherokee leaders that he had sent word to the Virginia governor for redress. For much of the letter Lyttelton appealed to reason and calm. He then offered a carrot by saying, "I do hereby promise to give presents to the relations of your people that have been slain, sufficient to hide the bones of the dead men and wipe away tears from the eyes of their friends."[133] The offer of goods was tied to a request that the Cherokees recall the war parties they had already sent out to Virginia. In closing, the South Carolina leader resorted to the threat of withholding trade from the Cherokees if they resorted to retributive justice to settle the matter of slain kin in Virginia. "The English are the only Nation that can furnish you," he wrote, "and are willing to continue to do it, if you do not prevent them by your own faults, but if you do, you will remember by words and repent your rashness when it is too late."[134]

Back among the Overhills Cherokees, Attakullakulla had recently distributed trade goods at South Carolina's Fort Loudoun as a part of a new recruiting effort. Yet most Cherokees were not interested in new war efforts in behalf of the British. Those who were interested were already in battle on the frontier or coming home from it.[135] By early August 1758, on the verge of Green Corn Ceremony time, the few remaining Cherokees finally abandoned the war effort. Only one group made it back to Cherokee country without experiencing violence or robbery at the hands of frontier whites. One group of Estatoe warriors lost six of their horses on the way home. Later on their way home, a force of some eighty frontier whites confronted them in Bedford County, Virginia, and ordered the Cherokees to disarm. The group eventually attacked the Estatoe warriors and killed three of them, resulting in a three-hour standoff. The survivors arrived in Estatoe on September 8, 1758.[136]

Similarly, wounded Cherokees began to arrive home in other towns. They bore wounds inflicted not by the French enemy or French-allied Indians such as the Shawnees. These injuries were sustained in conflicts with frontier whites in Virginia. Wounded warriors arrived in Quaratchee on September 15, 1758; two days later, the Lower Towns learned of a second attack on their people as they passed through Bedford County, Virginia. These deaths began to mobilize the Cherokees from the Lower, Middle, Overhills, and Valley towns in a way that had not happened before. The new sense of unity was not in favor of continued war alongside the British allies, but rather a sense of justice for the indignity, injury, and death experienced by the Cherokees at the hands of frontier whites while helping their British allies.[137] As Cherokee historian Tom Conley has noted, if a Muskogee Creek Indian killed a Cherokee, that victim's clan was entitled to kill the Creek perpetrator or a member of his clan.[138] This is the very nature of retributive justice and was often called the law of blood at the time. Thus, retaliatory raids against frontier whites by the Cherokees should have surprised no one accustomed to dealing with the tribes. However, few could have predicted the breadth of devastation that British armies would soon visit on Cherokee communities.

Notes

1. Francois Furstenberg, "The Significance of the Trans-Appalachian Frontier in Atlantic History," *American Historical Review* 113, no. 3 (June 2008), 660.
2. Ray, *Before the Volunteer State*, 36.
3. Ray, *Before the Volunteer States*, 36.
4. Ray, *Before the Volunteer State*, 36.
5. Furstenberg, *The Significance*, 657.
6. Mooney, *Myths of the Cherokee*, 35.
7. Articles of Friendship, Lords Commissioners for Trade and Plantations, CO 5, 4, Nos. 46, 46i, ii.
8. Articles, C.O. 5, 4, Nos. 46, 46i, ii.
9. Articles, C.O. 5, 4, Nos. 46, 46i, ii.
10. Articles, C.O. 5, 4, Nos. 46, 46i, ii.
11. Articles, C.O. 5, 4, Nos. 46, 46i, ii.
12. Articles, C.O. 5, 4, Nos. 46, 46i, ii.
13. Articles, C.O. 5, 4, Nos. 46, 46i, ii.
14. Articles, C.O. 5, 4, Nos. 46, 46i, ii.
15. Mooney, *Myths of the Cherokee*, 35–36.
16. Ray, *Before the Volunteer State*, 52–53.
17. Paul Kelton, *Cherokee Medicine, Colonial Germs: An Indigenous Nation's Fight against Smallpox, 1518–1824* (Norman: University of Oklahoma Press, 2015), 45–46.
18. Kelton, *Cherokee Medicine*, 51.
19. Kelton, *Cherokee Medicine*, 87.
20. Kelton, *Cherokee Medicine*, 88–89.
21. Kelton, *Cherokee Medicine*, 93.
22. Kelton, *Cherokee Medicine*, 85.
23. Kelton, *Cherokee Medicine*, 94.
24. Mooney, *Myths of the Cherokee*, 36.

25. Mooney, *Myths of the Cherokee*, 36.

26. Kelton, *Cherokee Medicine*, 97.

27. Mooney, *Myths of the Cherokee*, 36.

28. Emperor of the Cherokees to Governor Glen, October 10, 1744, CO5/371: 6.

29. Emperor of the Cherokees to Governor Glen, October 10, 1744, CO5/371: 6.

30. Glen to the Board of Trade, September 29, 1746, CO5/371: 104.

31. Articles of Friendship, C.O. 5, 4, Nos. 46, 46i, ii.

32. Glen to the Board of Trade, September 29, 1746, CO5/371: 104. A guinea, last issued in 1813, was worth 21 shillings. One hogshead by the mid-eighteenth century was equivalent to 52.5 imperial gallons. An imperial gallon was 20 percent more than a standard U.S. gallon. Thus, one hogshead contained the equivalent volume of sixty-three gallons.

33. Glen to Board of Trade, April 28, 1747, CO5/371: 133.

34. Glen to Board of Trade, July 26, 1748, CO5/372: 67.

35. Glen to Board of Trade, December 23, 1749, CO5/372: 168.

36. Kelton, *Cherokee Medicine*, 95.

37. Glen to Board of Trade, December 23, 1749, CO5/372: 168.

38. Gregory Evans Dowd, *A Spirited Resistance: The North American Indian Struggle for Unity, 1745–1815* (Baltimore: Johns Hopkins University Press, 1992), 24.

39. Brown, *Old Frontiers*, 53–54.

40. Paul Kelton, "The British and Indian War: Cherokee Power and the Fate of Empire in North America," *William and Mary Quarterly* 69, no. 4 (October 2012), 763.

41. Dowd, *A Spirited Resistance*, 25.

42. Dowd, *A Spirited Resistance*, 25.

43. Articles, C.O. 5, 4, Nos. 46, 46i, ii.

44. Articles, C.O. 5, 4, Nos. 46, 46i, ii.

45. Glen to Tacite of Hiawassie, Colane of Eurphorsee and King of the Valley, *Colonial Records of South Carolina: Documents Relating to Indian Affairs 1754–1765*, ed. William L. McDowell Jr. (Columbia: South Carolina Department of Archives and History, 1970), 26.

46. Kelton, "The British and Indian War," 766.

47. Ludovic Grant to Glen, March 27, 1755, Colonial Records of SC 1754–1765, 42–45.

48. Brown, *Old Frontiers*, 55.

49. Brown, *Old Frontiers*, 55.

50. Brown, *Old Frontiers*, 55.

51. Brown, *Old Frontiers*, 55.

52. Tortora, *Carolina in Crisis*, 43–44.

53. Brown, *Old Frontiers*, 56.

54. Brown, *Old Frontiers*, 57.
55. Conley, *The Cherokee Nation*, 46.
56. Conley, *The Cherokee Nation*, 46.
57. Conley, *The Cherokee Nation*, 46–47.
58. Brown, *Old Frontiers*, 58.
59. Kelton, "The British and Indian War," 769.
60. Brown, *Old Frontiers*, 57–58.
61. Lachlan McGillivray to Glen, May 13, 1755, Colonial Records of SC 1754–1765, 72–73.
62. Demeré to Lyttelton, October 13, 1756, Colonial Records of SC 1754–1765, 214. Ammonscossittee, a younger leader of the Overhills Cherokees resided at Tellico, though Connecorte, known to the British as Old Hop, considered himself the more fitting leader of the nation and his Overhills town, Chota one of the Mother towns, the more proper seat of power. Politically and economically, a rivalry of sorts existed between the towns of Tellico and Chota. See E. Raymond Evans, "Notable Persons in Cherokee History: Ostenaco," *Journal of Cherokee Studies* I, no. 1 (Summer 1976): 42.
63. Kelton, "The British and Indian War," 767.
64. Demeré to Old Hop and the Little Carpenter, October 3, 1756, Colonial Records of SC 1754–1765, 222. Like Attakullakulla, Old Hop had an English name and his own Cherokee name, Connecorte. Colonials called him Old Hop because of his lameness.
65. Colonial Records of SC 1754–1765, 222–223.
66. Old Hop's Reply to Captain Demeré, October 3, 1756, Colonial Records of SC 1754–1765, 223–224.
67. Old Warrior to Demeré, November 9, 1756, Colonial Records of SC 1754–1765, 244–245. Chatuga was located on the Tellico River, near Tellico, in modern Monroe County, Tennessee. Hiwassee was located on the Hiwassee River at Savannah Ford in modern Polk County, Tennessee. See Goodwin, *Cherokees in Transition*, 153–156.
68. Kelton, "The British and Indian War," 767.
69. Demeré to Lyttelton, November 18, 1756, Colonial Records of SC 1754–1765, 249.
70. Judd's Friend, known otherwise as Ostenaco, was a Cherokee leader noted for both diplomatic and military accomplishments. He most likely was born in the town of Hiwassee. In addition to his given name, he earned the right to be called "Mankiller" for his military prowess. He was called Judd's Friend because of his close association with a Euroamerican named Judd. Often based at Chota, Ostenaco used his diplomatic skills for many years to maintain amicable relations between the Overhills Cherokees and the government of colonial South Carolina. See Evans, "Notable Persons," 41–53.

Possibly more than other Cherokees, the Mankiller of Tellico was firmly identified by the English translation of the great war title Outacite, at least in colonial records. Born in the town of Tellico, this Cherokee leader did try to establish an alliance between the French at Fort Toulouse (Alabama Fort) and the Tellico Cherokees. Though close scrutiny indicates this alliance was possible because British traders so badly mismanaged the trade with Tellico, the South Carolina government came to view the Mankiller as an unreliable mercenary. See Fred Gearing, "Priests and Warriors: Social Structure for Cherokee Politics in the 18th Century," *American Anthropologist* 64, no. 5, part 2 (October 1962), 64.

71. Evans, "Notable Persons: Ostenaco," 42.

72. Evans, "Notable Persons: Ostenaco," 44–45.

73. Intelligence from Judge's Friend [Ostenaco] to Captain Raymond Demeré, December 10, 1756, Colonial Records of SC 1754–1765, 265. In *Empire of Fortune: Crowns, Colonies, and Tribes in the Seven Years War in America*, Francis Jennings noted that British soldiers at Fort Pitt deliberately infected enemy Indians with smallpox in 1763 (see 200).

74. Colonial Records of SC 1754–1765, 265–266.

75. Intelligence from Indian Nancy to Captain Raymond Demeré, December 12, 1756, Colonial Records of SC 1754–1765, 269.

76. Intelligence from Nancy Butler to Captain Raymond Demeré, December 20, 1756, Colonial Records of SC 1754–1765, 276.

77. Talk of the Blind Slave Catcher of Chatuga, January 2, 1757, Colonial Records of SC 1754–1765, 305–306.

78. Known alternately as the Alabama Fort and Fort Toulouse, the French enclave was lcoated just north of the modern Alabama capital of Montgomery.

79. Demeré to Governor Lyttelton, January 4, 1757, Colonial Records of SC 1754–1765, 306–307. Thomas Leaper and James Kelly were two packhorse traders who worked out of Tellico. See David C. Corkran, *The Cherokee Frontier: Conflict and Survival: 1740–1762* (Norman: University of Oklahoma Press, 1962), 104.

80. Demeré to Governor Lyttelton, January 15, 1757, Colonial Records of SC 1754–1765 315. Unfortunately for researchers, some of the Indian traders of the late colonial period are mentioned briefly or indirectly, and little other information is available on them.

81. Report of Lieutenant Robert Wall to Captain Raymond Demeré, January 13, 1757, Colonial Records of SC 1754–1765, 321–322.

82. Demeré to Governor Lyttelton, February 5, 1757, Colonial Records of SC 1754–1765, 333–334.

83. Colonial Records of SC 1754–1765, 333–334. Elliot's other questionable trade practices included the use of a shortened yardstick for measuring and a rigged scale that consistently measured two pounds less than actual weight.

84. Colonial Records of SC 1754–1765, 334.

85. Colonial Records of SC 1754–1765, 334. Lead poisoning occurs when the substance is ingested or absorbed through the skin, resulting in anemia, constipation, colic, paralysis, or muscular cramps.

86. Furstenberg, *The Significance*, 653.

87. Colonial Records of SC 1754–1765, 335.
88. Dowd, *A Spirited Resistance*, 26.
89. Kelton, "The British and Indian War," 767.
90. George Washington to Robert Dinwiddie, November 5, 1757, http://founders.archives.gov/documents/Washington/02-05-0028.
91. Kelton, "The British and Indian War," 770.
92. Kelton, "The British and Indian War," 773.
93. Demeré to Lyttelton, April 2, 1757, Colonial Records of SC 1754–1765, 360. Keowee was located on the Keowee River, adjacent to Fort Prince George in modern Pickens County, South Carolina. See Goodwin, *Cherokees in Transition*, 154.
94. Demeré to Lyttelton, April 11, 1757, Colonial Records of SC 1754–1765, 366.
95. Abstract of a Talk Between the Governor of New Orleans and the Cherokee and Shawnee Indians, n.d., Colonial Records of SC 1754–1765, 369.
96. Daniel Pepper to Demeré, June 27, 1757, Colonial Records of SC 1754–1765, 390. Pepper is again one of those figures whose name surfaces in connection with the Indian trade but who is hard to identify further against the backdrop of Anglo-Indian conflicts in the 1750s.
97. Tortora, *Carolina in Crisis*, 44.
98. Tortora, *Carolina in Crisis*, 43–44.
99. Kelton, "The British and Indian War," 773.
100. Kelton, "The British and Indian War," 773.
101. Kelton, "The British and Indian War," 775.
102. Governor Lyttelton to Old Hop and the Cherokee Head Men and Warriours, n.d., n.p, Colonial Records of SC 1754–1765, 478–479.
103. Governor Lyttelton to Old Hop and the Cherokee Head Men and Warriours, n.d., n.p, Colonial Records of SC 1754–1765, 478–479.
104. Governor Lyttelton to Old Hop and the Cherokee Head Men and Warriours, n.d., n.p, Colonial Records of SC 1754–1765, 478–479.
105. Tortora, *Carolina in Crisis*, 45–47.
106. Brown, *Old Frontiers*, 81.
107. General John Forbes to Richard Peters, August 28, 1758, *The Pennsylvania Magazine of History and Biography* 33, no. 1 (1909), 87.
108. Brown, *Old Frontiers*, 83–84.
109. Brown, *Old Frontiers*, 84–85.
110. Brown, *Old Frontiers*, 86–87.
111. Brown, *Old Frontiers*, 88.
112. Forbes to Peters, September 16, 1758, *The Pennsylvania Magazine*, 93.
113. Forbes to Peters, September 16, 1758, *The Pennsylvania Magazine*, 93.
114. Conley, *The Cherokee Nation*, 46–47.
115. Kelton, "The British and Indian War," 776.

116. General Forbes to Colonel Byrd, November 19, 1758, *The Pennsylvania Magazine*, 95.
117. Tortora, *Carolina in Crisis*, 52.
118. Brown, *Old Frontiers*, 89.
119. General Forbes to Colonel Byrd, November 19, 1758, *The Pennsylvania Magazine*, 96.
120. Kelton, "The British and Indian War," 779.
121. Kelton, "The British and Indian War," 780.
122. Kelton, "The British and Indian War," 781–782.
123. Kelton, "The British and Indian War," 783.
124. Tortora, *Carolina in Crisis*, 48–49.
125. Conley, *The Cherokee Nation*, 51.
126. Evans, "Notable Persons: Ostenaco," 45.
127. George Washington to Francis Halkett, May 11, 1758, *Founders Online*, National Archives, http://founders.archives.gov/documents/Washington/02-05-02-0133. [Original Source: *The Papers of George Washington*, Colonial Series, vol. 5, *5 October 1757–3 September 1758*, ed. W. W. Abbot (Charlottesville: University Press of Virginia, 1988), 175–177.]
128. "To George Washington from Francis Halkett, June 25, 1758," *Founders Online*.
129. Tortora, *Carolina in Crisis*, 49.
130. Conley, *The Cherokee Nation*, 46.
131. Governor Lyttelton to the Lower and Middle Cherokee Headmen and Warriors, September 26, 1758, Charles Town, South Carolina, Colonial Records of SC 1754–1765, 481.
132. Governor Lyttelton to the Lower and Middle Cherokee Headmen and Warriors, September 26, 1758, Charles Town, South Carolina, Colonial Records of SC 1754–1765, 481.
133. Governor Lyttelton to the Lower and Middle Cherokee Headmen and Warriors, September 26, 1758, Charles Town, South Carolina, Colonial Records of SC 1754–1765, 481.
134. Governor Lyttelton to the Lower and Middle Cherokee Headmen and Warriors, September 26, 1758, Charles Town, South Carolina, Colonial Records of SC 1754–1765, 481.
135. Tortora, *Carolina in Crisis*, 50–51.
136. Tortora, *Carolina in Crisis*, 54–55.
137. Tortora, *Carolina in Crisis*, 54–55.
138. Conley, *The Cherokee Nation*, 51.

Cherokee Diplomacy after Easton
A Coming Storm

2

I N THIS SAME SEASON OF FATEFUL DEEDS, the war in the North—at least for French-aligned Indians—was winding down. British officials met with over five hundred tribal leaders at Easton, Pennsylvania, on October 7, 1758, with negotiations lasting the next nineteen days. Signatories concluded the document on October 26, 1758. Though not present at the signing with the Mohawks, Senecas, Oneidas, Onondagas, Tuscaroras, and Cayugas, a small group of Cherokees caught up with Christian Post and Delaware and Six Nations representatives shortly afterward. They wished to smoke a peace pipe. The Delaware representative responded positively to the gesture and left with the understanding that the Cherokees were no longer his enemies.[1] Historian Paul Kelton credits the Cherokees in general and the rising leader, Attakullakulla, as the reason the Shawnees, Delawares, and Mingos abandoned their French allies, which all but secured a French loss in the conflict.[2]

Far from the diplomacy of Easton, news of the atrocities committed against returning Cherokees was beginning to filter through the Cherokee towns. This newfound antipathy against the British was not wasted on a few French agents. Such men had influence among the Overhills Cherokees in towns like Settico and tried to use them artfully against the British during the still ongoing French and Indian War.[3] A well-known Creek leader, the Mortar, visited Chota in early 1759 and shamed the Cherokees for being allies of the British rather than fighting them.[4]

It had been some of the pro-French Cherokees under the Moytoy who had carried out attacks on the frontiers of Virginia, North Carolina, and South Carolina in 1758 and 1759. They killed nineteen whites alone on the Yadkin and Catawba Rivers. In response, the South Carolina governor immediately cut off trade in weapons and ammunition to all Cherokees.[5] Pro-British Cherokee leader Attakullakulla quickly sent requests for forgiveness and peace to the governors of the affected colonies.[6] He then appeared before the expedition commander, Brigadier General John Forbes, the man who had called him little more than a consummate dog. Attakullakulla also met with Lieutenant Governor Francis Fauquier of Virginia and South Carolina's Governor Lyttelton. Relations with the Cherokees were so shaky that colonial officials decided not to press the matter further.[7] While still in Virginia, Attakullakulla sent word back to Connecorte (Old Hop) in the Overhills town of Chota that he had cleared up the trouble with the Virginia governor and that "the path is now clearer than ever, & that he was going to see his elder brother in Charles Town [Governor Lyttelton], & would soon return, & everything should be easy & quiet & no more bad talks going amongst them."[8]

Despite Attakullakulla's good words, troubles would continue in Cherokee country. In April 1759, Lieutenant Richard Coytmore assumed command of Fort Prince George, succeeding Lachlan McIntosh. McIntosh was well liked by the Cherokees, but Coytmore's relationship with them would be problematic until the end. Not long after assuming command, he celebrated with a drinking bout with an Ensign Bell under his command. In a drunken state, the two men made their way into a Cherokee woman's home while her husband was away fighting for the British and abused her. Days later, Coytmore and Bell repeated the offense on another Cherokee woman's home.[9] As historian William Ramsey noted in his 2008 work titled *The Yamassee War*, that conflict from forty years earlier was preceded by trader abuse of native women.[10] Tribes often interpreted outsider treatment of native women as a bellwether of what those people felt toward the entire tribe.

Further contributing to cultural stress were the efforts of a Frenchman named Louis Lantagnac. He had been taken prisoner by the Chickasaws when he thirteen years old and ransomed to the English at Charles Town for trade goods. As an adult, he was licensed by the English to trade with the Cherokees and married one of their women, with whom he had a child. Those acts gave a non-Indian as much political currency among the tribes as was possible. Now, in the early months of 1759, he came among the Cherokees trying to recruit them for service in the name of France since the tribe had suffered multiple bad experiences with the British of late.

His rousing talk elicited the desired response from Saloue of Estatoe, later followed by Wauhatchie, leader of three lower towns. Lantagnac inspired the formation of war parties from the lower towns, who were directed by their leaders to attack the same Virginia frontier communities where the violence first began. Instead, the warriors attacked frontier settlements on the Carolina frontier. Governor Lyttelton received a report on these events marking the deaths of twenty-two settlers with two scalped but surviving victims.[11]

In mid-May 1759, Fort Loudoun commander Paul Demeré wrote William Henry Lyttelton with an update on the situation. He mentioned the fact that Attakullakulla had sent his people a message to remain "easy and quiet until he came home, & that he had made everything up in Virginia."[12] However, Cherokee warriors were not remaining easy and quiet. In the same letter, Demeré told the governor that three parties of warriors left Settico for the Virginia frontier intent on revenge and returned with three scalps. The Moytoy of Settico, third of the British-proclaimed Cherokee emperors, led his own retaliatory gang, which returned with twelve scalps. Demeré sent word that he wanted to speak about these matters with the Moytoy, Connecorte (Old Hop), and his nephew Cunneshote (Standing Turkey). When they appeared at the fort, Demeré engaged them in conversation to reveal that the Settico people had committed these raids on the pretext of going to their hunting grounds. Their people did this because they believed the Virginians were at fault for the prior Bedford County attacks on Cherokees returning from the French and Indian War. The Cherokee leaders asked for Demeré to wait until the return of pro-British Attakullakulla from Charles Town before addressing the Settico people about these crimes.[13]

In early June 1759, Paul Demeré wrote Governor Lyttelton reporting Attakullakulla's return to his fort. Demeré mentioned that the Cherokee leader apologized for his people's entertainment of so many anti-British talks delivered in his absence, and he stated that he had given pro-British talks among his people as he made his way back to the Overhills country. With the return of Attakullakulla, Demeré went ahead with his planned meeting about Cherokee attacks on the backcountry with a group he assembled at the fort. In a public forum, Demeré confronted Connecorte about the talks given against the British, which Old Hop denied. Further, Demeré mentioned that the pro-French Muskogee Creek chief, the Mortar, had been warmly received at Chota and allowed to speak.[14]

In such perilous times, the older Cherokee leader, Connecorte, was losing his currency with British officials like Demeré. Propelled either by opportunity alone or by fear of where Old Hop's actions might lead, Attakullakulla was trying to eclipse the older leader with the British.

Ironically, Demeré wrote Governor Lyttelton that, in his opinion, neither of the two leaders would be able to resolve the current Cherokee dilemma of the murders on the frontier.[15] Finally, Demeré used the open forum to warn the Cherokees against allowing the creation of a new French settlement of which the commander had heard rumors. He couched the warning in terms that would resonate with the Overhills Cherokees—he told them that the establishment of a French settlement nearby would endanger the trade path between Forts Loudoun and Keowee. Demeré even planned to appeal to Attakullakulla to send a reconnaissance party. Attakullakulla agreed and promised to attack the French Creek allies if found there. Of course, the Cherokees did not fail to mention that they would need to be supplied with ammunition for such a venture.[16]

In August 1759, Paul Demeré of Fort Loudoun wrote the South Carolina governor about the trade embargo's effects. He started by saying that Fort Prince George Commander Coytmore had stopped sending trade goods up, particularly ammunition for hunting to the Overhills towns near him such as Chota, Tellico and near nearby Chatuga. He had done so because the Cherokees near his own fort were giving "bad talks" and bringing in scalps of frontier settlers every day, as he put it. He feared things might be the same for his counterpart at Fort Loudoun and stopped the trade, a fairly routine reaction on the part of the British to any violence in Indian country.[17] Demeré noted that a Cherokee man named Corn Tassel, whom he considered a friend, had come to speak with him about the trade embargo and wanted to know who had initiated it—the South Carolina governor, the Great Warrior of Fort Prince George, or Demeré himself. Demeré explained the trade stoppage without identifying who had initiated it, focusing on the fact that it was done because the Lower Towns were misbehaving. Corn Tassel told him that the Overhills men were planning to hunt after concluding the Green Corn Ceremonies. He promised to relay the explanation to the other Cherokee hunters that night.[18]

Demeré also reported to the governor that another Cherokee man named Great Warrior (Oconostota) had visited him. The Great Warrior reminded Demeré that the commander had asked him to stay in his community and try to quell bad talks, which the man had done for Demeré. Like Corn Tassel, he asked the Fort Loudoun commander which leader had stopped the trade, and Demeré repeated the explanation of why the trade had been stopped instead. The Great Warrior then relayed that he had heard that Attakullakulla had gone to the Alabama fort to make peace with the French; when he returned, the Cherokees would go to war against the British. After relaying the rumor, the Cherokee man admitted that there were many rogues in the Lower Towns, but he did not believe there were so many among the Overhills. The Great Warrior reiterated his commitment to keeping the peace with the British, and then he made a rather bold move. He told Demeré that he had been sent by the people of Chota and other towns to request that Demeré give orders for their hunting ammunition to be brought over. He told Demeré, "these last two winters I have been at warr [sic], and my people are almost naked, I therefore intend to go a hunting, a little while after the Green Corn-Dance that they may be cloathed."[19] While he did not mention it, the Cherokee man probably owed his trader for last year's debt on top of the clothes he needed to get for his family. Demeré ended his report with his own request for supplies from the governor—bags of flour for the soldiers and trade items such as knives, white shirts, and flints for the Cherokees.[20]

In late September 1759, Fort Prince George Commander Richard Coytmore wrote Governor Lyttelton about the state of affairs at his own fort. He told the governor that events in the South Carolina backcountry had reached a crisis stage and mentioned somewhat prophetically that he felt time until consequences was short. He also told the governor that the Cherokees had intercepted the fort's first messenger to Charles Town but that he made another attempt with a man named Charles Lamore. He further relayed that a Cherokee delegation composed of the Great Warrior and the independent chief, Ostenaco, also known as Judd's Friend, had arrived with a letter from Captain Stuart at Fort Loudoun. Coytmore told the governor that the Cherokee traders had sought refuge with him at the fort, save one man, presumed dead during the building crisis. Coytmore closed his letter saying, "I have no more to add but assure your excellency that affairs here are blacker than my pen is able to paint them but we are no ways apprehensive."[21]

Despite diplomatic attempts to negotiate the frontier violence, the new South Carolina governor declared war on the Cherokees a few days after Coytmore's letter in October 1759 and sent militia troops against them.[22] In 1757 and 1758, the Cherokee people had helped the British to strike a mortal blow against France's Indian alliances in the Ohio River Valley. Now the recent Anglo-Cherokee cooperation was washed away, in large part because a general who needed prunes could not supply the Cherokees when they were in war service to Britain.

In a letter to General Jeffrey Amherst, Commander-in-Chief of British Forces North America, Lyttelton recapped the situation for Amherst. Lyttelton haughtily admitted that it was he, with the backing of the South Carolina Assembly, who had decided that the Cherokees must put to death twenty-four of their own people as compensation for Cherokee murders on the South Carolina frontier or turn over to him twenty-four Cherokees "to be disposed of, as I should think fit."[23] This situation, combined with the rumors about an upcoming attack on Fort Loudoun, prompted Governor Lyttelton to dispatch reinforcements to Fort Loudoun and to order replacements for its dwindling food supplies. The colonial governor also initiated an embargo on trade goods, including arms and ammunition, against all of the Cherokee people. The cessation of trade was so drastic that the Cherokees sent a small delegation, led by Oconostota, to reason with Lyttelton. In early October 1759, Ostenaco and Oconostota set out with a group of the most esteemed among the Cherokee leadership. When the group reached the Lower Town of Keowee, the leaders decided that Ostenaco should return and help keep the peace among the Overhills communities.[24]

In November 1759, Attakullakulla sent a translated talk directly to Governor Lyttelton expressing his fealty to the governor and to the British people. He opened the letter by telling Lyttelton that he had just completed meetings with the head men of Chota. He confirmed that he was one of the original leaders who had wanted the forts and British soldiers among his people in the first place. The Cherokee leader acknowledged the soldiers were there to defend his people, and he pledged that he would defend the soldiers. He told Lyttelton it was his desire that "the fire would forever burn clear between us."[25] Trade always found its way into Attakullakulla's talks, and, of it, he noted that it had always been his mission to obtain supplies of necessary trade goods for his people and to see that the South Carolina governor had no complaints against his people. He hoped to be invited down to Charles Town soon, where he would give Lyttelton back the same beads that the governor had once given him. Attakullakulla's expressions of loyalty were strong. "My thoughts are constantly bent on going to war against his [the governor] and our enemies and any talk to my people is that they behave so to keep things straight and good, I hope to near nothing but good talk."[26] He went further to tell the governor that Willanawaw, the Warrior of the Overhills town of Toqua, felt the same way as himself. "We look upon Fort Loudoun as the place we are to receive our orders and be fitted out to war, and we esteem the garrison as our brothers."[27] He mentioned that both he and his counterpart from Toqua had always wanted the path to Charles Town to remain clear. Attakullakulla further mentioned that he would always remember the orders sent over by the great King George.[28] Recent events had strained Anglo-Cherokee relations, to be sure, but Attakullakulla mentioned the

Articles of Friendship with reverence. That 1730 document was made between the British and the original Moytoy, but Attakullakulla was leveraging himself as the leader of this new age with its new challenges that seemed to be threatening the alliance.

In late November 1759, Paul Demeré sent a rather routine letter from Fort Loudoun to Governor Lyttelton. In it he reported reading the governor's comments to Attakullakulla. He noted that the Indian leader seemed pleased to learn the governor had taken away the black beads from a string of white beads, symbolizing a white path of peace between the Overhills towns and Charles Town. The Cherokee leader was disappointed at first to learn that Lyttelton was not sending for him right away, as he had hoped, but rather would send for him to come to Keowee when the governor traveled there. Demeré mentioned in his letter that Charles McCunningham, his translator at Fort Loudoun, would not come when called. Otherwise, Demeré had little to report except that a Settico man called the Smallpox Conjurer had been conjuring daily and threatened to bring the young hunters in an attack against the fort. Demeré did not seem to take it seriously, instead sending a message to the Settico man to stop his foolish talks or he would regret it.[29]

In December 1759, Governor Lyttelton advised his council that he was planning to lead an army to force the Cherokees, through violence, into a lasting peace. The council agreed to the governor's plan, authorizing an army of 1,500 men under Colonels Rivers, Pawley, Beal, Hayward, and Byrne.[30]

Oconostota and his group of fifty-five delegates arrived in Charles Town in December 1759. Governor Lyttelton's council advised him not to offer the Cherokee dignitaries their customary honors and comforts, though the delegates were assured of their safe passage while in the low country. After performing preliminary ceremonies with the Cherokees, Oconostota spoke to the governor in council.[31]

Oconostota told the Carolina officers of government that he had been sent by Old Hop, his governor. He admitted that he had begun the atrocities on the frontier, but, as a warrior, he wanted no conflicts with the English. After extolling some elegant words, he laid deerskins at the governor's feet and mentioned that young men, acting more like boys, had committed grave errors on both sides of the frontier. He referenced King George II, saying that he knew the great king across the water wanted good relations between both sets of people. Oconostota concluded his attempt at healing the breach, giving Lyttelton the chance to respond.[32]

Governor Lyttelton replied that he allowed Oconostota to place the furs but that he did not accept them in token for the acts committed against white settlers in the backcountry. He asked the Cherokee leader whether he spoke for the Cherokee nation as a whole, and Oconostota replied that he did, though other chiefs of Keowee, Estatoe, and Hiwassee wanted to speak. Tiftowe of Keowee in particular spoke of Lieutenant Coytmore's molestation of Cherokee women in his town.[33]

The governor and his advisors dismissed the chiefs and began to deliberate on their words. Lyttelton in particular pushed the point that Oconostota did not speak for the nation as a whole and only wanted ammunition and supplies out of the visit since there was currently a trade embargo in place. He wanted council permission to start military actions against the Cherokees while holding the peace delegates hostage until the Cherokees surrendered those who had murdered white settlers in the backcountry. As both the Cherokees and the Carolinians considered ambassadors to travel under a protected status, the idea was controversial at best. When the council voted, they returned a tie vote of four in favor and four against, leaving the governor to cast the tie-breaking vote that would change Anglo-Cherokee relations and weaken the old chain of friendship.[34]

The next day Governor Lyttelton rejected the peace overtures, particularly telling Oconostota he did not represent the whole of the nation. The governor informed them they would be traveling under guard of the army. He blamed the armed escort on the mischief done by the Cherokees in the backcountry, stating that the army was the only way he could guarantee the peace delegates' safety.[35]

When Oconostota rose to give response, he was denied the right to drive home the point about British displeasure with their Cherokee allies, but it also illustrated the lack of equality between the two allies. Lyttelton then sent for Attakullakulla, the new preferred diplomat. By shutting down the spokesperson for Old Hop and choosing to dialogue with Attakullakulla, Lyttelton was showing his preference of the leaders among the Cherokee triumvirate.[36]

Though firmly planted within the British orbit, even Attakullakulla was horrified by the decision. Attakullakulla did persuade Lyttelton to release Oconostota, Tiftowe, Ostenaco, Saloue, and two other Cherokees.[37] The Cherokee diplomat claimed this act on the part of British authority would help him build consensus among the Cherokees to accept the temporary detention of their peace delegates at Fort Loudoun. Attakullakulla did turn in two Cherokee men who had committed violent acts in the backcountry, including one man whose wife had been molested by Coytmore.[38] Oconostota concealed his outrage, for a time, at his temporary imprisonment and for the hateful demand of the surrender of twenty-two Cherokees to meet certain death.[39] The trip from Charles Town to Fort Prince George under armed escort most surely was a tense one.

Enroute Lyttelton dispatched a messenger with the trader John Elliott to reassure the Cherokees that the measures of the armed escort were for the party's safety in the unsettled backcountry. Unfortunately, the messenger, at Oconostota's suggestion, told the Cherokees enroute that the delegation were indeed slaves and their colonial escorts planned to destroy their homes and enslave their women and children.[40] Jeffery Amherst's follow-up response to the South Carolina governor's letter echoed a common sentiment among British commanders stationed in North America. He wrote, "from the little experience I have of Indians I find the only way to deal with them is to reward or punish them according to their deserts, this maxim I have laid down to myself, I let them know it and I keep to my resolution."[41]

In December 1759, Captain John Stuart wrote Governor Lyttelton from Fort Loudoun, noting a major shift in the power dynamics among the Overhills Cherokees. In his letter, Stuart told the governor of a long-standing jealousy between Connecorte (Old Hop) and Attakullakulla (Little Carpenter) for leadership among the Overhills. Stuart reported that the conflict had finally reached an open breach, with Connecorte calling a public forum at the Chota Town house, where he told the people that Attakullakulla was an enemy of the Cherokee people and "a servile dependent upon the English."[42] Connecorte stated that Attakullakulla constantly thwarted his own efforts to make peace with the French. The elder statesman also disparaged the Little Carpenter's abilities as a warrior. Stuart further relayed that, in response, an angry Attakullakulla had told the Cherokee people to turn against Old Hop and that he, Attakullakulla, would now be their Beloved Man. Stuart closed his letter by telling the governor to expect a visit from Attakullakulla, wanting to be confirmed by South Carolina in the role of Beloved Man.[43] The practice of Europeans elevating native peoples to positions of prominence, such as what Attakullakulla desired, was not a new phenomenon. However, it was a destabilizing influence on Cherokee traditional society, as it often pitted the British-picked leader against one who had risen through the ranks by Cherokee methods.

A few days after his first letter to Governor Lyttelton, Stuart followed up with a letter that Attakullakulla carried to Charles Town for

Stuart himself. In it, the British Indian superintendent gave the governor a heads-up that the Cherokee leader who carried his letter already knew the governor's plan to demand that the Cherokees turn over those among them who had committed murders of settlers on retaliatory raids. Stuart told the governor that the Attakullakulla was prepared to fulfill the demand after a perfunctory show of resistance to it at first. Stuart suggested that the resistance was more of a show for the benefit of the Cherokee people by a leader hoping to replace Connecorte (Old Hop). After making the political gesture, Stuart predicted, Attakullakulla would then fall in line with what the governor wanted. Stuart further noted that Attakullakulla had not consulted with Connecorte, nor did he intend to carry any talk by him. Stuart closed the brief letter saying only that Attakullakulla desired to carry out the governor's orders.[44] Attakullakulla may have been exercising agency over Cherokee affairs in the face of a very powerful British official like Stuart, courting his support as new leader of the Overhills while planning a different strategy than the one of which Stuart was aware.

In mid-December, Fort Loudoun Commander Paul Demeré wrote Governor Lyttelton with an update on the situation at the Overhills fort. He told the governor of a recent letter from Coytmore at Fort Prince George relaying Lyttelton's orders that Attakullakulla and other head men should come down to the Lower town of "Keowee . . . to make things straight."[45] The fort commander then sent for Connecorte (Old Hop) to come down to his fort from Chota to help settle the conflict with the Cherokees. In response, the elder statesman sent word that he was unable to travel due to the cold weather and because he was, at the time, serving as a caregiver for a small child. Coytmore then sent word to Old Hop through the Warrior of Tennessee and his nephew. In the message of rebuke, Coytmore told the two Cherokees to tell their leader that he had made the path bloody and it was not Coytmore's business to chase after him. Coytmore wanted Connecorte to know that his reasons for not coming down to the fort looked foolish. If Governor Lyttelton could come to Keowee from Charles Town, then the least Old Hop could do was come down to Keowee and meet with him. The Warrior of Tennessee then relayed the fact that Attakullakulla had passed through his town without informing the Warrior of his plans or destination. The Warrior told Coytmore that he (the Warrior) was the man who should go down to Keowee and wait on Governor Lyttelton.[46] Apparently, others besides Attakullakulla were jockeying for position amid the new, troubling times.

As these events unfolded, there was a second outbreak of smallpox in both South Carolina and Cherokee country. Colonial soldiers returning from the Great War for Empire, also known as the French and Indian War, brought the disease back with them in January 1760.[47] Similarly, another group of soldiers brought it back to Cherokee country, Catawba warriors returning from the Pennsylvania frontier in 1759. By some accounts, it reduced the Catawba population to 4 percent of what their numbers had been at the time of colonist settlement at 1670. Catawba raids spread the disease once more into Cherokee towns like Keowee. Soon, it swept through the other Lower Towns as well, and many adults fled to the woods to avoid the sickness. Oconostota appeared at Fort Prince George on February 14, 1760, to exercise his power to free the hostages on Cherokee terms. Soldiers inside the fort had smallpox as well, and all members of the Cherokee party, save Oconostota, stopped outside the fort. Oconostota, through linguister John Caldwell, told Coytmore that he had come for the hostages because the Overhills towns, unlike the Lower Towns, had remained peaceful. He leveraged that fact, telling Coytmore the towns would remain quiet as long as the hostages were released. Coytmore refused to negotiate, and Oconostota left in agitation.[48]

By April 1760, smallpox had decimated the Middle settlements as well. Lieutenant Richard Coytmore, at Fort Prince George, saw the contagion as an ally, writing that he wished the disease could do "its deadly work among the whole population [of Cherokees]." Although such statements are the product of an eighteenth-century military mind that obviously saw Indians as obstacles, they are revelatory in the depth of the utter contempt Coytmore showed toward the Cherokees. The Overhills towns near modern Loudon, Tennessee, refused to admit people from the Middle Towns as a response to the threat. Their caution spared the Overhills settlements the deaths of the lower communities.[49]

Some within Cherokee society blamed themselves for the plague, or, rather, they blamed their youth, whom they said dishonored the tribe with the sexual indiscretions of couples taken to excess. The Cherokees believed these liaisons, often carried out in corn fields, had polluted both their society and their planting grounds. Cherokees and Catawbas, once infected, often threw themselves into the river, sometimes in a drunken state.[50] Some historians have speculated that those Cherokees who survived the epidemics may have learned to cast off deference to authority figures since they had seen their shaman class rendered powerless in the face of the deadly European disease. Tsyu-gun-sini (Dragging Canoe), son of pro-British chief Attakullakulla, was one such survivor, and witnesses reported that his face clearly bore smallpox scars. In Charles Town, colonists began to use inoculation to ward off the plague. Period reports indicate a frenzy or mania on the part of towns people to try the new treatment by which most avoided the smallpox epidemic.[51] Sadly, Cherokee shamans never found their miracle treatment for the disease.

The original Cherokee delegates who had gone to see Governor Lyttelton about the Carolina trade embargo in fall of 1759 made it back to Fort Prince George under armed escort in December 1759 without incident. Attakullakulla gave the South Carolina governor a French prisoner as a token of Cherokee fealty.[52] On December 26, 1759, the governor and Attakullakulla concluded a peace treaty with the Cherokees in which the chiefs promised to surrender twenty-four of their people responsible for the murders of Euroamericans in the backcountry. While awaiting the arrival of the guilty, twenty-two (two murderers had been turned in already) of those Cherokee diplomats recently returned from Charles Town, including Oconostota, would be held hostage at Fort Prince George and then released as the remaining twenty-two murderers surrendered or were brought in to the forts.[53] Led by Attakullakulla, others including Kittagusta, Oconostota, Oconeca, Otassite, and Killianca signed the treaty.[54] Though Oconostota signed the hated treaty, he had no intention of keeping it. In fact, these recent events soon sent him back to Fort Toulouse to court the French for help in ammunition and supplies.[55] The Cherokee leader was resorting to an old diplomatic policy of trying to balance the British by using the French and a possible alliance as a threat. Such a tense diplomacy took place amid the backdrop of the smallpox epidemic.

According to article 4 of the new treaty, those leaders signed away diplomatic hostages by the names of Chenshe, Ousanatah, Tallichama, and Tallitahe. Further detainees included Quarrasattahe, Connasoratah, and Katactoi. Other Cherokees included Otasitey of the Middle Town of Watauga, Ousanoletah of the Middle Town of Jore, Ousansletah of Cowatchee, Woejah, and Oucah. Cherokees such as Chistanah, Nicholche, Tony, Koi, Shalileshe, and Chistee rounded out the group of hostages. Article 5 of the treaty, in the meantime, authorized the return of the Cherokee traders to their trade outposts with instructions to resume normal trade, thus ending the embargo. The treaty required the Cherokees to execute any French subjects who came among them, in light of the ongoing state of war with France. Article 6 of the treaty went to great lengths to clarify that the Cherokees should turn over such a person, if they could not kill him, either to the South Carolina governor or to a military commander. This directive included French messengers and considered all such persons and messages a threat to the continuance of the current peace treaty.[56] Not to be missed in the various articles, holding diplomats as hostages was a provocative step on the part of the South Carolina governor. It was certainly not a step taken between good allies and was even an extreme measure to carry out on subject peoples. Surely the Cherokee hostage delegates must have wondered what had become of the spirit of the Articles of Friendship.

Many Cherokees soon came to despise this treaty for its provision requiring the deaths of those Cherokees who had attacked backcountry residents on the way home from the Fort Duquesne expedition. Some Cherokees came to blame those of their leaders who had signed it, and, to be sure, it would not be the last unpopular treaty that Attakullakulla signed. Complicating the hostage situation, smallpox soon appeared at the fort among both soldiers and hostages. Governor Lyttelton quickly wrote to General Amherst with news of his diplomatic handiwork and a copy of the Cherokee Treaty. The governor never mentioned Attakullakulla by name in his report. However, he noted that the treaty required the Cherokees to turn in twenty-four murders to obtain the release of specific warriors who were held as diplomatic hostages. The number of Cherokees required to die was tied to include the number of settlers killed in Virginia since November 19, 1758.[57]

Attakullakulla, a lead signatory, was one of the seven Cherokees who went to London in 1730, and that accomplishment brought him a measure of diplomatic currency that Oconostota lacked. Consistently pro-British for most of his career, he mentioned the 1730 trip in official documents ending the Cherokee War of 1760–1761. In that peace treaty, he spoke of his visit with King George II in which he promised the Great King to "love the English." He further recalled that King George had told him that he, the king, looked "on the Cherokees & the English as one people."[58] His support of the treaty secured the release of some Cherokees, but he also had effectively condemned others to death in a treaty despised by many of his people for what it conceded to the British. The British had come to the bargaining table armed with the trade goods desperately needed by the Cherokees but would not release those items until the murderers surrendered. Incensed over the treaty and the taking of hostages, many Cherokees turned against the most readily available Euroamericans in their midst—the traders who handled their merchandise. Shortly after the treaty was signed, two groups of Cherokees from Overhills town of Hyawassee and from the Valley town of Nottely killed and dismembered the trader John Kelly in a preview of the violence that was to come.[59] He was but the first sacrifice in venting social pressure that began to escalate when the Virginians first killed the Cherokees returning from war.

Commander Richard Coytmore of Fort Prince George reported the trader's death to Governor Lyttelton in a late January 1760 letter. He told the governor that the Cherokees of Hyawassee and Nottely wanted the Tellico people to kill traders Isaac Atwood and Thomas Hayley. Having received advance warning, Atwood and Hayley made their escape and sought refuge with Coytmore at the fort.[60] Fairly quickly, Governor Lyttelton, who had demanded such an extreme treaty, now wrote to Jeffery Amherst in early February 1760 telling him that the recent treaty was already in abeyance. He reported that the Cherokees had killed whites near or in Cherokee towns, and he feared the violence would spread beyond his province. He requested that Amherst send troops "to protect this colony & secure Fort Prince George & Fort Loudoun."[61]

Cherokee attacks reached Georgia colony in December 1759 with the death of trader Thomas Williams, whose home was some seventy miles north of Augusta. The Cherokees killed both the trader and his wife and child and took scalps. Williams's crime, if he had one, was selling rum to the Cherokees. A few days later, the Cherokees launched an offensive against the Long Canes region of South Carolina, forcing 150 refugees to flee toward the coast. The Cherokees killed some twenty-three settlers and took captives as well before driving settlers from the Stevens Creek settlements.[62] The Cherokees effectively rolled the frontier back and down toward Augusta as refugees headed in that direction for safety.

Governor Lyttelton's request for military aid set events in motion that would result in a delayed but deadly military reprisal by the British and using the theme of excessive violence to achieve an end goal, which fit the Amherst model of Indian management style. Among the Cherokees, less obvious forms of public anger over the treaty surfaced in most villages as people crowded into their central townhouses to discuss the controversial document that had transformed their delegates into hostages. Disease (or, rather, fear of disease) affected the emotions of this issue as well. One of the Cherokee hostages became ill in January 1760, and the fort commander, Coytmore, isolated the Cherokee man.[63] Soon, the surrounding Cherokee settlements learned of the outbreak and knew that it could easily terminate the lives of the hostage Cherokees held at Fort Prince George just as surely as any failure of diplomacy could do.[64] When a Cherokee woman from the lower town of Keowee visited the fort on January 20, 1760, she, too, came down with symptoms shortly after her visit. Coytmore had the woman moved outside the fort, whereupon she soon died.[65] When the commander learned of possible planned attacks on the fort, he began to use his detainees as a bargaining chip against Cherokee leaders of the Lower

Towns who might not be able to control their upset people. Coytmore told them that if the Cherokees harmed the fort in any way, he would kill the hostages personally.[66] Statements like these were in keeping with the Amherst style of management, but they must have deeply shocked leaders who considered themselves allies due to the Articles of Friendship treaty of 1730. Coytmore's earlier abuse of Cherokee women, now coupled with his threats against the Cherokee hostages in his fort, matched Governor Lyttelton's escalation by calling on Amherst for a military intervention. Since an expected attack might come from the Lower Cherokee town of Estatoe, a Cherokee man named Slave Catcher of Stecoe went to Estatoe (Dillard, Georgia) to try to quash the attack.[67] Sixteen years before the Dragging Canoe Rebellion, the Cherokees began to retaliate against both their own ineffective governance and British "imperial arrogance."[68] What they lacked in this earlier conflict of the Attakullakulla era was a well-defined leader such as they would have in the 1776 uprising. The triumvirate leadership of Ostenaco, Oconostota, and Attakullakulla, minus Old Hop (Connecorte), now kept trying to manage this latest crisis.

In January 1760, a series of Cherokee leaders came to Fort Prince George from various Lower Towns hoping to negotiate, albeit unsuccessfully, for the release of the hostages. One hostage, Chistannah of Estatoe, successfully escaped under a hail of musket fire. Subsequently, Lieutenant Coytmore ordered the soldiers to shoot any more hostages who challenged the guards.[69] On January 7, 1760, warriors from the Lower, Middle and Valley settlements left for Fort Prince George. A week later, warriors from the Overhills towns followed them as well. Their intent was to secure the release of the Cherokee hostages, peacefully if possible, or by whatever means necessary if peaceful methods failed.[70] Back at the fort, Coytmore learned of the activities of the Cherokee war parties that struck at frontier settlements like those at Long Canes Creek and Stevens Creek in South Carolina, killing twenty-three people at each community. Although the settlers at Ninety-Six, South Carolina, drove off their Cherokee attackers on February 3, 1760, the raids effectively rolled the settlement line back one hundred miles toward the coast.[71]

By January 17, 1760, native women connected to the fur traders had warned the men of the impending violence so that the traders could evacuate the backcountry.[72] More than likely, these traders were intermarried with some of the women, as this pattern repeated itself frequently in backcountry conflicts—prior warnings to esteemed non-Indians, giving them time to escape. Two days later, some eighty Cherokee men and a few women assembled at the Lower Town of Estatoe in Georgia and determined to intervene on behalf of the hostages. They convinced trader Thomas Beamer, a mixed-blood Cherokee, to interpret for them as they moved to address Lieutenant Coytmore at the fort.[73]

They were led by a man named the Young Warrior of Estatoe (or Seroweh) and several other men. While approximately thirty Cherokees remained in reserve, the rest of the group, secretly armed, approached the gate during heavy rains around 4:00 p.m. Seroweh requested admittance to the fort for his whole group in order to check on their friends, since there was smallpox outbreak, and to turn in two of the murderers. In a follow-up report later submitted to the South Carolina governor, Coytmore noted that it was easy to see that the group was armed with a tomahawk, pistol, or knife. In his note to the governor, Coytmore admitted that he did not trust Seroweh or his group and so limited their access to the fort.[74]

Coytmore, expecting trouble, allowed in only small groups of three or four people at a time. Seroweh decided to enter the fort with a small group including some murderers to be turned over to the British. Twelve Cherokee men also pushed their way inside. Coytmore and Seroweh talked, and the Cherokee man agreed to go outside the fort to bring in the murderers.[75] Coytmore wrote the governor that the talk was a good one and that Seroweh acted friendly toward him.[76] Soon after, Seroweh returned but without the murderer he claimed to be turning in for the release of hostages. When he did, two of the hostage Cherokees, both from Overhills towns—Tullatahee of Toqua and Yellow Bird of Watauga—escaped, and Seroweh returned without the murderer he had promised to exchange. At that point, Coytmore had the Cherokee delegation escorted out of the fort.[77] Not long after the departure of the Cherokee delegation, a soldier named John Lowlin came to the fort to report that he had passed a group of fifty Cherokees headed for the home and storehouse of long-time trader John Elliott. Lowlin reported there were thirteen white men at Elliott's home, ostensibly for its defense.[78]

As it turns out, the group of Cherokees, reported by Lowlin, had gone to John Elliott's home roughly a mile and a half from the fort during negotiations. There, they killed Elliott, who was guilty of overcharging them, along with nine other Euroamerican men.[79] One of the men targeted was an interpreter who had signed Attakullakulla's treaty. The Cherokee party divided up Elliott's goods among themselves as compensation for their losses. Later, a group of Cherokees hiding in the woods near the fort opened fire on three soldiers sent out to chop firewood. They killed one of the men and wounded another.[80] The next day, Coytmore wrote that a Cherokee woman had come to the fort and reported that Seroweh had intended to attack the fort if he could have gotten his entire group inside, which Coytmore did not allow. She relayed the facts about John Elliott's death as well. Because the Chreokees liked trader Thomas Beamer, his safety and that of his family's was guaranteed by the group.[81]

The Cherokees were exerting their own form of pressure on the British during the hostage crisis. They had successfully helped two hostages escape, and they exacted their own justice on the trader Elliott, who had been a treaty signatory. Then they laid siege to the fort, cutting it off from Charles Town. Thus isolated, the Cherokees could prey on the fort, pressing for the release of the remaining hostages.[82] The pro-French leader Oconostota, also known as Agan'stat, led this action and was furious with the British at this point.[83] Perhaps this was his own personal revenge for initially being imprisoned as a delegate to Charles Town.

Of the three leaders jockeying for power among the Cherokees, Oconostota first shows up among the Overhills around 1736. While Attakullakulla was known for his talks and diplomacy more so than his military prowess, Oconostota was the opposite—he was known for his military skills more so than his speeches. By 1738, his battle prowess had earned him the title of Raven of Chota, great warrior status. While Ostenaco tried to remain independent and Attakullakulla was pro-British, Oconostota was drawn to the French, first visiting Fort Toulouse in the 1740s.[84] When the French and Indian War came, he ultimately chose the British side until the incidents of murdered Cherokees returning home pushed him, like other leaders, to desperate measures.

As the Cherokees expanded their war efforts, the Lower Town Cherokees contacted the Muskogee Creek upper towns for help, and the Creeks actually sent two war parties at the request of the Lower Town chiefs. The pent-up aggression found release as the Cherokees continued to kill more traders, as they were relatively easy targets. The Overhills people of Hiawassee and Nottely killed their trader, John Kelly, and dismembered his body. The Middle Town people of Nequassee put five other traders under arrest. Cherokee people sometimes beat their local traders but let them go; however, the Cherokees killed some thirteen traders during the extended hostage period at Fort Prince George.[85]

Cherokee leaders initiated similar tactics at Fort Loudoun in the Overhills region. They started with negotiations with its commander, Captain Paul Demeré. Both the pro-British Attakullakulla and the pro-French Oconostota visited the fort during the month of January 1760. Attakullakulla, or Little Carpenter, was short and slight of frame. Oconostota was a bear of a man, and his face bore the scars of smallpox. On January

6, 1760, Attakullakulla told Captain Demeré in an initial visit to expect a return of peaceful relations. The next day, however, a Cherokee fired on soldiers outside the fort chopping firewood. Oconostota was less hopeful of peace when he spoke to the fort commander, noting that the families of those Cherokees who had gone on retaliatory raids were unwilling to give them up. If the clans did not volunteer these men, he told Demeré that Cherokee government could not compel the extradition of the murderers that British government wanted.[86]

When the two sets of negotiators met again at Fort Loudoun on January 23, 1760, diplomacy yielded little results except an escalation in tension. Both Attakullakulla and Oconostota met with Demeré again. The captain opened the dialogue by asking whether they had any murderers to turn in. After a long silence, Attakullakullah explained that anti-British sentiments had spread among his people due to the hostage situation at Fort Prince George, to which Attakullakullah had agreed in the name of the Cherokee people. The Cherokee leader asked that a letter be sent to Fort Prince George by way of Oconostota. It would command that the Cherokee hostages at the fort be released with no one else turned in. Instead, it pledged the Cherokees to send war parties against the French or their Indian allies in the spring offering to recommit the Cherokees to participation in the French and Indian War. Cherokee soldiers would return with a number of scalps equal to the number of colonial settlers lost in 1758 and 1759. Attakullakulla exerted agency by offering a comparable sacrifice of blood in service to his British ally. It was clever and took the topic of Cherokee executions off the table. The British fort commander declined the counteroffer, partly because he knew that some Cherokees, such as the Overhills people, were making overtures to the French during this crisis with the British over Cherokee hostages at Prince George.[87]

By the end of January 1760, the social pressure of the unresolved hostage situation at Fort Prince George led the people of the Middle and Overhills settlements to prepare for war. The Overhills towns, more distant from the source of pressure and often the last to react in a given situation, finally began to prepare for conflict in two ways. They agreed to stop all travel by non-Indians in their territory, and they began to send representatives to Fort Prince George to demand the release of four Overhills Cherokees being held there.[88]

During these tense events, the Overhills leader, Connecorte or Old Hop, died, ending the first triumvirate of Cherokee leadership. His passing actually stimulated more resistance to the British. Oconostota and Ostenaco supported the choice of Cunneshote (Standing Turkey) as his successor, who appears to have been little more than a figurehead.[89] In the resulting leadership vacuum, Attakullakulla, who was pro-British, now competed with the pro-French Oconostota, who championed greater sovereignty from the British. Ironically, Cherokee leadership reflected the two nations then fighting for hegemony over North America. The British, not surprisingly, chose Attakullakulla as their new representative for the Cherokee people, while the Cherokees themselves turned to Oconostota. Oconostota went to Fort Loudoun, where he met with Captain John Stuart, called Bushyhead by the Cherokees, on January 29, 1760, and then on to more meetings at Fort Prince George.[90]

Attakullakulla accompanied Oconostota to Fort Prince George in early February 1760 but may not have known the backup plan that the Great Warrior had, should negotiations fail. Speaking with Coytmore at Fort Prince George, Oconostota lobbied for the release of the four Overhills hostages there on Feburary 14, 1760. Coytmore stood firm on his orders not to release the delegates unless exchanged for the murderers of frontier settlers, and he also reminded Oconostota of his treaty obligations. The Great Warrior repudiated the treaty at that juncture and told Coytmore plainly that neither he nor their British-designated chief could deliver up these men.[91] The Cherokees also warned that the Overhills towns had now joined the war movement of the Middle and Lower Towns. John Calwell, one of the interpreters, confirmed to the fort's officers the statement about the growing Overhills war movement. Coytmore stood firm, and diplomacy on the part of the Cherokees came to an end.[92]

War parties from three Overhills settlements had already set out for the frontier, and roughly eight hundred Cherokees were taking up positions near Fort Prince George. Five of the original twenty-two hostages had died already—four from smallpox. The Out Towns Warrior of Stecoee died on February 8, 1760. Two days later, Tony of the Overhills town Chotee, another hostage, died of smallpox, as did a South Carolina soldier. On February 11, Chisquatalone joined the other hostages, dead from smallpox. The next day, February 12, 1760, Ousonaletak of the Middle Town of Joree died from smallpox as well. Two days later, Skalitoskee, a mixed-blood Cherokee and son of David McDonald, died.[93] Four British soldiers had died from the pox, and eighteen were critically ill with it at the time. The Cherokee strike force attacked the fort, which survived the initial attack, but Coytmore dispatched an enslaved man named Abram requesting reinforcements for the fort, which was nearing the end of its ability to resist siege.[94]

Attakullakulla also worked to diplomatically resolve the impasse, but another crucial figure was leaving the colony, adding to the difficulties. Governor Lyttelton had received an appointment as governor of the Jamaica colony on February 13, 1760. Earlier, he had requested military aid against the Cherokees and now waited on the arrival of Colonel Archibald Montgomery and some 1,300 men of the First and Seventy-seventh regiments.[95] By the time the Cherokee leaders made their visit to Prince George, the Middle Town Cherokees had killed some fifty-six people from the Long Cane and Stevens Creek settlements in South Carolina. Finally, John Caldwell, the interpreter, confirmed that a group of Cherokees had gone to attack Ninety-Six, South Carolina.[96] A Mr. James Francis later wrote to Governor Lyttelton on March 6, 1760, confirming an attack on the fort at Ninety-Six a few days earlier. He estimated that some two hundred Cherokees had attacked them. Francis noted that the fort had only twenty men inside at the time of attack but that luckily reinforcements arrived during a lull in the fighting.[97]

Real negotiation attempts on the part of the Cherokees had now ended, though Oconostota used a diplomatic ruse. On February 15, 1760, he placed thirty Cherokees in hiding in the cane field near the fort. Next he sent two Cherokee women to the fort, requesting a meeting with Coytmore.[98] The Cherokee women had previously served as informants to the fort, lending validity to what seemed like another diplomatic attempt to resolve the hostage situation. When they came to the Keowee River, Cornelius Dougherty from Fort Prince George went out to speak to them to obtain any information they might have. Oconostota appeared soon afterward and told Dougherty he wished for a white escort to accompany him to Charles Town to speak with Governor Lyttelton. Coytmore, with two soldiers, came to the banks of the Keowee River, and Oconostota stood on the opposite side of the river. He told Coytmore that he hoped to catch a horse for the distant journey to Charles Town. He then swung a horse bridle over his head three times. In response to that signal, the concealed Cherokees opened fire on Coytmore, wounding him fatally through the left side of his chest and hitting two others. Ensign Bell, who had also molested Cherokee women, was one of the escorts as well as a translator named Foster.[99] Another soldier pulled Coytmore inside the fort as its surgeon Alexander Miln assumed command. From the viewpoint of a Cherokee sense of balance, Coytmore had been the cause of the deaths of Cherokee diplomats inside a fort with a smallpox outbreak. His execution now restored balance, or duyvktv.

Miln noted that the Fort Prince George soldiers wanted to execute the hostages themselves on the spot because of Coytmore's shooting, though Miln gave orders against such a move. To pacify his men, Miln did order that the Cherokee captives be put in irons and tied with ropes. However, when the soldiers called the Cherokees to come out of their holding cell to receive their restraints, the Cherokee men did not budge.[100] As the soldiers went in to walk out the captives, Miln reported that the hostages attacked the soldiers with knives and tomahawks previously buried in the dirt. When the Cherokee hostages attacked two soldiers, the other soldiers opened fire on the Cherokees, with Miln admitting it was impossible for him to control his men or to stop the works of death once set in motion. Dr. Miln also said the men found a bottle of poison hidden by the Cherokees, which he presumed would have been used to poison the fort well.[101] Most likely it was liquor, but the soldiers rationalized the actions dictated by their emotions. Miln ordered the cannons to open fire on the town of Keowee as Cherokee snipers kept targeting the fort.[102] Those snipers remained around the fort, successfully cutting it off. Soon, the Cherokees would isolate Fort Loudoun as well.

Miln reported that around 8:00 p.m. that same night, the Cherokees outside the fort fired two guns, which Miln believed was meant to be a signal to the hostages to start an attack inside with their concealed weapons, not knowing the fate of their people at the time. Miln stated it plainly when he wrote Governor Lyttelton that "the men after seein [sic] their officer shot before their faces, was so exasperated, that immediately they put them every one to death, in spight of all I could either say or do, though I threatened them very hard . . . so I was obliged to put up with the massacre."[103] With those actions and words began the Cherokee War of 1760–1761. Oconostota left soon after in another of his visits to French Fort Toulouse, seeking to balance British power with possible French influence.[104]

Miln continued with his report, noting that Coytmore's injuries had rendered him speechless and the doctor did not expect him to last the hour. He also told Lyttelton that, to that point, he had fourteen deaths from smallpox at the fort, but the remainder of the sick were expected to recover.[105] Unfortunately, Coytmore was not so lucky and died from his wounds the next day on February 25, 1760. His death signaled a general war between the two cultures now occupying the southern backcountry. The trader Thomas Beamer carried the news to Charles Town, and Carolina officials hurried to organize a colony ill prepared for war. Governor Lyttelton summoned troops from North Carolina and Virginia, while Georgia governor Henry Ellis tried to marshal the Creeks to fight on the side of the colonists against the Cherokees, who had been their traditional enemies up until peace in 1755. Of major concern were the two forts isolated in a now hostile environment. The next day, on February 26, 1760, General Jeffery Amherst wrote Governor Lyttelton that he was sending 1,300 men from two different regiments under the command of Colonel Archibald Montgomery to South Carolina's aid.[106]

In Cherokee country, Oconostota led an attack against the fort at Ninety Six, South Carolina. Commander James Francis had been forwarned of a possible attack, and the fort repulsed the Cherokees.[107] At the same time, Ostenaco, who had been sent back from the original peace delegation, received the news of the murder of the Cherokee hostages at Fort Prince George. He was senior military leader among the Overhills communities and immediately mobilized the Cherokee men there. On March 20, 1756, his men, led by Willenawah and Cunneshote, surrounded Fort Loudoun and cut it off. The British had held Cherokee leaders hostage inside Fort Prince George. Now the Cherokees held British officers, soldiers, and assorted civilians hostage inside Fort Loudoun, though the British would never understand that the Cherokees were attempting to achieve duyvktv once more.

Cherokee troops fired on the fort for four days. The siege was interrupted by news that the British were massing an army at Ninety-Six, South Carolina, to move against the Cherokees. Ostenaco redirected his warriors against the direction of Ninety-Six, but the intelligence proved to be false. When Oconostota returned, he did not deploy enough troops for an all-out attack on Fort Loudoun but enough to keep the fort's soldiers pinned inside and starving.[108] During the attack, Oconostota forbid Cherokee women to provide food or supplies to the men of the fort with whom they might have been involved. Conversely, Attakullakulla encouraged such aid.[109] Attakullakulla apparently moved his wife and children out of the Overhills Towns in fear of their lives.[110] During this initial emergency, Ostenaco had reformed the triumvirate of Cherokee leadership, replacing the now-deceased Old Hop and joining Attakullakulla and Oconostota as the independent leader between his pro-British and pro-French counterparts respectively.

Of the Cherokees detained at Fort Prince George, three Cherokee hostages had escaped their confinement at the fort while four had died during it. Fort Prince George soldiers killed fourteen more Cherokee men at the massacre on February 16. Runners among the Cherokees carried the news of these events to all of the towns, although it only reinforced an already-existing commitment to expel the British from Cherokee territory.[111] Cherokee fighters renewed their attacks on the South Carolina backcountry, seeking revenge for their losses and adoption of a select few to replace their own lost people.[112] Once retributive justice was achieved and captives were selected to replace dead Cherokees and restore a population balance, the matter was concluded from the Cherokee point of view. However, from the British point of view, a righteous war of revenge had not even begun yet.

Governor Lyttelton, the man whose fateful and harsh decisions about the Cherokees had caused so much bloodshed, received news in April 1760 that he had been granted the governorship of Jamaica. He was replaced in the interim by Lieutenant Governor William Bull.[113] The plans that Lyttelton had set in motion continued unabated with the arrival of Colonel Montgomery's troops, who had sailed from New York on March 14 with some 1,373 Regulars. They landed in Charles Town on April 1, 1760. Those troops took a full two months before they arrived at the Cherokee Lower Towns.[114] In addition, Governor Bull placed all militia forces at Montgomery's disposal. They were further aided by Chickasaw and Catawba warriors under the direction of James Adair.[115] These forces arrived in spring into a Cherokee nation that had moved on from both the attack on Fort Prince George and the retaliatory raids of February and March 1760. Once the need for revenge was settled, the Cherokees were done with it. By the time that Colonel Montgomery reached Charles Town, the Cherokees had returned to plant spring crops, which the British soldiers noted had yielded results in abundance, as well as remarking on the neatness of their towns, before putting both towns and crops to the torch. British forces bayonetted those Cherokee people found in areas outlying Lower Towns like Estatoe. Some Lower Town residents were too sick with smallpox to fight, and so the troops burned them alive in their homes in a mind-boggling display of violence.[116]

In his report on the attack to Jeffery Amherst, Archibald Montgomery noted that the Cherokees had abandoned the town about thirty minutes before the British attack. He confirmed his troops had burned alive some of the sick people in their homes, and he estimated about two hundred houses were burned to ashes. Montgomery speculated that his men had killed some sixty to eighty Cherokee men, women, and children and had taken forty people as prisoners. While Montgomery admitted that some Cherokees had escaped, he noted that they had abandoned any supplies along with their town.[117]

British troops made it to the outlying Middle Town settlements by late June 1760. Here Oconostota led an offensive force of Cherokees outside the town of Etchoe, just south of modern Franklin, North Carolina. These warriors gave the British hard combat and made their stand against Montgomery's troops at a place called Crow's Pass, six miles south of Etchoe. Montgomery sustained one hundred dead or wounded troops in this engagement.[118] When British troops finally reached the town, they found the town abandoned but with many supplies carried off this time by the Cherokees. After a few days' respite, Montgomery pulled out of the town and made the decision not to move deeper into the mountains. Instead, his troops made their way to Fort Prince George, arriving on July 2, 1760. Montgomery wrote to the commander of British Forces, North America, Jeffrey Amherst, that he was abandoning his attack because of the casualties inflicted near Etchoe.[119] The results of the battle both added to Oconostota's war record and convinced Montgomery that he had sufficiently punished the Cherokees.[120] He wrote Governor Bull in Charles Town that he felt he had sufficiently carried out General Amherst's orders by destroying the lower towns.[121]

Military officials had managed to organize a relief expedition for Fort Prince George, though Fort Loudoun was completely surrounded. Montgomery had failed in his attempt to crush the Cherokees, leaving Fort Loudoun at the mercy of its enemies. A message smuggled out of it dated June 6, 1760, indicated the soldiers were in good spirits, though living on reduced rations. Trader Cornelius Dougherty had brought in four cattle, which allowed the soldiers a departure from their quarts of corn meal.[122] In addition to British efforts, local Cherokee women who had relationships with some of the British soldiers at the fort brought beans and pork to these men, both in defiance of Oconostota's orders and as a direct challenge from Willenawah.[123] Attakullakulla relayed word to the fort of the destruction of the towns Estatoe and Keowee.[124]

Lieutenant Governor William Bull wrote Jeffery Amherst in early May with a report on the siege of Fort Loudoun. He told Amherst it had begun with a barrage of gunfire that went on for four days and four nights. Further, he told Amherst of reports the Cherokees had asked other tribes like the Ottawas and some French-aligned Indians to enter the conflict. Cherokee leaders, like Oconostota, had also reached out to the French officers of Fort Toulouse and the governor of New Orleans.[125] To the British mind, this act was indicative of Cherokee treachery while to the Cherokees it was action to restore balance.

By late July, Fort Loudoun was on the verge of collapse. Captain Demeré got a courier through to Charles Town relaying the information that life inside the fort was without the hope of rescue or the prospects of food. On August 6, 1760, Demeré called a council of officers, who voted that trying to hold the fort was no longer tenable. They voted to ask for surrender terms from the Cherokees in order to abandon the fort. The officers agreed that Captain John Stuart, who had personal connections within Cherokee society, would go to Chota with a fellow officer to obtain surrender terms.[126]

The surrender terms given at Chota by Oconostota and Cunneshote were generous by comparison with what the British army had just done to the Lower Towns. Soldiers would march out with the arms and ammunition they could carry, plus whatever baggage they could manage. They were given safe passage to march either to Fort Prince George or to Virginia unmolested, though they would receive a Cherokee escort. Sick or wounded men would be treated in the nearest Cherokee towns. The fort's big guns and ammunition that could not be carried were to be left behind for the Cherokees. This amounted to some twelve cannons, one thousand pounds of ammunition, and eighty small arms. Paul Demeré signed the capitulation on August 7, 1760, surrendering Loudoun to Oconostota and Cunneshote. When the men took down the British flag at Loudoun, they forever changed British military history.[127]

They granted Demeré the right to march his 108 troops, plus sixty women and some children, out for a 140-mile journey to the lower fort. The defeated British troops left the fort on August 9, 1760.[128] When the Cherokees entered the fort, they found several bags of gunpowder and some buried musket balls. The Cherokees then discovered a cannon and other small arms thrown in the nearby river. Angered because a surrender of all weapons was a part of the agreement, some Cherokees followed the British soldiers and attacked them early on the second morning of their journey to the lower fort.

Paul Demeré's survivors had made fifteen miles that first day and camped on Cane Creek. That night, Ostenaco entered their encampment and had a verbal exchange with Demeré and then left. The next morning, as the commander briefed his troops on the day's agenda, gunfire erupted from the forest. When the British returned fire, some seven hundred Cherokees responded with intense barrage of gunfire before charging the troops.[129]

The Cherokees killed Captain Paul Demeré, who had replaced his brother Raymond, for a total of twenty-nine other soldiers—three officers, twenty-three soldiers and three women. The Cherokees first scalped Demeré and made him dance for them. Then they cut off his arms and legs and stuffed his mouth with dirt, symbolically wanting to give all British through their victim as much land as they could take.[130] Such a horrific death is hard to justify despite the passions of war. Perhaps it can only be balanced with remembrances of Colonel Montgomery's army burning Cherokee smallpox victims alive in his attacks on the Lower Towns.

These deaths were the rough equivalent of the Cherokee hostages who had died while detained at Fort Prince George. The remainder were made prisoners of war.[131] Ostenaco ordered the attack to stop once Demeré was killed.[132] With the death of Demeré, the killing, it seems, was over. John Stuart's life was spared when Onatoy, brother of Chief Round O, took Stuart and got him across Cane Creek, away from the others.[133] Attakullakulla took one of Fort Loudoun's sole surviving officers, John Stuart, and a small group of others into the woods, ostensibly on a hunting trip to obtain meat for them in their weakened condition. By this ruse, Attakullakulla spirited away Stuart, the fort doctor, an elderly man, William Shorey, a Cherokee interpreter, and others to Virginia, where he ransomed the British officer.[134] Attakullakulla had adopted Stuart into his clan; plus Stuart had a relationship with his Cherokee consort, Susannah Emory. Both factors probably saved his life that day, as Stuart had a child with the woman.

When Jeffery Amherst, the commander of British forces in North America, heard of the surrender of Loudoun, he wrote that he was ashamed, for it was, to his knowledge, the first surrender of a British fort to native peoples.[135] He reacted by ordering Colonel James Grant, who had served under General Montgomery, to take an army of two thousand men to invade Cherokee country to "wipe out the disgrace the Indians had inflicted upon his Majesty's arms."[136] As Cherokee author Robert Conley points out, to the Cherokees, the conflict had ended at this point, because enough British soldiers had died to balance the number of Cherokees killed by British soldiers.[137] A few weeks later, Ostenaco and Oconostota held a meeting with over two thousand Cherokees at the Middle Town of Nikwasi to formally end hostilities. Oconostota raised the British flag there. The two leaders gave orders that British colonials should pass through their territory unharmed. They also released another Fort Loudoun prisoner, Samuel Terron, who was to go to the new South Carolina governor, William Bull, with a message. Ostenaco told Terron that if Governor Bull could arrange a peace, he would have no war with the Cherokees.[138] To the Cherokee leadership and people, this conflict was now ended because balance in pain and suffering between the Cherokees and British was once more restored.

To the British military and the government of South Carolina, however, this conflict was now resumed because the Cherokees had attacked the Fort Loudoun survivors after they were granted safe passage following their surrender.[139] In reality, South Carolina was ill prepared for this optional war, due to the smallpox outbreak. One Charles Town doctor estimated that at least four thousand people in the city at that time were infected with smallpox. Nonetheless, the South Carolina Assembly authorized a payment of £25 per scalp that a colonist would receive for a Cherokee scalp. Georgia governor Henry Ellis offered the Muskogee Creeks of his colony a lesser bounty of £5 per Cherokee scalp if they would assist. The British also hoped smallpox would wreak the havoc on the Cherokees that their soldiers were unable to do.[140]

From the Cherokee point of view, the Anglo-Cherokee War of 1760 was concluded because retributive justice had been served. However, far away, the commander of British forces in North America, Jeffrey Amherst, had been both livid and incredulous that the Cherokees had conquered Fort Loudoun among the Overhills Towns. Amherst did not even believe initial reports of the fort's surrender until confirmed by South Carolina's new lieutenant governor William Bull. Bull had also asked him to plan second invasion of Cherokee country with a mission based on the theme that Indians only understood brutal violence as a deterrent to future hostilities. Amherst planned the raid to coincide with late growing season so that the Cherokees would not have the opportunity to plant a late corn crop to help them survive the winter. Thus, only after inflicting a second wave of total devastation would the British government seek a lasting peace with the Cherokees.[141] As always, the planned destruction of Cherokee food supplies by British armies meant a later death by starvation for some survivors of combat with the British. Of course, the Cherokees would also have their share of deaths on the battlefield. Some of Cherokee survivors driven out of destroyed towns would seek shelter among the upper town Muskogee Creeks and unfortunately spread smallpox to them.[142]

Notes

1. Kelton, "The British and Indian War," 786–787.
2. Kelton, "The British and Indian War," 790.
3. Edward J. Cashin, *Lachlan McGillivray, Indian Trader: The Shaping of the Southern Colonial Frontier* (Athens: University of Georgia Press, 1992), 197–198.
4. Brown, *Old Frontiers*, 89–90.
5. Cashin, *Lachlan McGillivray*, 190.
6. Conley, *The Cherokee Nation*, 46–47.
7. Colonial Records of SC 1754–1765, xxx–xxxi.

88 CHAPTER 2

8. Captain Paul Demeré to Willian Henry Lyttelton, April 6, 1759, Fort Loudoun, Letterbooks of William Henry Lyttelton.
9. Brown, *Old Frontiers*, 90.
10. William Ramsey, *The Yamassee War: A Study of Culture, Conflict and Economy in the Colonial South* (Lincoln: University of Nebraska Press, 2008), 24.
11. Brown, *Old Frontiers*, 90.
12. Captain Paul Demeré to Willian Henry Lyttelton, May 12, 1759, Fort Loudoun, Letterbooks of William Henry Lyttelton.
13. Captain Paul Demeré to Willian Henry Lyttelton, May 12, 1759, Fort Loudoun, Letterbooks of William Henry Lyttelton.
14. Captain Paul Demeré to William Henry Lyttelton, June 1, 1759, Fort Loudoun, Letterbooks of William Henry Lyttelton.
15. Captain Paul Demeré to William Henry Lyttelton, June 1, 1759, Fort Loudoun, Letterbooks of William Henry Lyttelton.
16. Captain Paul Demeré to William Henry Lyttelton, June 1, 1759, Fort Loudoun, Letterbooks of William Henry Lyttelton.
17. Captain Paul Demeré to Willian Henry Lyttelton, August 28, 1759, Fort Loudoun, Letterbooks of William Henry Lyttelton.
18. Captain Paul Demeré to Willian Henry Lyttelton, August 28, 1759, Fort Loudoun, Letterbooks of William Henry Lyttelton.
19. Captain Paul Demeré to Willian Henry Lyttelton, August 28, 1759, Fort Loudoun, Letterbooks of William Henry Lyttelton.
20. Captain Paul Demeré to Willian Henry Lyttelton, August 28, 1759, Fort Loudoun, Letterbooks of William Henry Lyttelton.
21. Lt. Richard Coytmore to Governor Lyttelton, September 26, 1759, Fort Prince George, CO5/57, Folio 167.
22. Kelton, *Cherokee Medicine*, 102.
23. Governor Lyttelton to General Amherst, October 23, 1759, Charles Town, CO5/57, Folio 173.
24. Evans, "Notable Persons: Ostenaco," 46.
25. Attah Kallah Kallah to Governor Lyttelton, November 2, 1759, Letterbooks of William Henry Lyttelton.
26. Attah Kallah Kallah to Governor Lyttelton, November 2, 1759, Letterbooks of William Henry Lyttelton.
27. Attah Kallah Kallah to Governor Lyttelton, November 2, 1759, Letterbooks of William Henry Lyttelton.
28. Attah Kallah Kallah to Governor Lyttelton, November 2, 1759, Letterbooks of William Henry Lyttelton.
29. Captain Paul Demeré, November 23, 1759, Fort Loudoun, Letterbooks of William Henry Lyttelton.
30. Brown, *Old Frontiers*, 91.
31. Brown, *Old Frontiers*, 91.
32. Brown, *Old Frontiers*, 91–92.

33. Brown, *Old Frontiers*, 92.
34. Brown, *Old Frontiers*, 92.
35. Brown, *Old Frontiers*, 92–93.
36. Brown, *Old Frontiers*, 92–93.
37. Evans, "Notable Persons: Ostenaco," 46.
38. Brown, *Old Frontiers*, 93.
39. James C. Kelly, "Oconostota," *Journal of Cherokee Studies* III, no. 4 (Fall 1978), 234.
40. Colonial Records of SC 1754–1765, xxxii-xxxiii.
41. General Amherst to Governor Lyttelton, New York, CO5/57, Folio 175.
42. John Stuart to Governor Lyttelton, December 3, 1759, Fort Loudoun, Letterbooks of William Henry Lyttelton.
43. John Stuart to Governor Lyttelton, December 3, 1759, Fort Loudoun, Letterbooks of William Henry Lyttelton.
44. John Stuart to Governor Lyttelton, December 7, 1759, Fort Loudoun, Letterbooks of William Henry Lyttelton.
45. Captain Paul Demeré to Governor Lyttelton, December 12, 1759, Fort Loudoun, Letterbooks of William Henry Lyttelton.
46. Captain Paul Demeré to Governor Lyttelton, December 12, 1759, Fort Loudoun, Letterbooks of William Henry Lyttelton.
47. Daniel. Tortora, *Carolina in Crisis: Cherokees, Colonists, and Slaves in the American Southeast, 1756–1763* (Chapel Hill: University of North Carolina Press, 2015), 82.
48. Brown, *Old Frontiers*, 94.
49. Tortora, *Carolina in Crisis*, 83.
50. Tortora, *Carolina in Crisis*, 83–84.
51. Tortora, *Carolina in Crisis*, 84–85.
52. Kelton, *Cherokee Medicine*, 117.
53. Ft. Prince George Copy of Treaty of Peace and Friendship Concluded by Gov. Lyttelton with the Cherokees, December 26, 1759, CO5/57, Folio 303.
54. *The South Carolina Gazette*, 1325, January 5–8, 1760, 1.
55. Kelly, "Oconostota," 224–225.
56. Ft. Prince George Copy of Treaty of Peace and Friendship Concluded by Gov. Lyttelton with the Cherokees, December 26, 1759, CO5/57, Folio 303.
57. Governor Lyttelton to General Amherst, December 27, 1759, Fort Prince George, CO5/57, Folio 301.
58. Copy of Journal of Conference with the Cherokee deputies, August 29–31, 1761, camp near Fort Prince George, CO5/61, Folio 457.
59. Corkran, *The Cherokee Frontier*, 189–191.
60. Richard Coytmore to Gov. Lyttelton, January 23, 1760, Fort Prince George, CO5/57, Folio 313.
61. Gov. Lyttelton to Gen Amherst, February 2, 1760, CO5/57, Folio 311.
62. Cashin, *Lachlan McGillivray*, 193–194.

63. Kelton, *Cherokee Medicine*, 118.
64. Tortora, *Carolina in Crisis*, 90.
65. Kelton, *Cherokee Medicine*, 119.
66. Richard Coytmore to Gov. Lyttelton, January 23, 1760, Fort Prince George, CO5/57, Folio 313.
67. Richard Coytmore to Gov. Lyttelton, January 23, 1760, Fort Prince George, CO5/57, Folio 313.
68. Tortora, *Carolina in Crisis*, 91.
69. Tortora, *Carolina in Crisis*, 92.
70. Tortora, *Carolina in Crisis*, 92.
71. Kelton, *Cherokee Medicine*, 120.
72. Richard Coytmore to Gov. Lyttelton, January 23, 1760, Fort Prince George, CO5/57, Folio 313.
73. Tortora, *Carolina in Crisis*, 92.
74. Richard Coytmore to Gov. Lyttelton, January 23, 1760, Fort Prince George, CO5/57, Folio 313.
75. Richard Coytmore to Gov. Lyttelton, January 23, 1760, Fort Prince George, CO5/57, Folio 313.
76. Richard Coytmore to Gov. Lyttelton, January 23, 1760, Fort Prince George, CO5/57, Folio 313.
77. Tortora, *Carolina in Crisis*, 93.
78. Richard Coytmore to Gov. Lyttelton, January 23, 1760, Fort Prince George, CO5/57, Folio 313.
79. Corkran, *The Cherokee Frontier*, 191–192.
80. Tortora, *Carolina in Crisis*, 93.
81. Richard Coytmore to Gov. Lyttelton, January 23, 1760, Fort Prince George, CO5/57, Folio 313.
82. Tortora, *Carolina in Crisis*, 93.
83. Conley, *The Cherokee Nation*, 47.
84. Kelly, "Oconostota," 221.
85. Tortora, *Carolina in Crisis*, 93–94.
86. Tortora, *Carolina in Crisis*, 94–95.
87. Tortora, *Carolina in Crisis*, 95.
88. Tortora, *Carolina in Crisis*, 96.
89. Kelly, "Oconostota," 227.
90. Tortora, *Carolina in Crisis*, 96.
91. Kelly, "Oconostota," 225.
92. Alexander Miln to Governor Lyttelton, February 24, 1760, Fort Prince George, Colonial Records of SC 1754–1765, 497–501.
93. Alexander Miln to Governor Lyttelton, February 24, 1760, Fort Prince George, Colonial Records of SC 1754–1765, 497–501.
94. Tortora, *Carolina in Crisis*, 97–98.
95. Cashin, *Lachlan McGillivray*, 199–200.

96. Alexander Miln to Governor Lyttelton, February 24, 1760, Fort Prince George, Colonial Records of SC 1754–1765, 499.

97. James Francis to Governor Lyttelton, Fort 96, March 6, 1760, Colonial Records of SC 1754–1765, 504–505.

98. Brown, *Old Frontiers*, 94.

99. Brown, *Old Frontiers*, 94.

100. Tortora, *Carolina in Crisis*, 99.

101. Alexander Miln to Governor Lyttelton, February 24, 1760, Colonial Records of SC 1754–1765, 499–500.

102. Brown, *Old Frontiers*, 94.

103. Alexander Miln to Governor Lytttelton, February 24, 1760, Fort Prince George, Colonial Records of SC 1754–1765, 497–501.

104. Kelly, "Oconostota," 225.

105. Alexander Miln to Governor Lytttelton, February 24, 1760, Fort Prince George, Colonial Records of SC 1754–1765, 497–501.

106. General Amherst to Governor Lyttelton, February 26, 1760, New York, CO5/57, Folio 320.

107. Brown, *Old Frontiers*, 95.

108. Evans, "Notable Persons: Ostenaco," 46.

109. Evans, "Notable Persons: Ostenaco," 46.

110. Brown, *Old Frontiers*, 95.

111. Tortora, *Carolina in Crisis*, 100–101.

112. Tortora, *Carolina in Crisis*, 101.

113. Brown, *Old Frontiers*, 96.

114. Kelton, *Cherokee Medicine*, 124–125.

115. Brown, *Old Frontiers*, 96.

116. Kelton, *Cherokee Medicine*, 124–125.

117. Col Montgomery to Gen Amherst, June 4, 1760, Camp near Ft. Prince George, CO5/57, Folio 71.

118. Brown, *Old Frontiers*, 97–98.

119. Kelton, *Cherokee Medicine*, 126–127.

120. Kelly, "Oconostota," 225.

121. Brown, *Old Frontiers*, 98.

122. Brown, *Old Frontiers*, 96.

123. Conley, *The Cherokee Nation*, 49.

124. Brown, *Old Frontiers*, 97.

125. Lt. Gov Bull to Gen Amherst, Charles Town, May 8, 1760, CO5/Folio 389.

126. Brown, *Old Frontiers*, 99–100.

127. Brown, *Old Frontiers*, 100–101.

128. Evans, "Notable Persons: Ostenaco," 46.

129. Evans, "Notable Persons: Ostenaco," 46.

130. Brown, *Old Frontiers*, 101.

131. Conway, *The Cherokee Nation*, 49.
132. Evans, "Notable Persons: Ostenaco," 46.
133. Brown, *Old Frontiers*, 101.
134. McDowell, Colonial Records of SC 1754–1765, xxxiv–xxxv.
135. Brown, *Old Frontiers*, 107.
136. Brown, *Old Frontiers*, 107.
137. Conley, *The Cherokee Nation*, 52.
138. Evans, "Notable Persons: Ostenaco," 47.
139. Kelly, "Oconostota," 226.
140. Kelton, *Cherokee Medicine*, 123.
141. Kelton, *Cherokee Medicine*, 130.
142. Kelton, *Cherokee Medicine*, 127.

Diplomacy after Fort Loudoun   3
"Till the Bloody Hatchet Is Buried"

As the British military renewed its plans for yet another strike against the Cherokees, the mood of the Cherokee people turned against further conflict as towns recalled their war parties and began to allow non-Indians unfettered travel through their territory, just as their leaders had ordered. Such behavior indicates the Cherokees were satisfied with the results of their actions under the laws of retributive justice. Cherokees began to visit Fort Prince George again, carrying gifts of food to its men, and they allowed supplies from Charles Town to reach the fort without conflict.

Just as war fever seemed to abate among the Cherokees, the French adventurer Antoine Adhemar de Lantagnac visited the Overhills town of Chota, ten miles southeast of modern Vonore, Tennessee, in late October 1760. He traveled with a small number of French soldiers and an equally small number of Shawnee Indians. Lantagnac, originally a soldier stationed at Mobile, became lost in the forest on a hunting expedition. Turned over to the British by their Indian allies, he remained in Charles Town for a time until he became a trader among the Cherokees. He acquired a Cherokee mate during his stay among them, though he traded among the Creeks as well. Aided by his Cherokee wife, he continued his efforts for many years to align the Cherokees with France.[1]

While a French officer distributed free goods, Lantagnac urged the Cherokees to return to war with the British. While Attakullakulla ignored these overtures, Seroweh, also known as the Young Warrior, traveled to Chota to meet with Lantagnac's party. Lantagnac left the French soldiers at Chota, promising, as he left, to return in three weeks with a full outfit of troops to take Fort Prince George. In this instance, Seroweh and his town were the lone Cherokees to take up this offer to renew the war.² Lieutenant Governor William Bull later wrote Jeffery Amherst of the results of the Lantagnac mission. His late December 1760 message noted that, in his opinion, while the French threat was not significant, the French were "enterprising and indefatigable in pursuing their schemes of discontent."³

When word of this low-level French intrigue reached the desks of British authority figures, they were already committed to resuming hostilities with the Cherokees as a precursor to create a lasting peace with them. It would be incorrect to say this latest news of French intrigue destroyed a growing peace effort on the part of the British; rather, it only confirmed their deep mistrust of Indians. They viewed Seroweh and his town's dalliance as if all forty Cherokee towns had taken up the French offer of war. Lieutenant Governor Bull certainly viewed matters this way, believing that the Cherokee peace overtures were merely a delaying tactic to give the Cherokees time to raise forces for an even larger attack than last time. He requested more British regulars from Commander Jeffrey Amherst, and the commander readied a mission under Colonel James Grant.⁴

While Lieutenant Governor Bull was requesting a military strike against the Cherokees, he was, at the same time, negotiating with the Choctaws. In November 1760, Bull notified the Board of Trade of a recent meeting with the Choctaws, who told Bull that the bulk of their people had few remaining ties with the French and wished to open diplomatic relations and trade with the British.⁵ Perhaps the governor hoped to replace the Cherokees as a favored tribe among the British during this time of conflict. Lantagnac's fateful visit certainly worked to alienate the Cherokees from the British. Two Overhills towns, intrigued by Lantagnac's proposal, sent delegations led by the pro-French chief Oconostota and by the Seed of Settico to the French forts to explore the relationship and to seek aid against the British.⁶

By contrast, in December 1760, other Cherokee representatives representing the major towns arrived at Fort Prince George. In particular, Mankiller of the Middle Town of Nikwasi led one delegation representing seven towns that lobbied for peace with the British. In terms of majority versus minority, the peace factions held the greater support among the Cherokee people. Isolated pockets, such as the people of Estatoe, held anger against the British, but they were the minority.⁷ The British representatives always sought unanimity among tribes like the Cherokees, which they never found among them or any other tribe. The differing political systems of Indian country and Europe always made the search for an all-powerful leader who could offer the total loyalty of his/her people a fruitless search. British officials also had a global war to consider, as well as their tenuous relations with other southern tribes.

Perhaps the major French defeats after 1756 and trade problems prompted the Choctaws to consider aligning with the British. In any event, more colonial officials began to report a correspondence with them. In October 1760, Georgia governor Henry Ellis reported to the board that the French had persuaded a small group of Choctaws to murder a British pack horseman. Another group of Choctaws, joined by some Creeks, pursued the original assailants until driven off by the gunfire from a nearby French fort. Ellis promised the Choctaws liberal trade and used the new relationship to discipline an old one. Ellis told the Creeks that traders bound for Choctaw lands would have to pass through their own. He warned the Creeks that if they molested these traders, they would have new enemies: the Choctaws.[8]

Meanwhile, British war plans for the Cherokees continued to take shape. General Amherst had chosen James Grant, now promoted to colonel, to head the follow-up invasion to Cherokee country. His orders were clear: to lay waste to Cherokee towns and follow the Cherokees as far inland as was practical to compel them to agree to a lasting peace.[9] The purpose was to punish Ostenaco for his actions against Fort Loudoun when the Cherokee leader was in charge during Oconostota's absence.[10] A late March 1761 letter to Virginia governor Francis Fauqier gave proof of Amherst's philosophy on Indian affairs: "They [the Southern Colonies] are of the same opinion I have long been that a peace with that misguided people [the Cherokees], is only attainable by the sword."[11]

Back in Cherokee country, Cherokee messengers came to Fort Prince George under a white flag on February 11, 1761. They carried the words of Attakullakulla, Ostenaco, and Cunneshote (Standing Turkey), who made peace overtures to the British and requested a meeting with Virginia governor William Byrd III. The British leadership at the fort had been replaced with Lieutenant Lachlan McIntosh, generally well liked by the tribes. In response, the Cherokees began to allow supply wagons to reach the fort. Starvation and hardship experienced by war-wrecked towns also stimulated many Cherokees to repair their relationship with the British.[12]

Under McIntosh's leadership, the Cherokees began to turn in large numbers of English prisoners taken in the recent hostilities to Fort Prince George in exchange for food. The pro-British leader, Attakullakulla, visited the fort in March 1761, and even the pro-French Cherokee, Seroweh, recommended peace with the British. Unfortunately, however, these changing sentiments could not overturn an order sent by General Jeffery

Amherst along with 1,200 troops sent to Charles Town in mid-December 1760. Their orders were for Lieutenant Colonel Grant to lay waste to Cherokee communities in an effort to bring Cherokee leaders to their knees. For the moment, French intrigue among the Cherokees was nonexistent, and so British military wrath turned full force on the Cherokees, and the antipathy mirrored how South Carolina people felt about the tribe.[13]

In the end, Grant's troops numbered almost three thousand, including South Carolina militia but also auxiliaries including the Catawbas, Chickasaws, and Mohawks. Colonel Grant's troops began the march from Charles Town to the Cherokees on March 20, 1761. His troops included several Haudenosaunee (Six Nations Iroquois) warriors, the very peoples with whom the Cherokee had made peace in order to fight for Britain in the Ohio River Valley. This army arrived among the Congarees on April 22, where it linked up with a unit of South Carolina troops as well as a battalion of Royal Scots. The combined forces headed for Ninety-Six, South Carolina, on April 23, 1761. Further Indian allies included the Lower Chickasaws and the Catawbas.[14] In late March 1761, Lieutenant Colonel Grant wrote Jeffery Amherst with his opinions about the growing peace efforts even as his troops moved deeper into Cherokee country: "I do not interfere about the peace, but I have wrote to the Lieut. Gov that we should not seem to be anxious to make one, that things have gone too far to think of terms, till the Indians have been corrected, and that we have them in some measure in our power."[15]

In early April 1761, Seroweh or the Young Warrior of Estatoe wrote to Lieutenant Lachlan McIntosh, the new commander of Fort Prince George. Part confession and part plea for an end to hostilities, Seroweh wrote, "it's true my people and I were hungry and we went to the settlements and got provisions and came home quietly. If I had a mind to spill more blood I might have done it then, tho I am blamed for everything both by white and red people, but if you and I were to meet you'd soon see there's greater rogues than me."[16] Seroweh continued with his mea culpa, rationalizing the events that had touched off the war, referencing his participation in the French and Indian War as requested by Virginia government. He wrote, "'tis true I was at the beginning of the mischief [as] it was owing to bad talks which made my young people mad; when you were here when did you know me a bad friend to the white people; did not I go to Virginia and did everything you desired me to help the white people?"[17] Seroweh ended his letter by stating that he was afraid to see McIntosh at that juncture but that he hoped to see him soon without fear.[18]

As Seroweh reached out to the British at Fort Prince George, other Cherokee leaders journeyed to Fort Toulouse in modern Alabama, near the confluence of the Coosa and Tallapoosa Rivers. The Seed of Settico (Overhills Town) and Oconostota returned with a few horse-loads of trade goods and only a few French soldiers to possibly use to counterbalance the overwhelming British presence in Cherokee country. At that point, the latter traveled to Fort Prince George along with Attakullakulla to try to neutralize the British military threat. Arriving at the fort shortly before Grant's army on May 27, 1761, Oconostota offered to lead Grant or another officer on a peace tour of the Cherokee towns so that he might observe their good will toward the British. When Colonel Grant declined this offer, the Cherokee military leader withdrew, as did most other Cherokee leaders except for Attakullakulla. The lone Cherokee diplomat remained at the fort, hoping to stop the impending violence and also hoping to boost his own status as leader. In response, Grant told the pro-British leader that he could not trust the Cherokee people, as they had broken agreements and their word too many times.[19] Essentially, Colonel Grant believed Attakullakulla's talk was merely a delaying tactic to give the Cherokees time for military pursuits, and so he set out on his attack mission on June 7, 1761.

Grant's armies then reached Etchoe in the Middle Towns in early June. Seroweh, who had previously pleaded for leniency, now met Grant on the battlefield on June 10, 1761, and the two armies engaged in combat. Grant attacked in a midnight raid on the town and then detached another attack force to hit the nearby town of Tassee. Grant's forces met less resistance this time, though the Cherokees fought until they ran out of ammunition and withdrew.[20] The battles took place in roughly the same area that they had a year before under Montgomery's attack. The Cherokees, armed with rifles, engaged the rear of the British combined army. Another group shot at the South Carolina militia near the Little Tennessee River. Still another group of Cherokees targeted the supply wagons as the main force began to retreat toward the Middle Towns. As they retreated, the Cherokees shot intermittently at the combined British army that followed them. The Cherokees' limited supply of ammunition would not allow for more sustained gunfire.[21] Grant and the British troops torched every settlement they found, always making sure to destroy crops in each town. The British troops even destroyed fruit trees as well as several hundred acres of crops. In Grant's journal of June 12 and 13, he noted that he sent his men out to burn all outlying houses, even stopping to pull up beans, peas, and corn in the field so that no viable crops would remain. Other Indian allies and his own troops destroyed the towns of Neowee and Kanuga.²² Some Cherokees evacuated ahead of the attack; others barely managed to escape Grant's troops. Because there were few Cherokees on whom enemy Indians could exact revenge, the Catawbas and Chickasaws soon lost interest in the mission, detached, and went home. Over a two-week period, Grant's troops attacked and destroyed some fifteen villages, always eliminating a town's crop supply as a part of the attack. On June 25, 1761, Colonel Grant returned to Nikwasi and left behind Lieutenant Colonel Henry Laurens with one thousand men. Grant then led his remaining Indian troops on a four-day march of destruction of Cherokee towns, including the mother town of Kituwah (between modern Cherokee and Bryson City, North Carolina). In this last mission, Grant's forces killed a man named Ocayulah from Kituwah, who had been a scout for the British at the battle of Fort Duquesne. On July 3, 1761, Grant's forces headed back to Fort Prince George, where they arrived on July 9, having completed their mission. He was confident that his handiwork would bring the Cherokees both to their knees militarily and to the bargaining table diplomatically. In a show of largesse, Grant permitted homeless Cherokees seeking refuge to settle near Fort Prince George.²³

In his raid, Grant and his troops had burned the towns of Lassee, Newcassee, Neowee, and Canuga. Other towns put to the torch included Wattoquiu, Ayoree, Cowhee, Cowitchie, and Ussanah. Another Cherokee town, Burning Town, was aptly named, as it became the tenth town to fall victim to Grant's raid. Alejoy, Stecoe, Kituwah, Tuckoritchee, and Tessantee rounded out the list of fifteen towns burned to the ground.²⁴ The next day after his return to Fort Prince George, Grant penned a letter to Jeffery Amherst. In it, he told his commander, "we have been lucky; everything has succeeded we have not met with a single rub; but I must observe to your excellency that the country we have been in is impenetrable if it was not defended by a very few men of any degree of spirit, they might have killed and wounded a great number of men every day without running the smallest risk."²⁵ The British officer admitted that if the Cherokees had been able to bring more warriors to the task, those numbers plus the terrain would have defeated his task force.

In the face of such devastation, Oconostota and other Cherokee leaders agreed to make peace on July 1, 1761. The Cherokee man sent word to Colonel Grant several times, but Grant insisted that the Great Warrior, Oconostota, appear before him in person, something that Oconostota was hesitant to do. The Cherokees decided, at that point, to turn lead negotiations over to Attakullakulla.²⁶ In September 1761, the pro-British chief, Attakullakulla, as well as the independent-minded Ostenaco, along with some seventeen other chiefs, met with Colonel Grant at Fort Prince George. Grant told the leaders that he wanted no less than four Cherokees turned over to him to be publicly executed, a demand Attakullakulla outright refused.[27] Attakullakulla's actions indicate sovereignty on the part of the Cherokees. The last time he was challenged with turning over Cherokee people for execution, Attakullakulla had offered an alternate plan of fighting against the French for Britain. This time, it was a quick and outright refusal. However, Grant told Attakullakulla that his people had to send a peace delegation to Charles Town, with which the pro-British leader did comply. Illustrative of how dangerous the Indian traders could be, a trader named McCunningham, for unknown reasons, told the Cherokees that the British planned to entrap them with smallpox in Charles Town should they go. The pro-British Attakullakulla refused to believe this talk, and in late August the Cherokee leader took the men he had spared at Fort Loudoun, John Stuart and William Shorey, plus a few other officers, toward Colonel William Byrd's army and ransomed them.

Byrd met with Attakullakulla on Reed Creek, a tributary of the New River in modern Blount County, Tennessee, between September 16 and 17 in peace talks in which the Cherokee leader promised a swift prisoner exchange. He pledged that the Cherokees would deliver up any Cherokee offenders that Byrd named before the full moon in October. He also pledged that the Cherokees would return any English prisoners they held by that same time. Attakullakulla promised that the Cherokees would give up control of Fort Loudoun with any cannons, balls, cohorns, or shells in their possession. Articles of the earlier Articles of Friendship treaty requiring them to expel any Frenchman were repeated in this latest treaty. Article 6 of the treaty named Attakullakulla as the "acknowledged Governor of the Nation, and that that he shall be obeyed as such."[28] This concession was a dynamic change in the Cherokee leader's status and one not granted by his own people. Some thirty-one years after the original Articles of Friendship Treaty elevated the original Moytoy to emperor status, this latest treaty did the same for Attakullakulla, though diminishing his title to that of "governor." If a comparison of titles means anything, it would seem his latest title for the Overhills leader indeed meant he was leader of a subject people and not true and sovereign allies.

The Cherokee leader left the meeting with a letter to take to the other Overhills leaders promising them fair treatment if they came to the peace talk in South Carolina. While Byrd promised their safety, he also pledged to level Cherokee country if they did not comply, even down to kernels of corn on the stalk.[29] Attakullakulla also met with Governor Bull that month. In the agreement reached by the two leaders, John Stuart, at Attakullakulla's request, was named Indian superintendent to replace the deceased Edmond Atkin, and so the Cherokees' friend, Bushyhead, returned to Cherokee country.[30] If indeed Attakullakulla's support resulted in Stuart's elevation to Southern Indian superintendent, it is indicative of the Cherokee man's status. It is also a good example of historian Francois Furstenberg's "tail wagging the dog" of empire theory—a regional figure affecting politics at the heart of the empire.

Surprisingly, Attakullakulla, the father of the leader of the Cherokee Rebellion of 1776, advised Colonel Byrd that, with the Cherokees, he must be prepared to "beat them into . . . a peaceful mode as they were over-confident about their recent battle successes."[31] The government of Virginia colony also continued to remain involved in Cherokee affairs seemingly in competition with South Carolina. Virginia leaders told the Cherokees they could not end the recent hostilities without a separate treaty with Virginia. When Lieutenant Governor Francis Fauquier wrote about these matters to a Captain Bullitt in the field, he urged the officer to let Attakullakulla know "that we cannot brighten the chain of friendship & make a peace to last forever till the bloody hatchett is entirely buried on all sides; and without the joint concurrence of the Carolinas on our side."[32] A group of Virginia militia moved south to build Fort Robinson near the Long Island of the Holston River, indicative of Virginia's desire to remained connected with the Overhills Cherokees.[33]

Thus, in November 1761, a delegation led by Cunneshote or Standing Turkey met with a Colonel Adam Stephens of Virginia and signed a separate treaty with them. If Cunneshote was a lesser dignitary than his deceased relative Connecorte, the Cherokees may have been sending the Virginians a message about their own status compared to that of South Carolina. From this agreement, the Cherokees also received a liaison, at their request: Lieutenant Henry Timberlake, who spent some time with them in Cherokee country in the months after the treaty.[34] Lieutenant Timberlake and a Sergeant Tom Sumter started out for the Overhills country by canoe on November 28, 1761, following the Holston River to the French Broad River juncture. From there, the two men followed the Little Tennessee River into the Overhills towns, where Ostenaco greeted them and escorted them to Chota.[35]

At this point, other Cherokee leaders viewed Attakullakulla with disdain. Some leaders, like Seroweh, also known as the Young Warrior and the Raven of Estatoe, wanted to unite with either the French or other

Indian tribes against the British. Seroweh wanted to force the British to evacuate Fort Prince George as they had done Fort Loudoun.[36] Obviously, Dragging Canoe in the 1770s was not the first Cherokee to desire conflict with white colonials and their military. However, many Cherokee people wanted peace, as did Attakullakulla, and were weary enough to do almost anything for it while saving a modicum of face, and Byrd's Treaty offered this. The number of Cherokee fighting men in the field had dropped by one-third, and smallpox, which had hit the Lower and Middle Towns, now ravaged the Overhills towns. Food was also scarce in many towns after Colonel Grant's raids. All of these factors combined to help the winds of peace to prevail.[37]

Jeffery Amherst responded fairly quickly to Grant's report. His early August 1761 letter echoed the sentiments that Grant had expressed in his latest letter. Amherst wrote, "if the burning of fifteen towns and destroying about 1400 acres of corns, beans and peas do not compel the Cherokees to sue for peace, nothing certainly will, but there can be no doubt of their submitting to terms; whatever they are, they must be preferable to starving."[38] Amherst ordered Grant to remain at the fort with his troops; he feared that a sudden departure by Grant's army might tempt the Cherokees to attack the frontier settlers, seeking revenge for their losses to Grant's raid.[39]

In July 1761, some of the Cherokee chiefs sent a messenger to Lieutenant Colonel Grant asking for peace terms. Chiefs such as Oconostota, Ostenaco, and Cunneshote (Standing Turkey) feared for their safety and did not make a personal appearance before him, sending a messenger instead. Other Cherokee leaders appeared by the end of the month offering Cherokee military services in a war against the Muskogee Creeks in exchange for ending the state of conflict with Great Britain and South Carolina. However, Grant refused to meet with these individuals and asked to negotiate with certain warriors only. As had been the case for over a decade, the Cherokees were conflicted as well on how to proceed and reacted with various strategies. Some wanted to use the old competition between South Carolina and Virginia by reaching out to the latter. Other Cherokees wanted French help, using Britain's greatest international rival.[40]

As peace negotiations were about to get under way in earnest, Jeffery Amherst wrote to South Carolina lieutenant governor William Bull in early August 1761. Speaking of Grant's mission, Amherst wrote, "the chastisement he has given those savages must compel them to sue for peace and if anything can, oblige them to the performance of these terms."[41] Amherst assured Governor Bull that the other Southern governors were in agreement that the peace should be concluded at Charles Town without the participation of the Indian commissioners like John Stuart.⁴² If the agenda of extreme violence toward the Cherokees in order to obtain an effective postwar peace seemed to be working out on paper, the same could not be said for matters on the Cherokee side.

In the end, peace negotiations took place between the pro-British chief Attakullakulla and Colonel Grant back where everything had started: at Fort Prince George near the end of August 1761. The Cherokees were not represented by their favorite leaders but by the British-elevated Attakullakulla, who had presented Grant with a bead necklace representing the peace wishes of the Cherokee people. Attakullakulla emerged from the war with a much more defined leadership position both by his own actions and due to the death of Connecorte (Old Hop). By contrast, Oconostota emerged from the war with the respect and admiration of the Cherokee people. Grant's devastating raids could not erase the pride the Cherokees felt in Oconostota's earlier defeat of Archibald Montgomery.⁴³

When Colonel Grant asked Attakullakulla whether he carried the authority to answer for all the Cherokee people, he answered that he was sent by the whole nation.⁴⁴ The deliberations opened with Attakullakulla passing around a peace pipe sent by the chief of Chokee, who could not attend. He also presented Grant with a string of beads from the warriors of Chokee. His summary statement noted that the warriors had "now found out that the white people are too many for them, by burning their towns but hopes that Colonel Grant will take pity on them & spare them."⁴⁵

Attakullakulla continued to present beads to Grant in the name of Cherokee leaders who were fearful of attending. He presented a string from the Overhills towns of Settico, one from Tellico and one from Chatouqu. Attakullakulla was not able to present beads from all the towns despite his claim to represent the whole nation. Continuing his opening speech, he told Grant that he had saved Captain Stuart and as many of the Fort Loudoun garrison as he could. Attakullakulla further recalled the story of his trip to London in 1730 for Colonel Grant. In remembering the past, he told Grant that he was the only one still living from that trip. Continuing, he told Grant that during that long-ago visit, King George II had told him to "love the English."⁴⁶ Attakullakulla continued his remarks, stating, "King George did bid him to always walk in the right."⁴⁷ The Cherokee leader stated that he wanted the path between the Cherokees and the people of South Carolina to be a straight one made of iron. He pledged that the Cherokees would only have good thoughts about the English.⁴⁸

Near the conclusion of his opening speech, Attakullakulla admitted that the Cherokees had stolen livestock from the backcountry settlers because they were hungry but promised to stop these activities. The cessation of the all-important Indian trade, Britain's ultimate power, made it into the Cherokee leader's closing remarks. He told Grant that the Cherokees "do not know how to make anything & they should be glad to see how soon the white people would come and bring them goods as before."[49] Since a desire for the restoration of trade was woven into initial peace overtures, it is clear how integrated that trade was into tribal life. Colonel Grant spoke second, after Attakullakulla, posing a series of questions for the Cherokee leader to answer. As mentioned earlier, the first question posed to Attakullakulla was whether he had the authority to speak for the entirety of Cherokee people. The second question reiterated the first point, asking whether the Cherokee people would adhere to what Attakullakulla agreed to in treaty. Grant's third statement indicated he would wait for any warriors still out in the field to receive news of the peace talks; in the meantime, Attakullakulla would have to deal with the South Carolina governor.[50]

The next day, Grant proposed the British side of the articles of the peace treaty to Attakullakulla. The first article demanded that four Cherokees be executed within sight of the camp or that four scalps of the same be brought to Grant within the same time frame. As it would turn out, this first article would be the most problematic for Grant even dealing with a pro-British chief who was accustomed to accommodating the British. The second article required all captured English people and livestock to be turned over by the Cherokees. Article 3 required the complete surrender of Fort Loudoun and its weapons back to the British. The fourth article was a familiar one, requiring the Cherokees to expel any French visitors to their nation. Article 5 required that the Cherokees to execute any of their own who murdered a white man. Since the war had begun with the slaughter of many Indian fur traders, such as John Elliot, the subject of article 6 forbidding the Cherokees from harming their traders is not surprising. The article also stipulated that they should not trespass on either pastures or gardens. Article 7 stipulated that the Chickasaws and Catawbas would be compensated in treaty negotiations. Article 8 stated that if an Englishman murdered a Cherokee, the Cherokees would deliver him to the commander of the nearest fort. Then the alleged murderer would be tried under English law in the nearest town. If he was found guilty, he would be put to death in the presence of the Cherokees if they desired it. Certainly article 8 would have given Cherokee leaders cause for concern. If article 5 required the automatic death sentence of a Cherokee who killed a colonial subject, article 8 required the Cherokees to give up automatic reciprocity to await the decision of a colonial official. Similarly, article 9 stated that if the Cherokees were abused by their traders, they were not allowed to harm them. Rather, the Cherokees were to make complaint to the governor of their province, who would "do them justice." Such trader abuse could take the form of enslaving members of a Cherokee family for debt owed by the husband or sexual abuse of Cherokee women. Both were quite serious matters to sovereignty as well as personal safety. This new requirement bypassed the role of Indian superintendent Edmond Atkin (later John Stuart) and commissaries. Normally the superintendent or the commissaries dealt with tribal grievances, but the new treaty put the governor in that role.

The tenth article stated that if a Cherokee injured a white man, that man would complain to the local chief, who would "do him justice." Finally, article 11 stated that when the articles had been mutually agreed to and the peace treaty was ratified at Charles Town, the Cherokee prisoners in English custody would be released and trade would be renewed, with trade items sent up for deerskins.[51]

The next day, August 31, 1761, Attakullakulla responded to Colonel Grant over the terms in the proposed peace treaty. The Cherokee leader promised that he had carefully considered each article and he hoped to give Grant as good a talk as was possible. He told Grant that he had been quite ill just before the negotiations and that the Overhills towns expected him back in only three days. In a somewhat rambling opening statement, he acknowledged that the people of the Middle towns had done wrong by the English. He also mentioned a concern that the Creeks would try to disrupt the Anglo-Cherokee peace treaty. Further, he told Grant that he had heard the Creeks would also try to attack the Chickasaws returning from English military service with their presents. In both of these matters, he feared his own people would somehow be blamed for the troubles.[52]

After opening remarks Attakullakulla cut to the heart of the matter by addressing article 1, the surrender of four Cherokees to be executed. Speaking of these people, Attakullakulla artfully stated "that he has looked all about but cannot see them for they are all grown better, but if any of them grow bad again they shall be killed."[53] Perhaps Little Carpenter hoped to communicate that wild, impetuous boys now had grown into wiser men, and the boys who caused the trouble no longer existed to be punished. However, he exercised agency as he crafted his answer, and he was clearly telling Colonel Grant that he would not agree to article 1 of the treaty. Attakullakulla mentioned that he approved of treaty articles 5 and 8, stating that whites or Cherokees who killed each other should be executed, though article 8 required due process for a white man accused of killing a Cherokee. After addressing these three articles directly, the chief returned to a recounting of his long journey to Keowee, his intent to drive the French out of Cherokee lands, and his hopeful return to peace with frontier whites so that the trade goods would return with the traders.[54]

Colonel Grant then commented on the Cherokee response, stating that he had been given full power to conclude the treaty and the Cherokees had been given full time to consider it. He noted that Attakullakulla had answered only two articles of the eleven. Further, Grant acknowledged that the chief had declined to perform article 1. Grant requested that Attakullakulla again speak, this time commenting on every article. The chief then listened as articles 2–11 were read aloud again, and he verbally agreed to each of them, in the name of the Cherokee people. Grant told the Cherokee leader that he could not alter the treaty by omitting article 1 and so encouraged Attakullakulla to go to Charles Town and treat with Governor Bull directly. In a surprising bit of encouragement, Grant told the chief that if the governor chose to drop article 1, Grant would not object, but it would be necessary for Attakullakulla and his warriors to deal directly now with the government in Charles Town.[55]

As Colonel Grant concluded his remarks, he promised that, while Attakullakulla attended these matters, no Cherokees would be harmed during the extended negotiation period of the treaty. Grant did require the chief to send representatives back to the Cherokee nation and acquaint them with the treaty articles in the meantime, and Attakullakulla agreed to these conditions. The next day, on September 1, 1761, Attakullakulla committed to Grant that he would travel to Charles Town with five warriors, who included Willanawa, Cappy, a mixed-blood Cherokee named Will of Nikwasi, and the Raven of Hywassee. These warriors and some attendants would make the journey for peace in the name of the Cherokee nation.[56] As Attakullakulla prepared for this trip, an Overhills trader based at Settico, Charles McGunningham, warned the Cherokees of a smallpox outbreak in Charles Town, telling them they would not live to return if they made the trip. Attakullakulla ignored the warning, and the Cherokees set out on September 2, 1761, escorted by South Carolina militia men who were also members of the assembly, and arrived in Charles Town on September 14, 1761.[57]

In a late September 1761 letter to Jeffery Amherst, Lieutenant Governor Bull recounted the details of the arrival of the Attakullakulla delegation and Bull's dealings with the Cherokees. The group arrived on

September 14, 1761, at Ashley Ferry; Bull had called the General Assembly into session to meet with the Cherokees there. One of his reasons for the changed location was due to an outbreak of yellow fever in Charles Town, not smallpox as reported by trader McGunningham. According to the governor, Attakullakulla produced several strings of white beads as his credentials, expressing the desire of the Cherokee people for peace. The governor told the Cherokee leader that he had to consult with his General Assembly over alterations to the treaty. Bull then produced for the Assembly the original conditions he had given Colonel Grant back in the spring; he followed with a report on Grant's recent negotiations with Attakullakulla, including the troublesome stalemate over article 1 and its demand for four Cherokee lives. Bull then finished his presentation with a report on his meeting with Attakullakulla the previous day and turned to his legislature for their advice on the discrepancies of agreement. Surprisingly, the Assembly returned a recommendation that article 1 be deleted so that more of the Cherokee people might adhere to a lasting treaty. They recommended that the treaty be confirmed by a delegation of chiefs from the Lower, Middle, Valley, and Overhills towns after Attakullakulla had returned to brief them. The Assembly gave these recommendations which Bull accepted on September 19, 1761.[58] Attakullakulla's obstinacy over article 1 was an example of a Cherokee leader exerting agency with the British ally—and it had paid off. If we consider this move from the British point of view—that the Cherokees were a subject people—then Britain backed down on this issue.

In a personal aside to General Amherst, Governor Bull observed that the meeting over the treaty produced a fuller house of delegates who possessed a great zeal for the topic at hand. He admitted the delegates moved reluctantly on the issues but, in the end, a great majority voted on the recommendation to delete article 1. Bull hoped that South Carolinians would accept the handiwork of such a majority of their representatives. He noted that South Carolina had secured the interests of both Virginia and North Carolina in their recommendations. He promised Amherst to get a copy of the deliberations back to Colonel Grant at Fort Prince George. Finally, Bull noted that Attakullakulla was anxious to leave the city, and he obliged the Cherokee leader's wishes.[59]

The long-standing belief among Indigenous people that colonial capitals held disease was not a new one. Though trader McGunningham had warned of the wrong disease, the city was still dangerous due to yellow fever, and the Cherokees did not tarry there. Governor Bull wanted Amherst to know that he gave Attakullakulla's group hospitality during their stay but not liberality. He did not want it to appear that he had achieved a peace by buying off the Cherokees. Rather, Bull reported that he had recognized Attakullakulla for his steadfast loyalty to the British and only gave plain clothes to the other members of his party. In Bull's opinion, the Cherokees were happy in what they had accomplished and had departed from Charles Town on September 24, 1761, concluding a visit of ten days. Bull had established a firm timeline of anticipated events to speed along the peace process. He had allotted the Cherokees a travel time of twelve days to reach Colonel Grant. The Cherokee chief was then to call his own assembly at the Overhills town of Chota on October 13, 1761, and allow up to four days to debate the terms agreed to in Charles Town. He was to send the result of the deliberations by October 21, 1761, to Fort Prince George, with Bull receiving the report by either October 27 or October 28. If all went well, Bull hoped to receive the headmen as outlined in the plan.[60] The Assembly chose to make Twenty-Six Mile Creek the new Cherokee boundary with South Carolina, beyond which the tribe could not travel without white escort. The boundary set by Colonel Grant had allowed them to travel out forty miles out from Keowee instead of the new limit of twenty-six miles. That new limit would severely diminish the hunting ground of the Lower Towns, whose trade with Charles Town might suffer.[61]

Attakullakulla returned from Chota on November 14, 1761, at Fort Prince George. He traveled with a few pro-British chiefs like himself. From there, he returned to Charles Town with a military escort from Colonel Grant. Virginia government once more sought to interpose its presence into the peace proceedings as well, perhaps snubbed from being left out of the initial meetings. In September 1761, the Virginians built Fort Robinson on the Great Island of the Holston, which put them in close proximity to the Overhills towns. Feeling the pressure from Virginia, one hundred Overhills delegates signed a separate peace treaty with Virginia Colony on November 20, 1761. Much simpler than its South Carolina counterpart, the treaty required the Cherokees to keep a firm peace with Virginia, North Carolina, and the Tuscarora Indians. Further, it required them to turn over any Cherokees who had murdered white people to the commander of Fort Robinson. Independent Cherokee leaders like Ostenaco were pleased to have this other source of trade and possible aid, separate from South Carolina.[62]

There is no record of something like a plebiscite vote among the Cherokees over the peace treaty ending the Anglo-Cherokee War. Rather, it seems to have been the handiwork of Attakullakulla powering through a series of diplomatic hoops. Connecorte (Old Hop) had once called him just a servant to the British. General Forbes, by contrast, had called him a consummate dog, full of demands, seeking to leverage them at critical junctures for Britain. Now the servant had made himself the preeminent diplomat among the Cherokees to British and South Carolina authorities. Was Attakullakulla a new Cherokee emperor rising from the ashes of the postwar period with Oconostota as his secretary of war? North Carolina governor Arthur Dobbs estimated that the war, the smallpox outbreak, and starvation had reduced the Cherokee population by one-third.[63] If Attakullakulla was the new Cherokee leader in British eyes, could he repair the damages to his kingdom?

Not to be left out, Virginia continued to maintain a presence among the Cherokees. Colonel Adam Stephens brought provincial troops to the Holston River to construct Fort Robinson. From North Carolina came Lieutenant-Colonel Hugh Waddell with a group of North Carolina provincials and Tuscarora Indians to widen a road between Fort Robinson and the Overhills town of Chota.[64] Virginia, it seems, intended to strengthen its position among the Cherokees in the postwar period.

The South Carolina Assembly took up the final ratification of the Cherokee peace treaty on December 14, 1761. The Cherokees and Assembly members smoked a peace pipe, and Attakullakulla distributed beads representing the peace wishes of several towns. Attakullakulla surrendered some nine English prisoners at the event but received only two Cherokee prisoners in exchange.[65]

As historian Walter Edgar observed, this treaty ending the Cherokee War was the last one that South Carolina colony negotiated with an Indian tribe. The war gave many young Carolina men both the honor necessary to move up in South Carolina society and the military experience they could call on in another conflict coming a few years down the road. The postwar era of peaceful relations was off to a rather bumpy start, however. As an even more discouraging omen, the Cherokee peace delegation was attacked on their way back to Cherokee country by a gang of frontier whites who relieved the Cherokees of some twenty horses.[66]

As an aging Cherokee leader returned home through war-damaged towns, another leader arrived in Charles Town. Thomas Boone arrived a few days after the peace treaty was signed. The new governor was relatively young but wise enough to see that the Cherokee War had polarized the Assembly and exacerbated rivalries among some of the assembly men over issues of honor.[67]

For the Overhills Cherokees, the presence of a Virginia fort within their territory signaled their need to negotiate with Virginia as well as

South Carolina if they hoped to enjoy a plentiful flow of trade goods to break the South Carolina monopoly. In early 1762, Virginia delegates and the Overhills Cherokees, a Settico delegation, reaffirmed the peace principles they had agreed on in November 1761. Lieutenant Governor Francis Fauquier offered a bounty of £200 to anyone who could provide evidence against any Virginian for the murder of a Cherokee during the late war.[68]

Yet soon after Governor Fauquier withdrew the militia garrison from the fort and dismantled Fort Robinson, citing expenses.[69] Now the Overhills Cherokees would not be able to force South Carolina to compete for their trade. Some Overhills Cherokees would also interpret the withdrawal of the Virginia presence as a sign of ill will by the Virginians for the Cherokees. By April 1762, Lieutenant Henry Timberlake had concluded his mission in service to Virginia among the Overhills Cherokees and was back in Williamsburg with Ostenaco, Cunneshote, and Woyi, along with a larger group of their countrymen. Though Governor Fauquier was not thrilled with the cost of maintaining this many guests, Timberlake knew enough of Cherokee culture to understand that he was repaying the hospitality he had been shown among the Cherokees. At a dinner given at William and Mary College by Professor James Horrocks, Ostenaco remarked on the portrait of King George III. "Long have I wished to see the king, my father," he stated, "this is his resemblance, but I am determined to see himself."[70]

Ostenaco spoke to Governor Fauqier about the trip, telling the governor that much of Attakullakulla's prestige had derived from his 1730 visit to London. Ostenaco further offered that he wished to see for himself whether Attakullakulla's stories were true. Ostenaco pressed his request until the governor relented and agreed to send Ostenaco, Cunneshote, and Woyi to London with Timberlake.[71] Timberlake noted the financial side of the deal: "the Indians having no money, expect the person who travels with them to treat them with whatever they take a fancy to."[72] One wonders whether the British ever thought of the cost of their stays among the Cherokees.

The party, including Timberlake, Sergeant Tom Sumter, and interpreter William Shorey, departed Virginia on May 15, 1762. The three Cherokee men suffered from seasickness, but translator William Shorey developed a cough that turned into pneumonia. He died at sea and was buried there.[73] Timberlake recounts the back story that, before departure, his Cherokee wife threw him in a river to counteract his drunken state. Unfortunately, he nearly drowned, having to be fished out by others, but his ailments soon set in. Timberlake esteemed him a "thorough master of their language."[74]

The next generation of Cherokee dignitaries arrived one month and one day after departing Hampton, Virginia, arriving in Plymouth, England, on June 16, 1762. Timberlake notes his Cherokee guests were curious about the British navy and seemed delighted to be able to tour the seventy-four-gun man-of-war *HMS Revenge* in Plymouth harbor. They arrived two days later in London and began a tour of both the hoi polloi in the city streets and some of the better set. Timberlake had difficulties arranging an audience with King George III while his guests enjoyed a theater performance.[75]

Not until July 8, 1765, did the eager Ostenaco get his audience with the new King George III. He wore clothes of rich blue, covered with lace and wearing a silver gorget bearing the king's coat of arms. Cunneshote and Woyi wore scarlet and gold lace, also wearing silver gorgets. Lord Eglinton, the same Archibald Montgomery whom the Cherokees had defeated in combat, now introduced them to his majesty as Timberlake struggled to translate for his Cherokee guests. Ostenaco was not confident in his abilities and yet praised Timberlake in a speech that Timberlake edited from a sense of modesty. Near the end of the ninety-minute visit, Ostenaco took out his pipe to offer a smoke to King George, as was the custom of the Cherokee man's country. Timberlake intervened, citing that the kind offer was contrary to local custom. Ostenaco agreed, putting away his pipe, stating that it would not be correct since the king had no equal under the creator.[76] In his memoirs, Timberlake wrote his visitors were taken with the king's youth and the grandeur of the power he commanded. Of the offer of tobacco, he advised Ostenaco not to offer the king a smoke or to take his hand, but rather to offer to kiss his hand, as it was considered the great honor in Timberlake's country.[77]

The remainder of July consisted of making travel plans for the Cherokee delegation to return. Timberlake was told that the returning vessel would take them to Charles Town as its port of origin despite the fact that Ostenaco wanted to return to Virginia. While Lord Egremont advised Timberlake to deceive them until later in the trip, Timberlake stood firm that he would not escort them back across the Atlantic due to exhausting the funds set aside for their visit. In the end, Sergeant Sumter agreed to escort the Cherokees back to North America.[78]

Ostenaco, Cunneshote, and Woyi departed Britain on August 25, 1762, and arrived in Charles Town on November 3, 1762. Today they are known among modern Cherokees as the "Emissaries of Peace."[79] Timberlake sent along a letter for Governor William Bull II, asking him to smooth over any hard feelings the Cherokee delegation might have had about any aspect of their visit. Yet, in receptions for the Cherokee party in Charles Town, Ostenaco gave the impression of being well satisfied with his trip. King George gifted Ostenaco with a new silver gorget, ingraved "Loyal Chief Outacite Cherokee Warrior."[80] Certainly the visit plus the medal had increased Ostenaco's stature among the Cherokees. The Cherokee chief received another gift from the English, but one that was given, probably without his knowledge, between November 1761 and March 1762. During his absence, one of Ostenaco's daughters gave birth to an Anglo-Indian child named Richard Timberlake. Apparently Ostenaco was delighted with his grandson, an ultimate expression of Henry Timberlake's acceptance of the Cherokee people.[81]

During the missions of the "Emissaries of Peace," the Shawnees had sent raiding parties back into the Overhills towns in early 1762. Attakullakulla's colleague Willanawa led a Cherokee party back to the Virginia frontier on a retaliatory raid but at a cost of losing the Raven of Toqua in the attack. As if these events were not draining enough, the war had reduced the number of Cherokee villages from forty towns before the war down to twenty communities afterward. Many Lower Towns, like Keowee, were not rebuilt. This region would soon receive an influx of new settlers, courtesy of the South Carolina government. Some Middle Settlements like Tassee and Nikwasi were abandoned for years before reoccupation. It is true the Cherokees built some new towns in better locations like Seneca (at modern Clemson) and, importantly, Malaquo among the Overhills.[82] An important warrior in 1776 would claim Malaquo as his base a bit later in time, and its population would increase as that warrior attracted more followers. As the Shawnee attacks continued through the year 1762, Attakullakulla informed the new commander of Fort Prince George, Lachlan McIntosh, that the Cherokees could neither rebuild nor hunt as they needed to do because of these attacks from the north.[83]

South Carolina took a proactive stance for its relationship with the Cherokees in the postwar years as the government unveiled its own plans for a new trade relationship. The South Carolina Assembly planned to take over the Indian trade to the Cherokees as a way to better manage relations with the tribe and to conveniently shut out the competing trade from Virginia. The colony had done something similar in the aftermath of the Yamassee War in 1715. The new governor, Thomas Boone, planned to make the Cherokee trade a public monopoly with a board of five directors to govern the trade and a resident factor to implement policy. A rough draft of this plan illustrated that the colonials well knew the source of many of their old problems. It also indicated they would no longer tolerate many traditional native practices that were becoming increasingly expensive. In a very bold opening statement, the draft noted that "neither the Indian traders nor Indians can be at all depended on; the first are the refuse of the Earth, [and] stick at nothing to obtain a temporary advantage."[84] The plan called for uniform policies in dealing with one group of Indians when two or more colonies were involved. Trade would take place at designated outposts located only so deep in the backcountry as could be readily defended in case of attack. The factors employed in the public trade were to be men of good character and even temper. Trade goods would consist of the usual items, and ammunition and rum were both included on the list. The authors of the plan deemed credit extension to the Indians to be the source of many past disputes and strictly forbade its use. The plan further called for factors to be authorized to seize persons trafficking in goods illegally in the Cherokee lands and to hold their wares as a guarantee that interlopers would appear at the proper time to answer charges. Punishments for Indian offenses were quite harsh. If a Cherokee killed a Euroamerican, then the government would be empowered to kill two members of his tribe. In order to prevent the Indians from engaging in retributive justice, all trade with the tribe would cease until the Indians accepted the judgment and punishment.[85] This last feature clearly contradicted the recent treaty ending the Anglo-Cherokee War.

Not surprisingly, the plan called for an end to Indian conferences, which it termed disgraceful. It asked that such practices "be forever laid aside, those ignominious tributes be utterly abolished, & that immense expense of provisions be saved."[86] Colonial Indian expenditures had risen steadily during the critical contest to gain the loyalty of the various tribes of the backcountry during the French and Indian War. Now officials were attempting to pare down those expenditures, a move bound to conflict with tribal values and with the custom of giving presents, long ago established by the Spanish and practiced by the British with the southern Indians for 150 years. Such a cost-cutting measure ignored the fact that gift-giving in native culture conveyed the wish to be a family member to the recipient. It was the only way the giver could expect to receive aid or military services from native people.

The South Carolina act for regulating the Cherokee trade was quite similar to its draft. The purposes of the act were to maintain the peace recently reestablished with the Cherokees and to encourage their withdrawal from French interests through a steady supply of needed goods. Honest, trustworthy men were to operate the trade out of a storehouse at Fort Prince George, adjacent to the nearby Lower Town of Keowee. The trade was to be governed by a board of directors that included Thomas Lamboll, Thomas Shubrick, Gabriel Manigault, John Savage, and Thomas Smith. South Carolina government planned to hire a resident factor for Fort Prince George at an annual salary of £300. That factor would take an oath and enter a bond pledging to enforce the trade regulations under penalty of a £1,000 fine.[87]

His duties included enforcing uniform prices for trade goods sold and skins received. Interestingly, the factor was to prevent the Indians from entering Euoamerican settlements for any reason whatsoever. No members of the governor's council or the assembly could be members of the board of directors.[88] In July 1762, the board chose Edward Wilkinson as factor and gave him instructions that covered weaknesses recognized by the colonials as detrimental to their relationship with the Cherokees. Neither Wilkinson nor any of his assistants was allowed to issue credit to the Cherokees. Nor was Wilkinson allowed to leave his post, except in extreme emergency. He and his associates had to maintain friendly relations with the Indians, though they were to avoid making them any promises. The factor had to record various aspects of the trade and notable events in Cherokee life.[89]

Ironically, this new policy had virtually no time to correct old ills. In 1763, King George III issued a royal proclamation opening the trade to all subjects. Thus, South Carolina's brief monopoly was illegal and was dissolved by an ordinance on October 6, 1764. Supervision of the trade in the South reverted to the office of Superintendent of Indian Affairs John Stuart. Stuart's ascendancy over the colonial governors, albeit incomplete and brief, ushered in a new age in Britain's relationship with the southern tribes. Private land transfers between native peoples and private individuals or corporations were illegal; tribes could only cede lands to the British government.

Of course, the preeminent news of early 1763 was the February 10 peace treaty between Britain and France ending the Great War for Empire. With negotiations beginning in the summer of 1762, the treaty resulted in a French commitment to evacuate from Louisiana by November of that year, with new ownership transferring to Spain. That would effectively eliminate the ability of the Overhills Cherokees to reach out to the French should they have continuing difficulties with the British. France also agreed to withdraw from its North American territory east of the Mississippi River. Further, while debating their diplomatic options, French negotiators chose to surrender Canada rather than the sugar cane islands of Martinique, Guadeloupe, and St. Lucia. In return, Britain would restore the French Caribbean islands it had taken during the war. Britain guaranteed the religious freedom of its new Catholic subjects in Canada while allowing France access to the fishing grounds off the coast of Canada.[90] Such transfers of vast territories between superpower nations certainly relegated events in Cherokee country to a subordinate position.

The postwar dynamics of British hegemony, especially in trade goods, only made the tribes more dependent than they were before the war. It would be more difficult for the tribes to play the three superpowers against each other with two of them relegated to minor positions.[91] The Overhills Cherokees would continue to interact with the French and occasionally court them when displeased with the British. The British government did not forget the Cherokees or other southern Indians for very long in these affairs.

The Proclamation Line was Britain's attempt to honor the 1758 Treaty of Easton in which the Cherokees were very involved. Britain, to be clear, was also giving itself time to figure out the problem of Indians and settlers. Though Britain had won the Great War, it lacked the resources to deal with Indian-settler conflicts. The Proclamation Line tended to view Indian peoples as subjects, not as the allies they were treated like in the Anglo-Cherokee Peace Treaty of December 1761.[92]

The idea for what historian Collin Calloway terms "a line in the mountains" came ironically from Henry Ellis, a former governor of Georgia colony. In documents written by Ellis, he postulated that the American colonial population would become ungovernable for Britain if allowed to spread beyond the Appalachian Mountains. Not only would the Proclamation Line prevent that possibility, but it would also honor the 1758 Easton Treaty with native peoples. Finally, the line would limit administrative costs of governing the American colonies.[93] The Earl of Shelburne, William Petty, was president of the Board of Trade when it deliberated the Proclamation Line. Petty had no plan to permanently stop westward expansion for the colonists; rather, he wished to better regulate it. The document was expedited through channels, and King George III signed it on October 7, 1763.[94] With the stroke of a pen, the Proclamation Line granted native peoples limited sovereignty as subject peoples. The next step was to communicate the change to both the colonists and the native peoples. Toward that end, the British government directed the Indian superintendents to hold congresses with the tribes to explain the change in policy.

Sir William Johnson, superintendent of Indian Affairs to the North, sent copies of the document and wampum beads to northern tribes for a conference at Niagara. Some two thousand native peoples assembled there in July and August 1764. The Indian superintendents knew both to distribute gifts, which made the English temporary family, and to exchange wampum belts recording the new Niagara peace treaty as well as the Proclamation Line. The British government validated Indian lands as inviolable, only transferable to the British Crown or its representatives in North America.[95]

Similarly, the British government instructed the superintendent of Indian Affairs in the South, John Stuart, to hold a series of congresses with the southern tribes to tell them the results of the Great War for Empire, or, rather, the British version of the results. At one such meeting, the Congress of Augusta in November 1763, Stuart told the Indians that the French and their Spanish allies had been defeated and were now banished from the Southeast.[96] He also reaffirmed existing treaties made between the British and those tribes present.[97] Johnson and Stuart were the British representatives to the major tribes. Both were important men with familial ties to the tribes. Johnson had married the Mohawk woman Molly Brant, and many diplomatic events were carried out from their home. Stuart had similar family ties among the Cherokees, though he had a legal wife back in Charles Town. One important power granted to these men in the Proclamation Line was their ability to make local adjustments to the boundary line to solve any human problems that might occur along the line drawn in the mountains.[98] At least on paper, the Proclamation Line seemed to solve previous problems between the tribes and settlers. Although it seemingly created an Indian reserve where colonials could not settle, it also opened the Indian trade to any British subject who could afford to pay a bond and obtain a trader license. The law thus nullified South Carolina's attempted monopoly of a Cherokee trade. It also severely curtailed the regulatory power of Superintendents Johnson and Stuart.[99]

As if there were not enough new rules and regulations to adhere to, the South Carolina Assembly legislated one final change that would affect the Cherokees in the postwar period. The Commons House of Assembly chose to appropriate land just south of the recent Cherokee border for a new immigrant community that would create a buffer zone between the Cherokees and backcountry South Carolina residents. Two plucky Scots-Irish entrepreneurs chose the postwar period as a time ripe for the establishment of a cluster of Scots-Irish communities in this location. John Rea and George Galphin, both partners in the Augusta-based firm of Brown, Rea, and Company, sponsored the legislation for the settlements. The original investors along with new members submitted a petition suggesting that a proper tract of forty thousand acres was sufficient to lure "good and faithful subjects of the Kingdom of Ireland [who] would cheerfully remove from thence to become settlers in this province provided they were favoured [sic] with proper encouragement."[100] The practical benefit of the phrase "proper encouragement" meant property tax exemptions which would certainly lure people away from the perpetually high taxes of Ireland. South Carolina government felt it prudent to plant the Scots-Irish between the Cherokee Lower Towns and Charles Town.

The triumvirate of Cherokee leaders—Ostenaco, Oconostota, and Attakullakulla—tried to manage Cherokee affairs during this critical time, each in their own way. The influence and prestige of Ostenaco was greatly increased after his journey among the British in London. A Cherokee man named Go-ohsohly, nephew to Oconostota, was taken prisoner in October 1765 by some of the Hodeeenosaunee in New York colony. The Cherokee-Haudenosaunee alliance had not lasted long without violation. Alexander Cameron, deputy of John Stuart, traveled to Charles Town with both Oconostota and Attakullakulla, plus their sons, to effect a rescue. They met with South Carolina's new governor, Charles Lord Montagu, on these matters.[101]

It was not until late November 1767 that a face-to-face meeting between the two sets of tribal leaders began to take shape. Both Attakullakulla and Oconostota, plus six others, departed by ship for New York. Their mission was to link up with Stuart's northern counterpart, Sir William Johnson, in order to effect the young man's release and a restoration of the peace treaty between the two groups. The Cherokees arrived in late December 1765.[102]

The meeting was with representatives of all six tribes, though primary dialogue occurred between Oconostota and the Senecas. Hodeeonsaunee represesentatives did not come to Johnson Hall until March 2, 1768. Though not known for his speeches, Oconostota spoke to the northern representatives as he gave out white wampum belts, speaking of his desire to bury the hatchet so deeply that it never rose again to hurt either group. Illustrative of the power held by Cherokee women, Oconostota distributed wampum belts sent by Cherokee women to their Haudenosaunee counterparts as well as belts sent by Cherokee boys to Haudenosaunee boys. The Cherokees finalized a peace treaty with the northern tribes on March 17, 1768, and the Cherokees were back in Charles Town with the nephew on April 28, 1768.[103] If their problems with northern tribes were settled for the moment, there were renewed issues with Virginia. Cherokee land claims stretched across much of the South, and in October

1768 the Cherokees were called to a conference at Lochaber, Alexander Cameron's estate, on Hard Labor Creek.

Cameron received the 2,600-acre grant off Little River in the Abbeville County region of modern South Carolina. The Cherokees had been called to water again for the purpose of negotiating a new boundary between the Cherokees and Virginia, which would change Cherokee history yet again. Superintendent John Stuart proposed a Cherokee boundary that covered much of what is modern West Virginia and the line surveying project was to be carried out in the winter. Oconostota took the lead and stated that the mountains would be full of snow and ice at that time and he believed the settlers would not accomplish the task. He offered that "early in the spring I promise my father [Stuart] that I will go and finish the line myself."[104]

Known as the Treaty of Hard Labor Creek, the Cherokees hoped once again that this latest offering would end the problem of colonial trespass. Only a year later, they were dismayed to learn that settlers had already crossed the new demarcation line. Oconostota set out with a party of Cherokees to survey the encroachments for a report to John Stuart. The Overhills military leader told Stuart that the Cherokees wished to keep the Virginians as distant as possible, for they loved to "steal horses and hunt deer."[105] For many decades, the Southern tribes had used the term "Virginian" to mean any greedy, land-hungry settler. In fact, as the decade of the 1760s was ending, the Cherokees were being called on, time and time again, to accept each new boundary as the last one, when only a short time later new settlers either knowingly or in ignorance trespassed on Cherokee lands. The triumvirate of Cherokee leaders, Ostenaco, Oconostota, and Attakullakulla, had learned to accommodate these transgressions, albeit often asking for major concessions in the transaction, though ultimately always giving in to the land requests of colonial governments as a way to maintain the peace. When the next transgression, land cession, or trespass occurred, they merely repeated the pattern of accommodating, asking for their own concessions, and returning to peaceful intercourse with their non-Indian neighbors. There was a new generation of Cherokee leadership waiting in the wings, discontented with this practice and ready to fault their own leaders, as well as the colonials, for this state of affairs.

Just before the transition came another boundary adjustment occurred in 1770. This time, warfare between the Creeks and the Cherokees disrupted the latter's trade access to Charles Town. Oconostota again took the lead as he reached out to the Virginia government to replace the Carolina trade vacuum. The two sides met at Alexander Cameron's estate of

Lochaber. Just prior to the Cherokee trade problems, Virginia leaders had contacted John Stuart, true to their reputation, desirous of more Cherokee land at the Holston River region. Oconostota led the trade negotiation, which gave up the land, but cautioned Stuart that his Cherokee hunters in the woods would have no way of knowing the boundary change this late in the year until they came home, typically in March. The Lochaber Treaty of October 15, 1770, formalized the transfer, but the land was not surveyed until the following year.[106]

During the negotiations at Lochaber, Oconostota mentioned that the young Cherokee men were likely to be angered by the treaty, negotiated while they were away, because it gave away more land. When they returned from the deer hunt, that was exactly the case, to the point that Oconostota wanted to redo the treaty. Stuart deputy Cameron warned the Great Warrior that he'd never be trusted again if he disavowed the agreement.[107] The new decade was beginning with a disaffected younger generation of Cherokee men who were angry both with encroaching settlers and with the older generation of leaders whom they had been taught to obey.

Notes

1. Lieutenant Governor William Bull to Board of Trade, November 18, 1760, CO5/7: 264.
2. Tortora, *Carolina in Crisis*, 135–136.
3. Lt. Gov. Bull to Gen Amherst, March 13, 1761, Charles Town, CO5/61, Folio 13.
4. Tortora, *Carolina in Crisis*, 136.
5. Lieutenant Governor William Bull to Board of Trade, November 18, 1760, CO5/7: 264.
6. Tortora, *Carolina in Crisis*, 138.
7. Tortora, *Carolina in Crisis*, 138.
8. Henry Ellis to Board of Trade, October 20, 1760, CO5/7: 270.
9. Kelton, *Cherokee Medicine*, 131.
10. Evans, "Notable Persons: Ostenaco," 47.
11. Gen Amherst to Lt. Gov Fauquier, March 25, 1761, New York, CO5/60, Folio 296.
12. Tortora, *Carolina in Crisis*, 138.
13. Tortora, *Carolina in Crisis*, 141–142.
14. Tortora, *Carolina in Crisis*, 142–144.
15. Lt. Colonel James Grant to Gen Jeffrey Amherst, March 30, 1761, Moncks Corner, SC, CO5/61, Folio 147.

16. Talk from Young Warrior of Estatoe to Mr. Mackintosh, April 1, 1761, Fort Prince George, CO5/61, Folio 262.
17. Talk from Young Warrior of Estatoe to Mr. Mackintosh, April 1, 1761, Fort Prince George, CO5/61, Folio 262.
18. Talk from Young Warrior of Estatoe to Mr. Mackintosh, April 1, 1761, Fort Prince George, CO5/61, Folio 262.
19. Kelton, *Cherokee Medicine*, 131.
20. Evans, "Notable Persons: Ostenaco," 47.
21. Tortora, *Carolina in Crisis*, 149.
22. Brown, *Old Frontiers*, 110.
23. Kelton, *Cherokee Medicine*, 130–131.
24. Copy of a List of Towns in the Middle and Back Settlements burnt by Grant, June–July 1761, CO5/61, Folio 385.
25. Lt. Col. Grant to General Amherst, July 10, 1761, Camp near Fort Prince George, CO5/61, Folio 377.
26. Kelly, "Oconostota," 227.
27. Conley, *The Cherokee Nation*, 53.
28. Col. Byrd Articles of Peace proposed to the Cherokees, September 17, 1761, CO5/60, Folio 20.
29. Tortora, *Carolina in Crisis*, 134–135.
30. Conley, *The Cherokee Nation*, 53.
31. Tortora, *Carolina in Crisis*, 135.
32. Lt. Gov. Fauquier to Capt. Bullitt, February 16, 1761, CO5/61, Folio 24.
33. Evans, "Notable Persons: Ostenaco," 47.
34. Conley, *The Cherokee Nation*, 53.
35. Evans, "Notable Persons: Ostenaco," 47.
36. Tortora, *Carolina in Crisis*, 135.
37. Tortora, *Carolina in Crisis*, 135–136.
38. Gen Amherst to Lt. Col Grant, August 1, 1761, Albany, NY, CO5/61, Folio 389.
39. Gen Amherst to Lt. Col Grant, August 1, 1761, Albany, NY, CO5/61, Folio 389.
40. Tortora, *Carolina in Crisis*, 155–156.
41. Gen Amherst to Lt. Gov Bull, August 1, 1761, Albany, NY, CO5/61, Folio 290.
42. Gen Amherst to Lt. Gov Bull, August 1, 1761, Albany, NY, CO5/61, Folio 290.
43. Kelly, "Oconostota," 227.
44. Copy of Journal of conference with the Cherokee deputies, August 29–31, 1761, Camp near Ft. Prince George, CO5/61, Folio 457.
45. Copy of Journal of conference with the Cherokee deputies, August 29–31, 1761, Camp near Ft. Prince George, CO5/61, Folio 457.

46. Copy of Journal of conference with the Cherokee deputies, August 29–31, 1761, Camp near Ft. Prince George, CO5/61, Folio 457.
47. Copy of Journal of conference with the Cherokee deputies, August 29–31, 1761, Camp near Ft. Prince George, CO5/61, Folio 457.
48. Copy of Journal of conference with the Cherokee deputies, August 29–31, 1761, Camp near Ft. Prince George, CO5/61, Folio 457.
49. Copy of Journal of conference with the Cherokee deputies, August 29–31, 1761, Camp near Ft. Prince George, CO5/61, Folio 457.
50. Copy of Journal of conference with the Cherokee deputies, August 29–31, 1761, Camp near Ft. Prince George, CO5/61, Folio 457.
51. Copy of Journal of conference with the Cherokee deputies, August 29–31, 1761, Camp near Ft. Prince George, CO5/61, Folio 457.
52. Copy of Journal of conference with the Cherokee deputies, August 29–31, 1761, Camp near Ft. Prince George, CO5/61, Folio 457.
53. Copy of Journal of conference with the Cherokee deputies, August 29–31, 1761, Camp near Ft. Prince George, CO5/61, Folio 457.
54. Copy of Journal of conference with the Cherokee deputies, August 29–31, 1761, Camp near Ft. Prince George, CO5/61, Folio 457.
55. Copy of Journal of conference with the Cherokee deputies, August 29–31, 1761, Camp near Ft. Prince George, CO5/61, Folio 457.
56. Copy of Journal of conference with the Cherokee deputies, August 29–31, 1761, Camp near Ft. Prince George, CO5/61, Folio 457.
57. Tortora, *Carolina in Crisis*, 159.
58. Lt. Gov Bull to Gen. Amherst, September 24, 1761, Charles Town, CO5/61, Folio 525.
59. Lt. Gov Bull to Gen. Amherst, September 24, 1761, Charles Town, CO5/61, Folio 525.
60. Lt. Gov Bull to Gen. Amherst, September 24, 1761, Charles Town, CO5/61, Folio 525.
61. Tortora, *Carolina in Crisis*, 161–162.
62. Tortora, *Carolina in Crisis*, 165–166.
63. Tortora, *Carolina in Crisis*, 172.
64. Tortora, *Carolina in Crisis*, 165.
65. Tortora, *Carolina in Crisis*, 166–167.
66. Tortora, *Carolina in Crisis*, 169.
67. Tortora, *Carolina in Crisis*, 170.
68. Tortora, *Carolina in Crisis*, 172.
69. Tortora, *Carolina in Crisis*, 174.
70. Duane King, ed., *The Memoirs of Lt. Henry Timberlake: The Story of a Soldier, Adventurer, and Emissary to the Cherokees, 1756–1765* (Cherokee, NC: Museum of the Cherokee Indian Press, 2007), 55.
71. Kelly, "Notable Persons: Ostenaco," 48.
72. King, *The Memoirs*, 56.

73. Kelly, "Notable Persons: Ostenaco," 48.
74. King, *The Memoirs*, 57.
75. King, *The Memoirs*, 58–62.
76. Kelly, "Notable Persons: Ostenaco," 51.
77. King, *The Memoirs*, 72.
78. King, *The Memoirs*, 72.
79. The Museum of the Cherokee Indian in Cherokee, North Carolina, has long maintained an exhibit of the Emissaries of Peace who visited London. In 2006, the museum published *Emissaries of Peace: The 1762 Cherokee & British Delegations: An Exhibit of the Museum of the Cherokee Indian*.
80. Kelly, "Notable Persons: Ostenaco," 51–52.
81. Kelly, "Notable Persons: Ostenaco," 53.
82. Tortora, *Carolina in Crisis*, 173–174.
83. Tortora, *Carolina in Crisis*, 175.
84. Rough Sketch of Plan for Management of Indians and the Conducting of the Necessary Commerce with Them, n.d., CO5/377: 273.
85. Rough Sketch of Plan for Management of Indians and the Conducting of the Necessary Commerce with Them, n.d., CO5/377: 273.
86. Rough Sketch of Plan for Management of Indians and the Conducting of the Necessary Commerce with Them, n.d., CO5/377: 273.
87. Documents Accompanying the Journal of the Directors of the Cherokee Trade 1762–1765, Colonial Records of SC 1754–1765: 557–560.
88. Colonial Records of SC 1754–1765, 560–562.
89. Instructions to Edward Wilkinson, July 19, 1762, Colonial Records of SC 1754–1765, 570–573.
90. https://history.state.gov/milestones/1750-1775/treaty-of-paris.
91. Dowd, *A Spirited Resistance*, 26.
92. Collin G. Calloway, *The Scratch of a Pen: 1763 and the Transformation of North America* (Oxford: Oxford University Press, 2006), 92–93.
93. Calloway, *The Scratch of a Pen*, 93.
94. Calloway, *The Scratch of a Pen*, 94.
95. Calloway, *The Scratch of a Pen*, 96–97.
96. Michael P. Morris, *George Galphin and the Transformation of the Georgia-South Carolina Backcountry* (Lanham, MD: Lexington Books, 2014), 41.
97. Conley, *The Cherokee Nation*, 54.
98. Calloway, *The Scratch of a Pen*, 98.
99. Tortora, *Carolina in Crisis*, 185.
100. Journal of the Council, June 9, 1762, South Carolina Department of Archives and History.
101. Kelly, "Oconostota," 227.
102. Kelly, "Oconostota," 227.
103. Kelly, "Oconostota," 227.
104. Kelly, "Oconostota," 228.

105. Kelly, "Oconostota," 228.
106. Kelly, "Oconostota," 228.
107. Kelly, "Oconostota," 229.

Snowball in the Sun
Dragging Canoe and the Spirit of 1776

4

BEFORE 1775, FEW PEOPLE outside of Cherokee society knew much about a rising warrior named Tsyu-gun-sini, or Dragging Canoe, except perhaps that he was the son of a revered chief, Attakullakulla. However, a series of events occurred between 1770 and 1775 that signaled a failure in the abilities of the previous generation of leaders to manage the relationship with the British. This failure caused Dragging Canoe and his followers to branch out on their own military agenda, contrary to the wishes of those Cherokee leaders. They chose to strike at American settlements, many of them Scots-Irish, in the backcountry of western North Carolina and eastern Tennessee at the time of the American Revolution. For a time, Dragging Canoe and his followers were like a fearful comet in the nighttime sky, forever changing the destiny of the Ani-yun-wiya, the Cherokees, and the American Patriots. Insatiable land greed on the part of American settlers and some Indian fur traders prompted Dragging Canoe and his followers to act as they did. His aggression was fueled by the deep fear that the incessant land cessions to American settlers that had never stopped during his father's generation would lead to the extinction of the Cherokee people. The appearance of Scots-Irish communities just below the Cherokee border with South Carolina in the early 1760s added new strains, as the communities further diminished Cherokee hunting grounds and offered the most ready supply of trespassers on Cherokee land. Dragging Canoe's raids also were influenced by his deep, personal family connections and loyalty to Scottish Indian agent Alexander Cameron, who was both his adopted brother and married to one of Dragging Canoe's sisters, Mollie Ollie.[1]

Known as the Chickamauga Cherokees, the Dragging Canoe campaign of seventeen years lasted as long as it did because the British wanted it to last. Indian superintendent John Stuart, and other British officials who followed after Stuart's death, supplied the rebellion with guns and ammunition because it destabilized Patriot forces. The Cherokee rebels pulled the Patriot forces into the backcountry instead of facing the British challenge from the coast. Dragging Canoe and his followers deviated from the wishes of older, established leaders, like his father Attakukllakulla, and their raids brought a swift and devastating retaliation on the Cherokee people by Patriot armies in a replay of the violence from the Anglo-Cherokee War. In fact, Cherokee attacks may have planted the seeds to rationalize Indian removal itself some forty years later, as President Andrew Jackson specifically wanted the Cherokees to be the first tribe to march west.

Tsyu-gun-sini (Dragging Canoe) was born to Attakullakulla and his wife Nionne Ollie of the Cherokee town of Echota. His father was Wolf Clan and his mother was Paint Clan.[2] Later called Little Carpenter by the English, who noted his small height, Attakullakulla's name meant Leaning Wood in Cherokee. According to at least one source, he was one of the Nipissing Indians, captured as an infant and later raised by the Cherokees. Dragging Canoe's mother was a daughter of Oconostota, another chief.[3]

Dragging Canoe was firstborn, one of several natural and adopted children of the couple, including several sons and daughters, all belonging to the Paint Clan. His siblings included brothers Tache, Dutsi Tarchee, The Badger (Oocumma), Little White Owl, Raven, and Turtle at Home and sisters Mollie Ollie, Hannah "Nikitie," Wurtagua Wa-Ta-Ge Watts, and Ama'itseyi Water of a New Green.[4] Attakullakulla also adopted a Scottish Indian agent stationed long term among the Cherokees, Alexander Cameron.[5] That adoption not only made Cameron a brother to Dragging Canoe but also covered him with an all-important clan affiliation. Cameron lived among the Cherokees starting in the early 1760s.

Correspondence about Cameron clearly indicates he had been adopted by the tribe in the late 1760s. On October 15, 1768, Cherokee Chief Oconostota made a petition to Cameron's boss John Stuart. In that report, Oconostota noted that Cameron had "lived long amongst us as a beloved man, he has done us justice & always told us the truth. We all regard & love him & we hope he will not be taken away from us; when a good man comes among us, we are sorry to part with him."[6]

The Chief further indicated how enmeshed Cameron had become within Cherokee society. He stated, "Mr. Cameron has got a son by a Cherokee woman, and we are desirous that he may educate the boy like the white people, and cause him to read & write, that he may resemble both red & white men & live amongst us when his Father is dead."[7]

Similarly, Attakullakulla adopted another, more important Scot, John Stuart, when Stuart was a soldier stationed at the Overhills British Fort Loudoun.[8] John Stuart was perhaps the most influential Scot working among the Southeastern Indians in the 1760s and 1770s. When Stuart later became superintendent of Indian Affairs for the South in 1761, he hired Cameron as his deputy or commissary among the Cherokees. Thus, British Indian policy was a bit more complicated than a mere bureaucracy of empire imposed on subject peoples by complete strangers. Men like Cameron and Stuart, connected to the tribe by adoption, marriage, and Cherokee children, presented those policies to the Cherokees. Dragging Canoe and his followers may have seen their later military actions as a defense of Cherokee rules.

Dragging Canoe was born in the Overhills town of Chota in the 1740s, perhaps between 1744 and 1746. At the time, his father was a preeminent diplomatic leader of the Cherokee Nation.[9] Attakullakulla was also part of an elite group of Cherokees who had visited Great Britain in May 1730. One of seven Cherokees, Attakullakulla and his party arrived at Dover on June 5, 1730. Their hosts presented them to King George II on June 18 in their traditional clothing, though their hosts later fitted them with English attire for the remainder of the trip. The group visited Canterbury Cathedral and the Tower of London, where they viewed the crown jewels.[10] The journey obviously made an impression on the Cherokee youth, as he told someone later in life that the English had viewed him as a "strange creature." However, they had given him the opportunity to view thousands of people while they had only viewed him (as one person).[11] The seven Cherokees were probably overawed by their trip to England, which was often the purpose of such visits. It may have helped the chief later in life to forge his close, familial bonds with the Scots Indian agents among his people.

As a young boy, Dragging Canoe earned his unusual name due to a boy's desire to accompany his father's war party against the Shawnees in the 1750s. Attakullakulla told the child he was too young to go, and so he hid inside a canoe placed along the route his father's group intended to take. When the boy intercepted the war party, his father told him that if he could lift the canoe to portage it, he could accompany the group. Unable to fully lift it, he dragged it along the ground, earning the name Tsyu-gun-sini ("he is dragging the canoe").[12] Unlike his shorter father, Dragging Canoe grew tall, six feet according to some sources. He was also one of the Cherokees to have survived smallpox. When he spoke out against Cherokee policy at the Treaty of Sycamore Shoals in 1775, his face clearly bore the deep scars of smallpox.[13] The Cherokees may have experienced a smallpox outbreak as early as 1711–1712.[14] Later, documented outbreaks occurred in 1738–1739. Some period observers noted the disease was brought by South Carolina fur traders on a routine trade trip to Cherokee country. The Cherokees named the disease Kosvkv Askini and developed a treatment ritual for it.[15] The Cherokees also experienced a well-documented outbreak in 1758 when the disease first appeared in the Lower Town of Keowee, possibly spread by Fort Prince George, near modern Pickens, South Carolina.[16] Most likely it was the 1758 outbreak that infected young Dragging Canoe.

As a young adult, Dragging Canoe became the Raven, or head warrior, of the village of Malaquo, located in the Little Tennessee River one mile below Fort Loudoun.[17] As a Cherokee man of the 1760s, his tribe fell under the jurisdiction of the superintendent of Indian Affairs for the southern colonies, his adopted brother John Stuart. The Scot was fiercely loyal both to the crown and to the Cherokee people. He was a survivor of the Fort Loudoun disaster, thanks to Dragging Canoe's father, Attakullakulla, and was integrated into Cherokee society in two ways. First, he had a biracial Cherokee child named Oo-no-do-tu, conceived during his time at Fort Loudoun.[18] Further, Attakullakulla had adopted Stuart as another of his sons, giving Stuart that clan affiliation to go along with his Cherokee child.[19] Stuart and Cameron had their own clan affiliations and Cherokee children with the clan affiliation of their Cherokee mothers. Both sets of connections were a powerful currency of influence among the Cherokees. Such familial ties moved a non-Indian as close into Cherokee society as an outsider could get. There were many more fur traders and Indian agents with native wives in place at the time of the American Revolution.

Though the Proclamation Line of 1763 had fixed the boundary between colonial subjects and native peoples, there were at least four communities of non-Indian settlers on the Cherokee side of the line, living in what would be modern Tennessee. The Indian superintendents like John Stuart and William Johnson had the power to make small adjustments to the line to fit human problems such as these four communities. Most likely, these communities contained their fair share of the Scots-Irish, as outside reports listed the settlers as poor and land-hungry, first entering Cherokee lands to work as Indian traders.[20]

The outbreak of the American Revolution caused nearly as much disruption in Indian country as it did among colonial settlements. The conflict disrupted the trade shipments and white-tailed deerskin sales on which the major tribes depended. British Indian agents, such as Alexander Cameron, normally distributed the merchandise from Georgia and South Carolina along with whatever instructions that John Stuart wished to convey. Now, however, Patriots began to seize such supplies either to arm themselves or to distribute among the tribes in order to win influence with them in the name of the Patriot government.[21] Much as it did among the Muskogee Creeks, the war caused factions to appear among the other great tribe of the Southeast, the Cherokees. Initially, however, the war played second fiddle to a growing land trespass problem that had troubled the Cherokee government since 1770. Ironically, the two sets of troubles highlighted a failure of the previous generation of leaders and made possible the rise of Dragging Canoe and his followers.

The British government implemented the Proclamation Line of 1763 as a temporary solution at best to growing land problems between backcountry settlers and native peoples. In truth, the British saw it as a stop-gap measure, giving themselves more time to develop a permanent solution to conflicts between colonial subjects and tribal peoples. Former Georgia governor Henry Ellis also envisioned the line as a way to hold down imperial expenses of governing settlers who moved past the mountains. Some colonial settlers had already moved west of the mountains at the time of the new boundary and faced the prospect of being shipped back east of the mountains. A survey commissioned by Virginia and carried out by John Donelson found at least four white communities living on Cherokee land. When Virginia government ordered the settlers to vacate, they did not. These white settlements on Cherokee lands by 1770 were indicative of historian Kristofer Ray's point, that Britain's administrative control of its North American empire was sometimes more theoretical than reality based.[22] As is often the case with frontier settlers, many of them were poor, some were escaped indentured servants, and most were land hungry. Early in 1771, a group of Cherokee leaders, led by Attakullakulla, requested that the boundary line be adjusted because they felt sorry for the women and children suffering in these illegal communities.[23] The proposed solution of Cherokee leadership would allow these whites to remain on the land south of the Holston River.[24] As had become the pattern now after the Anglo-Cherokee War, the Cherokee leadership accommodated the other side when settler expansion threatened peaceful relations with South Carolina and Virginia. To put it another way, the Cherokee traditional leadership practiced appeasement when it came to British colonial expansion—always hoping that each adjustment was the last. The British government complied with the adjustment request, and the Cherokee leaders hoped this charitable act also would stop further trespass on their lands by these illegal settlers.[25]

The boundary line adjustment did not encompass every white settlement made past the mountains, however. In 1772, a community of these settlers asked to lease their lands on the Watauga and Nolichucky Rivers directly from the Cherokees as a solution to the boundary problem. The Cherokee leadership again granted the request to grow food on the land on a temporary basis in exchange for rent. However, some of the original settlers then sold their leased lands fraudulently to newer arrivals who purchased the land, believing they possessed clear title to the property.[26] New arrivals were likely to be Scots-Irish immigrating into the region. Thus, a fairly magnanimous set of gestures on the part of the Cherokees only resulted in more complicated land troubles for them.

In the fall of 1773, a group of white settlers traveled through this region on their way to Kentucky when a war party of Shawnees ambushed them and killed several, including the oldest son of Daniel Boone, Israel Boone. The Shawnees tortured their victims before death, including young Boone. The sight deeply disturbed one survivor, Isaac Crabtree. A few months later, in summer 1774 at a horse race at the Watauga settlement, Crabtree killed a Cherokee man named "Cherokee Billy." Other visiting Cherokees quickly left the area and soon informed their leaders of the murder. Dragging Canoe's adopted brother, Indian agent Alexander Cameron, stepped in to avert a retaliatory war.[27] White settlers legally and illegally occupying Cherokee land meanwhile complained to John Stuart, the superintendent of Indian Affairs, again, for redress in these matters. The governor of North Carolina, Josiah Martin, ordered the white settlers to leave Cherokee country completely or to otherwise expect no further help from their government in recent matters.[28]

Dragging Canoe had his own stake in these disputed lands. A group of Cherokees from his town of Malaquo on the Little Tennessee established a settlement on Chickamauga Creek in 1770, near modern Chattanooga in Hamilton County, Tennessee. This group contained a mixed-blood Cherokee named Will Shorey and Scot fur trader, John McDonald, who had married Shorey's sister. McDonald originally arrived from Inverness, Scotland, at age nineteen. He initially traded with native peoples in Georgia but was sent to Fort Loudoun to trade with the Cherokees. There he married Anna Shorey, whose father was a deerskin trader himself. The couple had a child named Molly.[29] McDonald built a trading post where two travel paths crossed Chickamauga Creek and was able to influence events for some miles around through this trade post. Dragging Canoe established a hunting camp near the trade outpost and occupied it by 1776.[30]

Colonel Richard Henderson, also a judge, obtained a grant of some 20 million acres of land from both North Carolina and Virginia. He then organized the Transylvania Company to promote land sales. Because much of the land to be sold was claimed by the Cherokees, Henderson decided to try to obtain a clear title to this land from the Cherokees. To that end, Henderson enlisted the help of famed frontiersman Daniel Boone, whom he sent to the Cherokees in March 1775 along with six wagon loads of merchandise. Clearly, Henderson's actions were in violation of the Proclamation of 1763, which outlawed Indian land transfers to private subjects or their corporations.

White negotiators included John Sevier, Charles and James Robertson, Isaac Shelby, Jacob Brown, and Jesse Benton, among others.[31] Three of the interpreters for the Cherokees, who included Ellis Harlin, Thomas Price, John Vann, and Richard Pearis, had a financial stake themselves invested in the proposed Transylvania Purchase. Very few of the Cherokee leaders present there spoke fluent English.[32] Though no whiskey was supposed to be present during the actual talks, the Henderson representatives brought in large kegs of rum, and they feasted the Cherokee delegation.[33] Some of the Cherokee delegates believed that the banquets, rum, and merchandise were compensation for the actions of the illegal settlers on their lands.[34]

The chiefs, including the diplomat Attakullakulla, Savanoooka, Ostenaco (Outacite), Ookoooneka, and war chief Oconostota, assembled at Sycamore Shoals on the Watauga River in March 1775 in what is modern East Tennessee to consider the offer.[35] Another pivotal event in Cherokee history was about to transpire on a river running through Cherokee country. This older generation of leaders included the triumvirate of the 1760s—Ostenaco, Oconostota, and Attakullakulla. Young Cherokees present included Willanawaugh, the Tennessee Warrior, and Dragging Canoe.[36] Henderson and Boone provided a tempting incentive to sell away Cherokee lands—$50,000 worth of merchandise in the wagons, including guns and ammunition as well as more mundane items such as blankets and cloth.[37]

Such efforts violated previous British policy mentioned not only in the Proclamation Line of 1763 but also in the original 1730 Articles of Friendship. Both documents prevented land transfers from tribal peoples to private individuals or corporations; rather, they could only be transferred to the British crown or its colonies.[38] The outbreak of the American Revolution was providing a convenient excuse to violate that law, however. Both

Virginia governor John Murray, Earl of Dunmore, and Cherokee commissary Alexander Cameron tried to stop the transfer sought by Henderson.[39]

Like all complicated diplomatic ventures, the conference had many different sides. Some sources noted that Attakullakulla always gave in to requests from colonial governments and military officials in order to keep the peace. Yet there were several instances of him refusing to give in to British demands in his past service as diplomat. There were many times when he and Oconostota were on opposite sides. Yet, in this particular instance, Oconostota joined his side on the proposed transfer. Soon, the other chiefs fell in line behind these two men.[40] One source indicated that all the major chiefs present, except Attakullakulla, believed they were being offered goods for just an extension of the Watauga lease, quite a different proposition from permanent land transfer.[41]

During the negotiations, Dragging Canoe rose and gave a talk in which he reminded those present of the great past of the Cherokee Nation. He spoke of a never-ending expansion by white settlers that had caused the traditional lands of all tribal peoples to shrink steadily in the face of incessant demand. "Whole nations of Indians had melted away in their [whites'] presence, like snow in the sun, and had scarcely left their names behind, except as imperfectly recorded by their destroyers," according to Dragging Canoe.[42] Tsyu-gun-sini explained that the Cherokees, like other tribes, had assumed initially that white settlers would not move past the mountains because it would place them at such a distance from their commerce with Great Britain. Referencing the recent incursions onto the Watauga lands, Dragging Canoe noted that it was clear now that white settlers would continue past the mountains. Further, the Watauga settlers wanted their illegal presence on Cherokee lands validated by this latest treaty.[43]

Dragging Canoe predicted that this same "encroaching spirit" would lead settlers to continually demand more and more land until the Cherokees would be reduced to a mere fragment of the land they once claimed. Rather prophetically, he predicted the Cherokees would be compelled to remove to some distant land where they would remain until white society dictated they be moved again.[44] Dragging Canoe foresaw a cultural extinction for the Cherokee people, though he could not, of course, propose a timeline for this. When he finished his talk, the Cherokee Council, suitably impressed and possibly shocked, adjourned in disarray.[45]

Privately, the older chiefs, led by Dragging Canoe's father, favored the cession. As noted, some leaders may have believed they were agreeing to only an extension of the Watauga lease, although Attakullakulla knew otherwise. Dragging Canoe opposed the sale but was convinced by the older

Cherokee leaders to return for a second day of talks, where he continued to speak out against the transfer. Dragging Canoe warned Colonel Henderson that the lands he wanted had a "dark cloud" hanging over them, as the Northern Indians, including the Shawnees, claimed them and would show his settlers no mercy. Tysu-gun-sini predicted that Henderson would find the land dark and bloody.[46]

Treaty negotiations continued on over four days. On the fourth day, translator Joseph Vann read the transfer treaty out loud, word for word. At that point, Chief Oconostota warned Colonel Henderson that white settlers should go to the ceded land at their own peril and must not hold the Cherokees liable for any harm they might suffer. The chief noted that the Cherokees could "no longer hold them by the hand."[47] Then the assembled chiefs began to sign the document—Attakullakulla, Oconostota, and Savanuka all signed. At that point, Dragging Canoe withdrew from the conference and never negotiated with whites again.[48] The governors of North Carolina and Virginia issued proclamations against the Treaty of Sycamore Shoals or, as it became known, "the Great Deed."[49]

From a British legal standpoint, the Treaty of Sycamore Shoals was quite illegal. It violated the Proclamation Line of 1763, which forbade private transfers of land from Indians to private individuals (in this case, the Transylvania Company). The treaty also violated the much earlier agreement of 1730 between the Cherokees and the British stating that Indian lands could be transferred to the crown but not to private individuals or their corporations.[50] Both Virginia and North Carolina governments issued warrants for Henderson's arrest when word of the treaty spread; he and his associates left the area quickly.[51] John Stuart wrote William Legge, the Earl of Dartmouth and secretary of state for the American colonies, in late March 1775, acquainting him with Henderson's actions and his flight from arrest by Governor Josiah Martin of North Carolina. Stuart predicted that if the Sycamore Shoals treaty were not stopped, it would lead to danger in Anglo-Cherokee relations.[52]

Cherokees upset by the treaty made the legal and correct move of contacting Superintendent John Stuart, the chief mediator for the southern tribes and Dragging Canoe's adopted brother.[53] Superintendent Stuart had previously invalidated fraudulent treaties as a regular part of his job. Conversely, Henderson and his associates had attempted the treaty in the first place precisely because of the advent of the American Revolution, marked by civil disobedience of all British law, and the timing to attempt such a land grab was propitious.[54] A series of events made it impossible that spring for Stuart to overturn the treaty. In May 1775, a group of Catawbas visited Charles Town for a trade resupply that Stuart fulfilled as a normal part of his duties. The Catawbas had heard rumblings of the revolution before their visit. As they received their supplies from a local merchant, the Catawba leaders told Stuart that they could use their guns against King George's rebellious peoples as easily as against game animals. John Stuart immediately discouraged the idea, but the Charles Town merchant filling the order passed along the comment, which quickly stirred up Charles Town citizenry.[55] Charles Town Patriots soon ran Stuart, now seventy-five years old, out of his Tradd Street home and into an English ship in Charles Town harbor.[56] From there, Stuart found a temporary refuge in Savannah, Georgia, but local Patriots soon repeated his expulsion and forced Stuart into exile eventually landing him in Pensacola, West Florida. Because of this personal exodus, he was thus disrupted from performing his job with respect to the Treaty of Sycamore Shoals.[57] Since Stuart could not meet with Cherokees upset about the treaty, he dispatched his brother and deputy, Henry Stuart, to enter Cherokee country with a small resupply of ammunition on packhorses bound for the Overhills town of Chota.[58]

The government of the colony of South Carolina was also taking bold measures, as Governor William Henry Drayton contacted Cherokee commissary Alexander Cameron in late September 1775. Drayton began his letter rather melodramatically by announcing that it was a "time of public calamity, when the King's troops have unnaturally commenced, & continue to prosecute a cruel war upon the people of America."[59] Drayton bluntly requested that Cameron leave his post among the Cherokees to eliminate the fear held by South Carolina government that Cameron would use the Cherokees against the colony.[60]

Alexander Cameron wrote back rather quickly, telling Drayton that, while he could not abandon his post as commissary to the Cherokees, he regretted that his position caused South Carolina government such uneasiness. At that moment, Cameron could truthfully respond that he had never been ordered by his superiors to use the Cherokees against the people of South Carolina.[61] Two months later, Cameron received such orders. In December 1775, John Stuart wrote Alexander Cameron from St. Augustine, telling his commissary he had received orders to use the Southeastern Indians to "distress His Majesty's rebellious subjects by all practicable means."[62] Stuart clarified his instructions to Cameron by saying that he did not interpret his orders as authorization to indiscriminately attack backcountry residents but rather for groups like the Cherokee to assist the Loyalists in stopping the Patriots. Cameron was to deliver the message to leaders such as Attakullakulla, Kittagusta, the Great Raven, and others.[63] Ironically, Dragging Canoe would soon deliver a similar message to his own followers.

In early January 1776, John Stuart again wrote the Earl of Dartmouth from his new base of operations in St. Augustine, British East Florida. At the time of the letter, he informed the secretary of state that a large delegation of Cherokees was on the way to meet with him in St. Augustine. Stuart told Dartmouth that his commissary Cameron had been working tirelessly to promote the work of the superintendent's office among the Cherokees, despite threats against his life. He also assured Dartmouth that the Cherokees were firmly loyal to Britain despite "the trying circumstances of hunger and nakedness." Stuart remarked that the very long journey of such a large group to check on him proved their loyalty. Stuart told his superior that the Continental Indian Commissioners, newly created by the Patriot government, intended to arrest the British Indian superintendents and their commissaries. Of this, he told Dartmouth, "the complement I shall return if in my power."[64]

As diplomatic letters traveled between leaders on both sides of the Atlantic, Indian Commissary Henry Stuart passed from Pensacola, Florida, northward and learned that Dragging Canoe was waiting for him at Mobile in modern Alabama. Henry Stuart traveled to meet Dragging Canoe with Alexander Cameron in conference at Mobile on March 1, 1776.[65] Dragging Canoe complained bitterly to Stuart of the recent Sycamore Shoals treaty, which he stated had surrounded the Cherokees with white encroachment. Henry Stuart chastised the young Cherokee leader because the older generation of Cherokee leadership, including his father, had given the settlers an illegal permission to settle. Dragging Canoe disavowed the actions of the older leaders, saying that they did not represent his young followers, who were determined to hold onto Cherokee lands. He stated that the leaders, like his father and Oconostota, who signed the treaty were "too old to hunt or fight."[66] The younger Cherokee man rejected the leadership of the Cherokee triumvirate that had managed relations with the British since the 1760s by practicing appeasement when it came to tribal lands. Tsyu-gun-sini told Henry Stuart that his young followers believed it was the intention of the white people to destroy the Cherokee nation through land dispossession. Dragging Canoe also sought a better explanation of the recent trouble between the colonies and Great Britain, particularly as it concerned the cessation of regular trade shipments to Cherokee country.[67] The trade cessation caused dire concern among Cherokee leaders. The Cherokees had thoroughly integrated key British trade items like gunpowder and lead into their culture. Ammunition and powder was critical to successful hunting, much less defensive and offensive warfare.[68]

Finally, Dragging Canoe asked the deputy how the Cherokees could assist British authorities in suppressing the rebellion. The Cherokee man wanted to use strikes to both support the British and remove illegal settlers on Cherokee lands. John Stuart had anticipated such a move on the part of the Cherokees and had instructed his brother Henry to tell the Cherokees to remain neutral in the conflict for the moment. Henry Stuart told Dragging Canoe that his people were to hold themselves ready, as they "might" be asked to mobilize in conjunction with British Regulars who would arrive in their region soon. John Stuart feared that if the Cherokees waged war unsupervised, there would be the collateral damage of mistaken attacks on neutral or Loyalist settlers.[69]

Dragging Canoe then returned to Chota awaiting a shipment of thirty horse loads of ammunition that Henry Stuart was sending up to resupply the Cherokees. Dragging Canoe later met the shipment with eighty warriors to escort the goods so they would not be plundered by Patriots, who now regularly seized arms from Indian trade shipments to supply their own militias.[70] Once arrived at Chota, Henry Stuart dispatched letters to the illegal Watauga settlers urging them to voluntarily abandon the land they were currently occupying in exchange for free land in Florida. In doing so, he fell victim to some of the most destructive diplomatic manipulation of the conflict. Some of the settlers with patriot leanings altered Henry Stuart's letter by hand-copying a forgery to read that a large British army, bringing Creek, Choctaw, and Chickasaw warriors, was on its way to link up with Cherokees for an all-out attack on the backcountry settlers. Within weeks the altered letter was in the hands of Patriot leaders, who published it in newspapers to prove the duplicity of the British to the American public, further fueling a growing conflict.[71] The altered letter may have sealed the fate of the Cherokee people in the minds of leaders like Thomas Jefferson.

Fate further complicated the normal overturn of an invalid treaty when a delegation of northern tribes arrived in Cherokee country in the middle of May 1776. Diplomatic courtesy required that these visiting tribal leaders be greeted and heard with respect to their message. Their arrival exacerbated the war movement that already was gaining momentum in some Cherokee towns. The Cherokees received the delegates in Chota, which displayed a war standard for the occasion, with both the flagstaff and the posts of the town house painted red and black.[72] The group of fourteen representatives wore black-painted faces and represented the old Cherokee allies: the Haudenosaunee Confederacy (League of the Iroquois), Delawares, Shawnees, and Ottawas.

The representatives sought an alliance with the Cherokees to use the outbreak of the Revolution as a time to settle the score with colonial transgressors. The delegates carried wampum belts of shell as records of their proposed treaty and as a calling card of introduction. They spoke of a seventy-day journey to reach Cherokee lands from their home territory. Previously, Indian travelers covering the same territory had seen bountiful game animals, but this time the delegation saw only armed settlers along their route.[73] Alexander Cameron later told John Stuart that the Mohawk delegate recounted the gruesome tale surrounding the murder of the son of the northern superintendent Sir William Johnson. According to the account, a group of angry Patriots came into an Indian town the past winter and surprised Johnson there. When he would not switch to the Patriot side by taking an oath, they shoved his head into a large container of boiling tar, which killed him. Cameron noted that bit of information particularly inflamed the Dragging Canoe followers, whom he could not discourage from planning new raids.[74] Like John Stuart, northern Indian officials often had had relations with tribal people, in this case the Mohawks, and had advised the tribe in confidence for many years. The violence inflicted by northern Patriots on the northern Indian officials would have seemed threatening to the Cherokees, for John Stuart had those same Cherokee familial connections. Dragging Canoe frequently referred to John Stuart in translated correspondence as his father and alternately as their Great Man.[75]

Despite the gruesome tale, the northern emissaries found no interest in their cause from the traditional Cherokee leaders, who were unmoved by these stories and their pleas to join: the traditional leaders did not accept the northern wampum belts. One of the northern Indians gave a talk recounting a settler attack on one of their towns, killing their people and, in particular, the son of one of their beloved men.[76] However, the delegation did find interest among the dissident young Cherokee warriors, who accepted the wampum belt of the northern delegates.[77] A long silence followed the presentation until Dragging Canoe stood up and took the wampum belts of the northern representatives. After Dragging Canoe took the belt, other young men followed suit. Henry Stuart, a witness, said almost all of the young Cherokee men joined in and sang the war song. By contrast, the older Cherokee leaders sat in stony silence, properly shocked. The older leaders did not oppose the commitments made by their young counterparts, however. Stuart recorded that the northern delegates then came to the Indian agents and wanted them and other whites present to take the belts. Stuart refused, telling the northern Indians that he would not "give any sanction to a war that was likely to bring destruction on their nation."[78] In truth, the older chiefs told Stuart that a war decision rested with Oconostota, whose decisions over the years had shown he did not turn readily to the option of war. These older leaders had set a date for such a talk, but before it could occur, the Cherokee Lower Towns began the planned attacks.[79]

A few days later, Dragging Canoe met with Deputy Superintendent Henry Stuart and the Cherokee commissary, Alexander Cameron, his adopted brother. The meeting also included the Cherokee fur traders who were of special importance to Dragging Canoe. He gave them promises for their safety, hoping they would stay in the Cherokee Nation during the coming conflict. He told the traders that he considered them his own people. If any of them wanted to join his war parties, they would be welcome, but he did not expect it. He did expect them to keep bringing supplies like ammunition, however.[80] Dragging Canoe met them with his own face blackened and asked of them why the fur traders were evacuating Cherokee country.[81] As human barometers capable of sensing growing tension, Indian fur traders often escaped the backcountry when they sensed imminent violence, as they were often the first targets of native anger. Some sixty years earlier, the Yamasees had initiated their attack on Charles Town by killing as many of their traders as they could find. The Cherokees killed some of their traders in the Anglo-Cherokee War as well.

Dragging Canoe revealed to Henry Stuart that he planned to lead Cherokee war parties in simultaneous attacks on the backcountry regions of Virginia, Georgia and North and South Carolina. He would personally lead a party of three hundred to attack the Holston River settlements and, from there, move farther into Virginia. Abram of Chilhowie would attack the illegal Watauga settlements, and the Raven of Chota would attack Carter's Valley.[82]

Henry Stuart told Dragging Canoe that his war plans were the reason traders were evacuating and not to turn their departure into the problem at hand. He and Cameron both cautioned the Cherokee leader that the Cherokees were not prepared for war at this time, in the opinion of British Indian authorities.[83] Conversation turned to the whereabouts of messenger Isaac Thomas, and Dragging Canoe wanted an update on his mission to the illegal Watauga settlers. The next day, Cherokee scouts went out to look for Thomas when he returned, albeit with discouraging news.[84] Thomas reported that there were at least six thousand men on the Virginia and North Carolina frontiers who had organized originally to fight British forces. However, that military force was now determined to fight Indians on the frontier. Thomas also returned with the identity of Jesse Benton as the man who had hand-copied an alternate version of Henry Stuart's letter that had been delivered to the Patriot government as proof of British and Cherokee treachery. For a time, it seemed as if the Cherokees had decided to wait to consult some of their highest officials for an opinion on whether to make war about these circumstances. Then some small acts of violence occurred, further increasing the tension levels. A Cherokee man was put to death for his murder of a white man in Virginia, upsetting some prominent Overhills Cherokees. Then a group of whites entered the Lower Towns on a mission to remove two Indian traders guilty of misbehavior. The Lower Town leaders detained the party, and violence erupted. The Cherokees killed five of the men and seized all of their horses and weapons. Stuart reported that any chance of peace was hopeless at that point. He warned Dragging Canoe and his followers not to cross the Proclamation Line and not to injure Loyalist settlers in their raids, nor to harm women and children among the settlers.[85] Shortly afterward, Henry Stuart departed the nation and returned to his base in West Florida.

Once returned to West Florida, Henry Stuart wrote his brother, updating him on his mission to the Cherokees. He told John Stuart of his meeting with an agitated Dragging Canoe, whom he called Chincanacina. Henry Stuart reported that he had reassured Dragging Canoe that the encroachment on their lands by white settlers was contrary to the king's orders, but he also chastised Dragging Canoe's people for making these private land arrangements, which they had been told not to do by John Stuart and Alexander Cameron.[86] Henry told his brother of the threat from the illegal settlers on the Watauga land against his commissary, Alexander Cameron. Henry Stuart reported that he had Dragging Canoe to look after Cameron and all the king's friends in their country.[87]

As the report continued, Henry Stuart told the superintendent that, when he arrived in Cherokee country, he assembled the head men for a talk and gifted them with a small supply of ammunition, too low in quantity to distribute to other Cherokee communities. Dragging Canoe had sent messengers to many towns to survey the mood, and the majority opinion was a talk of war. Henry Stuart referred to the Patriots as the king's "obstinate children" and related his request to Dragging Canoe and his men to hold themselves ready to give help in the conflict. He also asked them to be on the lookout for Patriots hoping to harm Alexander Cameron and to prevent that from happening.[88] Henry mentioned the growing plan to unite the Lower Creeks and Lower Town Cherokees, but the effort was still in the planning stages.[89]

In the rather lengthy report to his brother, Henry mentioned a correspondence between himself and two men, John Carter and Aaron Pinson, speaking for the illegal inhabitants on the Nolichucky River. In a letter carried to their community by messenger, Henry told them of their illegal status on the land. In response, the settlers responded that they had paid rent for these lands to one Patrick Brown and also paid him for goods paid to the Cherokees supposedly to facilitate the rental process. They asked for a meeting with the Cherokees, who told the settlers that they indeed remembered the goods they had received from the settlers, but they thought these were payment for deer and buffalo the settlers had killed on Cherokee lands, payment for the grasslands their horses and cattle had consumed, and payment for the houses built on their hunting grounds. Henry ended the report with his admission that he could not stop Dragging Canoe from his planned attacks; he could only temper his actions.[90] Thus, Dragging Canoe and his followers would start a Cherokee rebellion within the American Revolution. Its targets would be outlying colonial subjects, especially those on contested lands.

Far from Cherokee country or Pensacola, Florida, the Continental Congress at Philadelphia reversed its original neutrality program for the tribes in May 1776 and authorized the use of military alliances with them.[91] In early June, the newspaper *Virginia Gazette* published Henry Stuart's letter, altered by Watauga settler Jesse Benson, which recounted a supposed British plan to send an army north out of Florida that would pick up Muskogee and Cherokee allies, who would wreak havoc on the backcountry. Patriots sent the letter to the governments of North Carolina and Virginia and sent a copy to the Continental Congress as well.[92] Few documents during the conflict probably had as much impact as Henry Stuart's altered letter. A few weeks later, Jefferson, tapped by Congress, had his Declaration of Independence ready on July 2, 1776. Not surprisingly, he listed Native Americans, mentioned as "the merciless Indian savages," as one of the numerous grievances against King George III.[93] The Congress edited the document, to Jefferson's chagrin, and approved it on July 4.

In the backcountry that month, Dragging Canoe and his followers organized to reverse the land appeasement policy of their government by committing an attack against three different backcountry targets. They were unaware that other Cherokees were going to warn colonials in the target areas. Though Henry Stuart and Alexander Cameron had advised against it, Dragging Canoe and his followers planned to strike against settlers. These young men seemed equally angered by settler trespasses against the Cherokees and against Patriot transgressions against Stuart and Cameron. The Raven of Chota was to lead one strike force while the two others were to be led by Abram of Chilhowie and Dragging Canoe. Dragging Canoe addressed his followers at a council meeting at Chota, where he echoed Stuart's instructions by telling his men they were not going to strike at backcountry whites indiscriminately, but rather only those who were Patriots engaged in rebellion.[94] On the surface, it appears that Dragging Canoe and his followers were trying to enforce Anglo-Indian trade laws for his brothers John Stuart and Alexander Cameron. Dragging Canoe told the many white traders present at the meeting that while he did not expect their participation in the Cherokee conflict, he did expect them to supply his troops with guns and ammunition.[95] Some of the traders and some of the Cherokee women, including Nan-ye-hi (Nancy Ward), warned the backcountry settlers ahead of time.[96]

Nan-ye-hi was Attakullakulla's niece and Dragging Canoe's first cousin. Her mother was Tame Doe of the Wolf Clan.[97] Nan-ye-hi had married a white trader, Bryan Ward, and so had definite connections to backcountry settlers. Called Nancy by these settlers, her role in this matter is noteworthy. She carried an earned status of a Ghighau and, as a Beloved Woman, she had a political voice. In this particular issue, she opposed the Dragging Canoe war plan. Nan-ye-hi was a part of the group that prepared the ritual Black Drink consumed by the warriors and chiefs prior to an important meeting. She was present during the discussion and remained resolutely opposed to the attack. When the men began their Black Drink ceremony, she slipped away, heading for the trading post of Isaac Thomas, Jarrett Williams, and William Fawling. The Ghighau helped them escape Chota and send warnings to settlers in the intended targets.[98]

The Raven attacked the settlements at Carter's Valley while Abram hit the Watauga and Chilhowie settlements. Dragging Canoe and his men attacked the Holston River settlements with their nearby fort, Eaton's Station.[99] The Raven of Chota experienced the most success, destroying several backcountry cabins, albeit with little strategic significance.[100] Dragging Canoe and his men reached the Holston River settlements on June 19 and camped overnight. Due to Nan-ye-hi's early warning, five companies of militia, along with some 175 other frontiersmen, protected the fort.[101] Though Dragging Canoe's group had the opportunity to seize two white women from the fort, bathing in the river, they did not bother them for fear of alerting the fort over two missing people. Soldiers from the fort knew the Cherokees were in the area later the same evening but were waiting to attack the next day. The soldiers from Eaton's Station decided to attack Dragging Canoe's Cherokees outside the fort in open space. When the Cherokees attacked from the forest, some of the soldiers retreated to the fort. Dragging Canoe's men eagerly gave pursuit but crossed into a volley of rifle fire from settlers shooting from behind trees. Dragging Canoe received a non-life-threatening wound, but the musket ball penetrated both of his thighs, and his men had to carry him from the battlefield.[102] His brother, Little Owl, was struck eleven times by gunfire. At first, people thought him dead instead of badly injured.[103] Thirteen of his men were not so lucky and lay dead on that same field of battle, reportedly scalped and mutilated by the militiamen.[104] Dragging Canoe thereafter abandoned conventional frontal assaults and returned to the guerilla-style warfare that tribal people usually employed.[105]

Abram of Chilhowie found his target of Watauga nearly empty due to the advance warning; most settlers had fled to the relative safety of Fort Caswell under the command of James Robertson with John Seiver as his lieutenant. Abram's forces stayed near the fort for two weeks, waiting out its inhabitants, who subsisted on a diet of parched corn. In time, Abram's patience was rewarded with the capture of a group of women who left the fort at daybreak to milk their cows. Abram seized several prisoners, including a child, Samuel Moore. At the same time, a woman named Lydia Bean rode into capture as she approached the fort.[106]

Abram's group burned young Moore at the stake outright, violating Henry and John Stuart's orders to leave women and children alone. The Cherokees took Lydia Bean to Toquo and tied her to a stake atop a mound for burning. The Cherokees had lit kindling around her already when Nan-ye-hi interrupted the execution.[107] She intervened as Ghighau, with the power to pardon prisoners, and kicked the burning logs away from Mrs. Bean's feet, freeing her on the spot from her death sentence. Nan-ye-hi took Mrs. Bean under protection to her own home, where she remained for a time.[108]

The Raven of Chota attacked his targets in Carter's Valley but, like the other two target areas, found the settlers had moved inside forts due to the advance warning. He burned some isolated cabins and stole what he could before returning to Cherokee country.[109] Thus the initial Cherokee rebel strike in mid July 1776 was off to a rather bad start with only limited results. Far more effective was the damage the Cherokees had done themselves in the mythology of the Revolution. They had turned against the Americans during the darkest hour of the American Revolution. Before this, settlers had perceived tribal peoples as a hindrance or an annoyance to colonial expansion. Now they had become true villains as British pawns at best; at worst, they were now devils in the dark.

Alexander Cameron soon notified John Stuart of the attacks in a late August 1776 report. He told the superintendent that the northward Indians had influenced Dragging Canoe to attack backcountry targets both for the king's cause and for their own reasons. Cameron confessed that he was at a loss as how to best advise the Indians at this point. Since they had already begun the effort, he had encouraged them to continue it until they received orders from Stuart to stop. Cameron boldly asserted his belief that the Cherokees could totally disrupt the rebellion in Georgia, both Carolinas, and Virginia, predicting a winter 1776 surrender by the Patriots.[110] Cameron informed Stuart in the report that he had sent along Captain Nathaniel Gist with Dragging Canoe on the raids. He noted the Cherokees respected Gist, who prevented the Cherokees from attacking women and children. Cameron observed that only Patriots were attacked on the raid except for one boy (young Moore), who was taken, tortured, and killed.[111]

Though the Cherokee attacks accomplished little, they had fulfilled the Patriot fear of an Indian attack from the backcountry directed by British efforts. The Cherokees did not have to wait long for a response from the Patriot military. In late summer, a Patriot army entered Cherokee country with a mission to destroy the Cherokee nation.[112] In September 1776, Colonel Andrew Williamson led over one thousand South Carolina troops into the Lower Cherokee towns (near present-day Pickens, South Carolina), where they leveled those communities. Major General Charles Lee, a continental commander in the South, gave voice to the new American attitude about the Cherokees stated after the attacks when he gave the opinion that the state of North Carolina could then go ahead and "with greatest justice make an example of the Cherokees."[113] Lee's comment indicates that the Chickamauga Cherokees had given North Carolina an opportunity to deal with what many considered a preexisting problem. Lee's attitude toward the tribe as problem long overdue for a solution was common now among frontier people.

Later Williamson's troops joined two thousand North Carolina troops who wreaked similar destruction among the Middle Towns (in the vicinity of current-day Cherokee, North Carolina). Many refugees of the Lower and Middle Towns flooded into the Overhills Towns to take shelter with their clans there.[114] However, an army of 1,800 Virginians soon after attacked the Overhills towns (close to present-day Loudon, Tennessee), wreaking havoc there as well.[115] Chief Old Tassel and other peace chiefs lost their homes in the Overhills towns because Dragging Canoe had lived there as well.[116] In a repeat of strategy from the earlier Anglo-Cherokee War, Patriots deliberately destroyed the food supplies, which meant the survivors would starve over the winter with no time to grow more crops in late summer. A large number of neutral Cherokees paid the ultimate price for the actions of the young Chickamauga Cherokees who eventually formed a camp at the base of Lookout Mountain in Tennessee.[117] Patriot leaders now blamed all Cherokees for these rebels. South Carolina Patriot William Henry Drayton, who had once politely asked Alexander Cameron to evacuate the backcountry, now voiced a common view among Patriots when he stated that the Cherokees should "be extirpated and the lands become the property of the public. For my part, I shall never give my voice for a peace with the Cherokee Nation upon any other terms than their Removal beyond the mountains."[118] Some sixty years later, the Cherokees would experience just that.

The Patriot army bound for the Overhills towns arrived in October 1776, led by Colonel William Christian and augmented with troops from North Carolina. They moved toward the Overhills Cherokee towns located near modern Loudon, Tennessee. Traditional leaders Oconostota and the Raven advised their people to make a peace treaty with the Americans rather than face the total destruction of any more Cherokee towns. Dragging Canoe was the lone voice of dissent. He urged the Cherokee people to take the almost unthinkable step of burning their own towns, sending their noncombatants out of the region, and then intercepting the Americans with a Cherokee attack force at the French Broad River.[119] Instead, the traditional leaders sent messengers to the Virginia army and then negotiated a temporary peace with the Patriot Army.[120]

Captain Nathaniel Gist was a spokesman for the Cherokees at that meeting. He had also accompanied Dragging Canoe's troops as they attacked Watauga. The violence of those campaigns had convinced him that peace was the only possible avenue for the Cherokees now.[121]

William Christian sent for Attakullakulla, Oconostota, and Dragging Canoe. When Attakullakulla arrived without his son, Christian told the elder peace chief he wanted to speak with young warriors and not old men. The American commander told Attakullakulla to send the scalp of his own son and to turn over Cameron to the Americans, or they would burn the rest of the Overhills towns.[122] Christian also extracted an agreement from the war chief, Oconostota, to turn over Dragging Canoe (his own grandson) and Cameron to the Americans. In final discussions, the arrangement was altered to include a reward of £100 each for Cameron and Dragging Canoe turned in alive or dead. The Cherokees turned over Lydia Bean to Christian at the conclusion of negotiations, agreeing to meet the following year in July to sign a peace treaty. Colonel Christian left the area in December 1776.[123] These agreements extracted from the Cherokee leaders under duress ruptured normal governance for the Cherokees as well as harmony within the clans. Though the Overhills leaders had their temporary peace treaty, the Americans were not able to supply them with trade goods. Further, white settlers continued to trespass on Cherokee lands just as before the start of hostilities.[124]

Throughout all of the initial setbacks, Dragging Canoe tried to remain in close contact with Alexander Cameron. The month after the Cherokee leadership effectively cut off their support to him, Dragging Canoe sent a translated letter to Cameron through interpreter William Thompson. Sentiments can be lost in translation; however, Dragging Canoe's commitment to his cause and his attachment to both Cameron and Stuart are stunningly clear in this letter. He began by recalling the past, saying, "I talk to you being my oldest brother from the first talk we had together to this day. I remember it good that you may tell it to our Father Mr. Stuart and was sent by men from the Heads of the Over Hills towns, Chollee excepted."[125] Dragging Canoe proceeded to give his own report to Cameron about the recent talks between his people and the American army. He told Cameron that the Americans had summoned the Raven, his own father, and himself but that he sent back word that he received no talks except for those from his father (Stuart) and from Cameron. He continued telling Cameron that the American negotiators wanted to speak with his young warriors and not the traditional Cherokee leaders. When Dragging Canoe did not attend, the Americans told the traditional Cherokee leaders that they wanted them to deliver up both Cameron and himself. The American negotiator threatened the Cherokees that unless he received Cameron and either Dragging Canoe or his scalp, he would "kill, burn and destroy every living thing they had."[126]

As Dragging Canoe's report continued, he included the details of various plans to capture both himself and Cameron. Then Tsyu-gun-sini told his brother, "I am glad you are where you are as the Virginians and our Great Man [Oconostota] wanted to take your life was well as mine, but you are a great way from them and I close to them, but while I live you never shall be hurt for I never will forget your talks to us, nor our Fathers [Stuart's] who find us in every thing we want, nor will I ever give my consent to a peace until our father and you agrees to it and makes it for us."[127] The Cherokee man's words definitely indicate familial ties and steadfast allegiance even in translation and fall just short of true passion in his commitment to his brothers in the British Indian Superintendency. We can judge the depth of the disturbance caused by the Transylvania Land Company purchase by its realignment of Dragging Canoe's allegiance to Cameron and Stuart, both born in Scotland, over the policies of Dragging Canoe's own biological father, uncle, and grandfather.

Dragging Canoe continued in his report about his own questioning by the Virginia army officials. The Cherokee man referred to the Virginia man as the Great Warrior of Virginia, otherwise known as Colonel Christian. The colonel, speaking of John Stuart's recent flight from Charles Town, told Dragging Canoe that the Patriots had made their great man (Stuart) "run away and jump into the great water; they had sent men after him to take him, but he was gone."[128] Dragging Canoe responded to the colonel's story that he would die alongside John Stuart if necessary. Colonel Christian had asked, "Who is this man you call your father?"[129] Dragging Canoe mentioned that Christian bragged that his side could beat King George's people by fighting behind trees or in any manner necessary to win. The colonel understood enough of how the trade in merchandise operated to tell Dragging Canoe that the Patriots had the means of making their own gunpowder and cloth. Christian bragged that Patriot goods could supply all of the Cherokee traders, using trade to try to sway Dragging Canoe back to a pro-Patriot alignment.[130]

Dragging Canoe told Cameron in the translated letter that the current price on both Cameron's head and his own was £100 apiece, and the amount was for their death and not their capture. Dragging Canoe noted that none of the Cherokees indicated interest in the offer, and so Colonel Christian then upped the reward by offering all the rifles his men had. Dragging Canoe reassured Cameron that no counteroffers would ever sway his loyalty. He told his brother, "I shall never forget your talk and your father's to us, you may be assured my ears shall always be open to receive your talk and our fathers."[131] The Chickamauga leader pledged that his "thoughts and heart is for war as long as King George has one enemy in this country."[132] As Dragging Canoe closed his letter, he told Cameron again, "I hold our Father [Stuart] and you fast by the hand and never will let go which I hope you will do the same by me."[133] His words paralleled the original Articles of Friendship, which linked a great chain from the breast of the king to the breast of the first Cherokee emperor. Dragging Canoe ended his translated talk with a pledge to send out his troops again once he returned to Chickamauga.[134]

The British continued to supply Dragging Canoe's Chickamauga communities with trade goods through trader John McDonald.[135] Dragging Canoe's efforts destabilized the American war effort, an added benefit to the British war effort at only the cost of trade goods. Soon after, Alexander Cameron relocated to the Chickamauga base camp, where he worked to supply the Chickamauga Cherokees with guns and ammunition and keep them in field against the Americans.[136]

By November 1776, Colonel Christian and his troops had withdrawn from Cherokee country, which was full of continuing war rumors. One, of course, was the reward for Dragging Canoe's death. Dragging Canoe countered those rumors by sending word to the towns along the Little Tennessee River that Alexander Cameron had given him encouraging talks recently and was sending reinforcements to help the Cherokees against the Watauga settlers. Rising leaders Young Tassel and Hanging Maw returned to Chota after a recent conference with Dragging Canoe at Chickamauga. While with him, the two Cherokee leaders saw the arrival of Indian trader John McDonald from Pensacola with a supply of ten wagon loads of ammunition as well as regular supplies. These supplies were then distributed to other Cherokee towns by other Indian traders.[137] Thus, the Chickamauga Cherokee attacks were being encouraged and supplied by British forces. McDonald often carried instructions directly from Cameron to Dragging Canoe. Of particular note was the arrival of some Creeks, frequent enemies of the Cherokees in the past, whose warriors came to the Chickamauga base camp desirous of joining the breakaway Cherokee movement against backcountry whites.[138]

Recent Patriot attacks had left towns like Chilhowie, Settico, Toquo, and Tellico depopulated, and dislocated Cherokees moved to find new homes. Some moved to the Chickamauga towns to live with the leader who they believed would fight for the Cherokees. When Settico refugees found a new home on the Tennessee River, they named it after their former home. Dislocated people from Toquo did the same with their new homesite among the Chickamaugas. Recent events had caused some Cherokee leaders to move their political positions into the Dragging Canoe camp as well. Ostenaco (Judd's Friend), Willenawah, Blood Fellow, Hanging Maw (Scolacuta), Kitegiska, Young Tassel, and Tsaladihi were now officially Chickamauga Cherokees. Around the same time, Attakullakulla died and one of the great voices of the Cherokee triumvirate went silent during a time of great turmoil.[139]

A few days after the British resupply of goods, Dragging Canoe, his son (Young Canoe), and thirteen supporters left the Chickamauga camp and met with traditional leaders at the Overhills town of Toqua on the Little Tennessee River. Dragging Canoe sent his son to collect information about a talk at Chota, and Dragging Canoe's group ultimately camped near Chota to learn what they could about this meeting. By this time, Cameron had authorized Dragging Canoe to scalp those backcountry inhabitants who were joining the Patriot army. The trader John McDonald was the messenger with the commission and was authorized to pay two hundred pounds of leather for each scalp.[140] McDonald's trade outpost was already located at the old settlement of Chickamauga, and he was a vital component of the continuing British effort to keep the Chickamauga Cherokees mobilized.[141]

In late December 1776, John Stuart wrote to General William Howe with a report of success relayed by the Cherokees. Dragging Canoe's attacks on the backcountry of North Carolina and Virginia had caused the Patriot army to pull out of Cherokee country. He bragged that the Americans now lived in fear of a perceived Creek and Cherokee alliance as well as suffering from a lack of supplies. Stuart had been accused of concocting this same plan, which had caused his hasty exodus from Charles Town courtesy of the Patriots. Stuart's same letter noted to General Howe that the Muskogee Creek leader Emistisiguo was reluctant to commit troops because of what the Cherokees recently suffered at the hands of the Americans.[142]

Patriot Indian officials were hard at work at the same time trying to keep the Muskogee Creeks neutral. That same month, Patriot leader General Lachlan McIntosh told Creek leaders, "we in Georgia and you Red men of the Creek Nation are and should be one people."[143] McIntosh went further stating, "we could wish and desire . . . your warriors and our warriors take up the hatchet as with one hand to keep our enemys the Red Coats and people over the great water out of our country."[144]

Despite American efforts with the Creeks, Stuart was able write to Sir William Howe in December 1776 that some Muskogee raiding parties had gone out against the people of Georgia and brought back two boys as hostages. Stuart closed his letter to his superior by voicing his confidence in the imminent reestablishment of peace in the colonies. The superintendent noted, however, that he did not think such a peace was possible "without their [Patriots] first being made sensible of the Superiority of Great Britain."[145] Stuart's comment reminds us that the conflict was, in fact, between the two sets of British people. Dragging Canoe and his people were just a sidebar in the greater story, although their breakaway movement was its own revolutionary event within Cherokee society.

January 1777 began with great uncertainty for the Cherokee people. Patriot leaders reached out directly to Cherokee leaders, like the Raven of Chota. In mid-January, Colonel Christian wrote the Cherokee leader explaining his actions in his recent, devastating raids through Cherokee country. He opened by assuring the Raven that "it was not the wish of the great men that sent me, that I should destroy the towns that were willing to be at peace . . . we did not want to hurt your women and children or your old people."[146] Colonel Christian continued, "I burnt the Canoe's town because he begun the war, burnt Chilowey because them people did not send the hostages that was by promised by their two warriors."[147] The Patriot leader told the Raven that he had taken pity on his people because Alexander Cameron had deceived them. Although the colonel offered trade goods for friendly behavior by the Cherokees, he also stated, "if any of your people are of a bad way of thinking they will be sorry for it if they do not change their opinions."[148] Christian ended his communication by warning the Raven against his people entertaining talks from Loyalist traders or British Indian commissaries. He saw no harm in the Cherokees buying the goods of these traders but warned them, "your best way is to lye still and let the white people fight out their disputes."[149]

Traditional Cherokee leaders like the Raven essentially had to accept a treaty from Colonel Christian if they wanted to prevent the kind of devastation visited on their towns the previous summer. In fact, several of the traditional Cherokee leaders met Christian in July 1777, as had been promised, to stop the earlier Patriot hostilities. Attakullakulla was now gone, and Oconostota was over seventy-five. The Cherokees chose Old Tassel and the Raven to speak for them.[150] Colonel Christian was joined by Colonels Preston, Shelby from Virginia, and Avery Winton and Lanier for North Carolina. The Patriots began by condemning the Cherokees for their part in the recent murders in the backcountry. They asked the traditional chiefs about the whereabouts of Dragging Canoe and other war chiefs.[151]

The Cherokee spokesmen responded with the explanation that Dragging Canoe and his people had seceded from the Cherokee Nation and relocated to Chickamauga Creek. In response, the traditional leaders stated that he refused to treat with the Patriots, and so the traditionalists disavowed any responsibility for his actions.[152]

The Raven met Colonel Christian at Fort Patrick Henry on Long Island in the Holston River in July 1777. At first, the Patriot leaders asked for a cession of all Cherokee land north of the Little Tennessee River. After negotiations, the Americans reduced the demand to all land north of the Nolichucky River. Not surprisingly, the cession included the transfer of the Watauga lands to the states of North Carolina and Virginia. The Patriots would have continued their attacks had the Cherokees not ceded the land.[153] In so doing, Cherokee leaders signed away some five million acres of land. That massive concession on the part of leaders, painted by the Chickamaugas as weak and concessionist, sent even more converts to the Chickamauga base camp at Lookout Mountain.[154] In South Carolina, the new treaty brought in the future western counties of Anderson, Oconee, Pickens, and Greenville.[155] Many among the Cherokees opposed the measure, especially as it ceded away prime hunting grounds on what would later become the Tennessee side of the mountains.[156]

While traditional leaders bargained away yet more land on another treaty by the river, Dragging Canoe showed his contempt for the peace negotiations by attacking targets fifteen miles from Fort Patrick Henry.[157] Dragging Canoe and his men began to fortify their base of operation in what later became Brainerd, Tennessee. His followers began building towns nearby, including one at modern Graysville, Georgia, another at Soddy Daisy, Falling Water, and Ooltewah in modern Tennessee. He also placed a camp atop Lookout Mountain, which signaled the valley floor towns when suspicious groups approached. Perhaps commanding one thousand men, Dragging Canoe received regular war supplies from trader John McDonald. Thus positioned and supplied, Dragging Canoe periodically sent out small raiding parties for lightning strikes on backcountry targets.[158] The breakaway Chickamauga group concluded an alliance with the Creeks for further planned attacks. The British kept the Chickamaugas well supplied with war materials while starving out the Cherokee towns that had made peace with the Americans.[159]

On the wider imperial stage, the British government began to formulate plans based on the active participation of groups like the Chickamauga Cherokees. In July 1777, Sir William Howe wrote to Governor Chester of New York informing him that John Stuart had been ordered to encourage the Southern Indians to form a confederacy to support the crown by protecting each of their tribes against Patriot attacks. Howe wrote that Stuart was to aid the (Chickamauga) Cherokees specifically with arms and ammunition as well as to bring in the Creeks and other tribes. Their mission, as detailed by Howe, was to attack Patriot parties scouting the frontier and to disrupt Patriot communications in rebel provinces.[160] At this juncture, the British government seemed to form a policy to support what Dragging Canoe's rebels were doing in the field, another case of the tail wagging the dog of empire. John Stuart's influence on his superiors was apparent near the end of Howe's letter, as the general remarked that white men

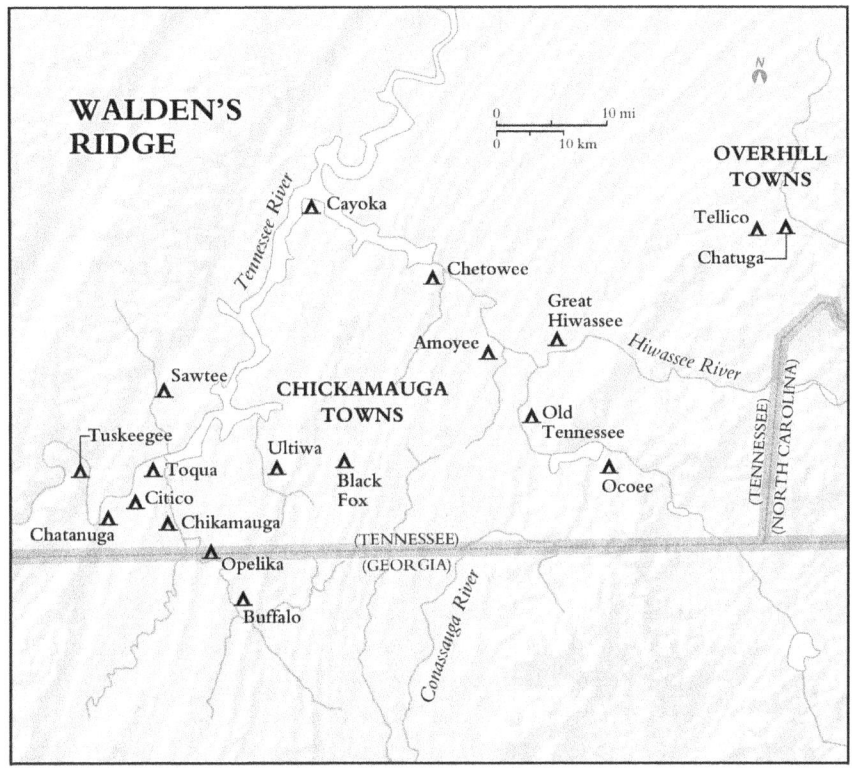

Figure 4.1. Walden's Ridge Chickamauga towns map (courtesy of Robert Cronan, Lucidity Information Design, LLC)

should conduct the Indian raids to make them more effective. Howe also remarked that regulation of the Indian traders should be given the utmost scrutiny during the conflict, with only those men who were licensed and who had given assurances for their behavior to be tolerated in the backcountry at that time.[161] Stuart long held the belief that unregulated traders were the cause of most trouble in the backcountry. He had never believed in sending the tribes out on a mission without British military supervision to prevent deadly mistakes and excessive collateral damage.

Cherokee relations with surrounding whites thoroughly divided Dragging Canoe's family. His father Attakullakulla sent word to the Patriots that he had five hundred Cherokee soldiers ready to join them in their fight against the British.[162] Meanwhile, the chief's son and his warriors withdrew from the area, returning to the base camp at Chickamauga Creek, where they continued to draw supporters from among the younger Cherokees, especially after the recent Treaty of Long Island. The group also gained the support of a venerable old lion, too old to fight, but not too old to give advice. Ostenaco or Judd's Friend, who had long been a voice calling for the independence of the Cherokees from British or French influence, now joined this movement. The elder chief had been part of the group to visit Great Britain like Attakullakulla but now cast his lot with the rebellious faction.[163]

The bulk of Cherokee people were pulled in many directions by this conflict. This recent treaty with the Americans gave the Cherokees new Patriot Indian agents—James Robertson from North Carolina and Joseph Martin representing Virginia. The Cherokees knew both men, whom they generally liked and respected. Robertson chose Chota as a base, and his presence there kept the highly influential town relatively quiet during the war.[164] When Dragging Canoe attacked Robertson's home, his father Attakullakulla reported the action to Captain Thomas Price.[165]

Backcountry settlers continued to use the war as an excuse to occupy Cherokee lands, and the Patriots kept the pro-Patriot Cherokee towns poorly supplied with goods during the conflict. By contrast, the British kept the Chickamauga Cherokee towns well supplied and continued to refuse to trade with the Patriot-aligned Overhills towns. This trade imbalance itself encouraged some Cherokees to join Dragging Canoe's side, illustrative of the power of the Indian trade to shape politics.[166]

The paucity of trade led to some incidents of starvation among the Overhills Cherokees, which prompted Virginia Patriot agent Joseph Martin to contact the enemy side, British Superintendent John Stuart, in February 1778, imploring that Stuart reopen the trade to all the Cherokee towns. Martin went so far as to admit to Stuart that the Cherokees were pro-British and only remained silent from fear of further American retaliatory raids like those of the summer of 1776. Martin even suggested a meeting between he and Stuart at Pensacola to restart the British trade.[167]

In summer 1778, Cameron dispatched the Chickamauga Cherokees to work in tandem with the British Army in their recent actions to retake Georgia. Dragging Canoe and his trader, John McDonald, led those missions, which took the Cherokees into Georgia and South Carolina battling Patriots for the rest of the year. Some Georgia settlers probably learned to hate the Cherokees for their part in the war to retake Georgia. Meanwhile, Patriot forces by year's end scouted the Chickamauga towns near Lookout Mountain and planned for a strike against them.[168]

In March 1779, the Dragging Canoe rebellion received a major setback, though not of the military kind. John Stuart, whose health had been failing for some time, died on March 21, 1779.[169] Stuart's death caught the British government off guard, and the Southern British Indian Superintendency was effectively neutralized for much of the remaining year. Peter Chester, the governor of West Florida, appointed a five-man commission to carry on Stuart's work after his death. Later that summer, George Germain appointed Lieutenant Thomas Brown of Augusta, Georgia, and Alexander Cameron as dual Indian superintendents for West and East Florida, respectively.[170] Thomas Brown received authority over the Cherokees and Muskogee Creeks while British government placed Cameron in charge of the Choctaws and Chickasaws.[171] Brown was a relatively recent arrival in North America and a sincere Loyalist. Patriots near Augusta, Georgia, had subjected him to physical torture for refusing to join the Patriot cause and, as a result, he lost several toes due to severe burns. Though a devoted Loyalist, he held no familial connections or influence among either the Cherokee or the Muskogee peoples. He had little to no experience dealing with tribal peoples. It was Cameron who held cultural currency with both groups but was assigned to the western tribes with whom he previously had little contact. Neither man would be able to command the loyalty that John Stuart had enjoyed. Dragging Canoe had lost his Scottish "father" for whom he had publicly stated he would willingly die. Dragging Canoe's other brother, Cameron, had been reassigned to different tribes. Though Cameron still lived, Dragging Canoe, in a sense, had lost both of his greatest supporters.

The Patriot saga with the Chickamaugas continued for a time. British agents kept these breakaway rebels supplied with arms from supply bases in West Florida for the next two years. Thus armed, the Chickamauga Cherokees eventually took control of the Wilderness Road, the main artery between Virginia and Kentucky. They launched attacks which sent the Watauga and Holston River settlers once more into their forts.[172] These strikes prompted Colonel Evan Shelby to raise a strike force to move against Dragging Canoe's base camp towns. In April 1779, Colonel Shelby led a Patriot large attack force of six hundred men down the Tennessee River for a strike against the Chickamauga base camps. Most Cherokee men were out on duty under Dragging Canoe and trader John McDonald. Most Cherokee women and children ran to the woods when the attacks came; the Patriots killed only four Cherokees, but they burned eleven Chickamauga towns in a similar pattern to previous wars. The Patriots seized what they did not burn, including McDonald's home and storehouse, costing him some £25,000 in damages to merchandise and property.[173]

Confusion within the British Indian superintendency itself, caused by Stuart's death the previous month, prevented follow-up attacks, allowing the survivors to regroup.[174] The Patriot army did such damage that Dragging Canoe retreated to the base of Lookout Mountain. American actions sent the bulk of the neutral Cherokees into the British camp for the rest of the war. In hindsight, the devastation launched against the Cherokees meant that the long-feared Indian apocalypse against the backcountry would never include the Cherokees now.

These attacks drew Dragging Canoe and McDonald back from the front to the Chickamauga camps. Alexander Cameron sent a party of Florida Rangers as support along with a pack horse train of replacement goods for McDonald. Despite a major loss of a base of operations, Dragging Canoe persevered to receive a Shawnee delegation who came to him in July 1779. Dragging Canoe acknowledged the loss of their towns, telling the Shawnees, "Now we live in the grass as you see us. But we are not yet conquered."[175] He returned a set of wampum beads they had given him during a meeting years earlier. The meeting was successful enough that the Shawnees and Cherokees exchanged peoples, with members of each group moving to live long term among the communities of the other.[176]

When Alexander Cameron took up his new role as Indian superintendent of West Florida, wrote Lord George Germain in mid-December 1779, he updated his commander on the handiwork of the Virginia troops in late April 1779, who had attacked the Cherokees while the Chickamaugas were on missions against Georgia. Cameron estimated a group of seven hundred men came down the Holston River by canoe for a surprise attack on the Chickamauga towns. Patriot forces killed numerous women and children, though survivors took to the woods. The Virginia troops made sure to destroy crops and homes while carrying off horses and cattle.[177] The American raids were particularly devastating in that they left behind no resources on which those attacked could soon rebuild or recover. Shelby took an estimated 150 horses and 100 cattle and even a quantity of deerskins owned by trader John McDonald. The confiscation included some twenty thousand bushels of corn; in total, the seized merchandise was valued at around $100,000 in Cameron's report.[178] The Cherokee commissary reported that his Patriot counterpart, Commissioner Martin, had offered relief supplies to loyal Cherokees if they would abandon the Chickamauga camps and return to a life of neutrality in their former towns.[179]

Cameron told Lord Germain that he believed the Cherokees would have taken the offer had he, Cameron, not arrived back in Cherokee country when he did. The British Indian agent observed that Commissioner Martin soon departed the area after Cameron had returned. Cameron also offered an opinion to his superior that speaks of a deep breach of familial connections among the Cherokees. Cameron observed that the Cherokees seemed "much dejected since they have been told that I have no more to do with them, and that they are not only determined to apply to General Prevost, but also solicit His Majesty for my return among them."[180]

In the report, Cameron made a passionate statement of Cherokee fidelity that also spoke of family connections. He told Germain, "I can venture to assure your Lordship that there is no Indian on the continent of America firmer in their attachment to His Majesty than the Cherokees."[181] The British Indian superintendent briefly recounted his own career with the Cherokees, noting that he had lived and worked with them since 1764. Cameron mused, "I have the vanity to think that they would follow me to any part of the Continent provided I could support them."[182] Was Cameron speaking of mere vanity or the strength of his family connections now being wasted in his new position?

The attack drew the Chickamauga attack force in Georgia back to their ruined base camps to survey the devastation, which prompted them to sue for a temporary peace with Colonel Shelby. Perhaps more long-term damage was the fact that the Patriot armies got to see how desirable the Chickamauga territory was. The Chickamaugas began to rebuild their communities and lay quiet for a time.[183] To prevent the odds of future Patriot attacks, Dragging Canoe moved his towns farther down the Tennessee River. Just as river networks once brought outsiders into Cherokee country, five new Chickamauga towns emerged at critical bends along the winding river, including Tuskegee Island town and Running Water town, from which Dragging Canoe personally operated. Then there were Nickajack town, Long Island town, and Crow town at the most distant point south. The river was its own warning system, with upper towns being able to warn lower towns; plus the river had some navigation hazards as well. The Chickamaugas controlled the access paths through the mountains to complete the security issues.[184] From these bases along the river, Chickamauga strike teams would launch against colonial settlements.

British forces continued to try to use tribes like the Cherokees to fight a backcountry revolution. Lieutenant Governor Henry Hamilton was both the head of Fort Detroit, a province of Quebec, and a superintendent of Indian affairs after Guy Johnston's death. He began to develop his own plan using the British-aligned tribes, including the Shawnees, the Muskogee Creeks, and the Chickamaugas. Using trader John McDonald, he assembled some £20,000 sterling in ammunition and other supplies to be used for a great springtime 1780 offensive. Hamilton was also going to bring together at the mouth of the Tennessee River a representation of all the tribes.[185] Before Hamilton could carry out his plan, however, Patriot forces captured his armies when they tried to liberate the Illinois country from George Rogers Clark and his Kentucky troops.[186]

As the summer of 1780 passed, the Chickamauga Cherokees began to plan retaliatory raids. Particularly appealing about the timing was the fact that Patriot Colonels John Sevier and Isaac Shelby had taken troops and marched to King's Mountain, some distance from Cherokee country. Dragging Canoe sent runners to the various towns in preparation. Backcountry fur traders also made a move. Isaac Thomas and Ellis Harlin gave prior warning to the towns being targeted, and they relayed word to Colonel Sevier. Sevier sent a group of soldiers back on forced march to reinforce a skeletal defense force he had left behind.[187]

As a Cherokee attack force got under way, Sevier brought a group of about one hundred men and headed for Cherokee country, and his group reached the Cherokee encampment before they launched their attack. Catching the Chickamaugas off-guard, the two sides exchanged gunfire until the Cherokees retreated under militia pursuit, which ended at Boyd's Creek with a Cherokee loss of twenty-eight men to Sevier's three wounded militiamen.[188] After the Patriot victory at the Battle of King's Mountain on October 7, 1780, the British trusted the Chickamauga Cherokees with launching diversionary attacks on the North Carolina and Virginia frontier to keep Patriot militia busy. Dragging Canoe and John McDonald led those diversionary raids, which were successful enough to prompt a devastating Patriot attack against traditional Cherokee towns.[189]

Pressing their advantage, Colonel Arthur Campbell and Major Joseph Martin arrived with troops, bringing Colonel John Sevier's forces up to seven hundred men. Their combined troops crossed the Little Tennessee River, missing a Chickamauga force while they moved toward the Hiwassee towns. Backcountry Patriots destroyed Nan-ye-hi's town of Chota while troops under Robert Campbell attacked Chilhowee. Although Nan-ye-hi went out to negotiate with Sevier, her talks landed on deaf ears. The Patriots laid waste to every town between the Tennessee and Hiwassee rivers.[190] Some estimates of inflicted damage include one thousand cabins lost and some fifty thousand bushels of corn destroyed.[191] The Cherokee leaders of Tellico made a successful peace talk that spared their town of forty houses, but the same could not be said of the majority of Cherokee towns. As before in the Anglo-Cherokee War, American troops raided livestock and food supplies by the end of December 1780.[192] The mission effectively neutralized the upper Cherokees but made the Chickamaugas resolute in their desire to wipe out the American settlements in the Cumberland.[193] Simultaneously, backcountry settlers used the attacks, which resulted in the Cherokees abandoning their towns, as an opportunity to move in and squat on the land. When the Cherokees lodged complaints with North Carolina governor Alexander Martin, he ordered Colonel John Sevier to tear down the squatter dwellings. Sevier, however, ignored such orders.[194]

Colonel James Robertson made his home at The Bluffs, one of the three outposts near Nashville. The Chickamaugas planned an attack to wipe out this station, and Dragging Canoe led the strike force which moved into position in early April 1781. When a diversionary small group of Cherokees charged the fort gates, a group of twenty mounted soldiers under Robertson charged out. Dragging Canoe then released a large number of Chickamauga troops who cut off the United States troops from their fort. While Dragging Canoe held the upper hand, fate intervened in the form of dogs released by Mrs. Robertson, which viciously attacked the Chickamauga ground troops. The noise and violence of the attacking dogs spooked the horses, which ran back toward the fort, breaking the line established by the Chickamaugas. Robertson's troops followed, carrying their wounded back inside the fort. Dragging Canoe's troops did not pursue further hostilities.[195] Fate and a resourceful woman denied Dragging Canoe his victory, but the targets of his retaliatory attacks were becoming less strategic with each mission.

For example, the Chickamaugas struck again in July 1782 in Powell's Valley, resulting in two settler casualties but the loss of a great number of livestock. Militia units responded, overtaking the Chickamaugas and retrieving many of the animals.[196] Thus, the conflict had become one of minor guerilla skirmishes with little consequential result. Later in the summer, the Chickamaugas sued for peace through trader Ellis Harlin, who responded with a call to meet. The Chickamaugas promised to bring their captives to Chota, where Governor Martin planned to meet with them. Colonel John Sevier had other plans, however. Where Martin sought diplomacy, Sevier planned for an attack on the Chickamauga towns to take the land by force.

Sevier led an attack force of two hundred men on horse through the Overhills towns but did no damage. Sevier's group began their initial attack on Indian towns on the Hiwassee River before moving outward to strike places like Vann's Town, Spring Frog Town, and Estanala.[197] The British war effort received a fatal blow in 1781 when Spain and France entered the conflict on the side of the United States. Afterward, a Spanish fleet seized the British West Florida capital of Pensacola. Dragging Canoe continued his strikes, undeterred in attacks against frontier settlements at what is now Nashville, taking out most farms on the Cumberland River.[198] Although Dragging Canoe definitely qualified as a pivotal frontier figure capable of wagging the empire, leaders at the heart of empire were deciding to end the war in spite of him.

On the global stage of the war, the Americans and British signed the Treaty of Paris on November 30, 1782. In the larger scheme of American history, the new nation celebrated the treaty as David's victory over Goliath, emboldening America's confidence in its own abilities. The treaty was less of a symbolic issue for the British and more one of practicality, cutting their losses and financial drain while they were behind. Loyalists began to evacuate the colonies that same month. For the Chickamauga Cherokees, the treaty meant the end of British support to their cause. Yet Dragging Canoe met a deputation of tribes in January 1783 at the Muskogee Creek mother town of Tuckabatchee in modern Elmore County, Alabama. There he led representatives of the Cherokees, Muskogee Creeks, Choctaws, and Chickasawas proposing a federation dedicated to stopping American expansion, and British Indian agent Thomas Browne gave his support to the plan. However, on June 1, 1783, Browne received orders to evacuate all Indian officials and traders from Indian country.[199] Britain's empire over the Cherokees was coming to an end, whether it had been real or just perceived as historian Kristofer Ray theorized.

The five Lower Towns of the Chickamaugas survived and, according to some, even flourished for a time after the war. For at least fifteen years, they were left to their own pursuits, and their women and children enjoyed a relative safety. Dragging Canoe dispatched ambush parties against white settlements on a frequent basis, though the missions have been described as both "vicious and small" in scope.[200] Before his departure, British agent Thomas Browne suggested that Dragging Canoe reach out to the Spanish for continued supplies for his missions. Dragging Canoe and his people were on their own now, with trader John McDonald as their sole support.[201]

In the wake of Dragging Canoe's efforts lay seven years of destruction vented on the greater Cherokee society in which American troops practiced deliberate overkill of destruction with their retaliatory raids. In short, some of the Chickamaugas were even ready to end the conflict by the mid-1780s.[202] At that time, the new United States government, confident in its defeat of Great Britain, made new treaties with tribes like the Cherokees and Creeks. As their tribal boundaries were redrawn, the new treaties ripped away thousands of acres of land from the tribes. United

States representatives met with the Cherokees on November 18, 1785, at Hopewell on the Keowee River in South Carolina. Nearly one thousand Cherokees attended the meeting, including Chickamauga representatives, though not Dragging Canoe himself. Treaty negotiations covered ten days and the resulting Treaty of Hopewell was ready on November 28, 1785. It formally ended hostilities between the Cherokees and the United States, and thirty-seven chiefs and principal men signed it. Those signatories included Chickamauga leaders Newota, Umatooetha, Wyuka, and Necatee.[203] Dragging Canoe was not one of them.

In fact, his movement received a booster shot of support in late 1787 when a small group of Shawnees came to visit him at Running Water. The lead warrior was Cheesekau, who brought along his younger brother, Tecumseh, both sons of Pukshinwa, who had been killed at the Battle of Point Pleasant on the Kanawha River in 1782. The two Shawnees may have been influenced by Dragging Canoe's idea of an Indian confederacy against white encroachment. Cheekeskau and Tecumseh stayed with the Chickamaugas for two years and participated in their raids that seemed to challenge the peace established by the Treaty of Hopewell. The Shawnees participated in a raid on Bledsoe's Station in February 1788, where Cheesekau was killed. When Tecumseh returned to the Ohio country in spring 1790, he left behind some forty Shawnee warriors who permanently joined the Chickamauga movement at Running Water.[204]

As with so many diplomatic solutions, there were nasty, residual issues that remained on the white side of the Hopewell Treaty as well, resulting in continued violence over the next few years. About three thousand illegal white settlers still inhabited land on the Cherokee boundary side created by the Treaty of Hopewell. The North Carolina government continued to issue land allotments of Cherokee land as well. These problems particularly aggravated the Chickmauga Cherokees, whose own arc of defiance had begun over the Treaty of Sycamore Shoals.[205] The Chickamaugas continued to receive foreign support in the form of ammunition by the British agent at Detroit, Alexander McKee, who hoped that the Chickamaugas could "shoot sense into the heads of the King's recalcitrant subjects."[206] The agent used Dragging Canoe's brother, The Badger, as a messenger, and Dragging Canoe communicated with this agent as late as 1793.[207]

The United States government and the mainstream Cherokee leadership continue to meet and sign diplomatic agreements in spite of the Chickamauga insurgency. Colonel James Robertson met with traditional Cherokee leaders in June 1791. Although Dragging Canoe did not participate and the Chickamaugas were attacking targets at the time,

Chickamauga leaders John Watts and Bloody Fellow did participate. The traditional Cherokees sent some forty-one leaders and 1,200 warriors. Tennessee governor William Blount presided. When negotiations ended on July 2, 1791, the resulting Treaty of Holston redrew boundary lines for the Cherokees in return for an annuity of $10,000 and certain trade goods. The treaty granted backcountry settlers right of passage on the Tennessee River, though the Chickamauga towns were in a position to stop access. In the grand scheme of things, the Ani-yun-wiya placed themselves under the protection of the United States government and pledged to return all U.S. prisoners held by them. The U.S. Senate ratified the treaty in November 1791. Supporters credited Governor Blount with achieving a final peace to end hostilities with the Cherokees, now reduced to a subject people some sixty-one years after the original Articles of Friendship.[208] They had made the long journey from a sovereign people to a "civilized" people under American authority—one of five such tribes in the South.

The conflict ended for Tsyu-gun-sini in March 1792 when he died at Running Water on the Tennessee River. Black Fox, a participant in the annual summer council of the nation at Eustanaula in 1793, memorialized him by stating, "The Dragging Canoe has left the world. He was a man of consequence in his country. He was a friend to both his own and to the white people."[209] Funeral tributes are perhaps left best unanalyzed; however, Dragging Canoe's probably deserves a brief commentary.

His eulogizer was absolutely correct on several points—Dragging Canoe was a man of consequence in Cherokee society. He was an absolute patriot to Cherokee society based on events occurring at the time. His convictions forced him to break with the path of his father and other accommodationist Cherokee leaders of the triumvirate of the 1760s. Such courage is remarkable and could not have been easy. His loyalty to his Scottish brothers Alexander Cameron and John Stuart would have been admirable had they been blood kin—the fact that they were adopted kin reveals a depth of attachment that is truly remarkable. His words to them and about them reveal a passion that even translation could not dim. Dragging Canoe's commitment to the British Indian authority and its vision for the Cherokee people was based on John Stuart's authority and wisdom. His death probably finished any slim chance the Chickamauga rebellion ever had for success. That rebellion could almost be best characterized as a revitalization movement similar to the Ghost Dance of the nineteenth century. It was not a pan-Indian movement, of course, and it involved a much smaller set of participants. For a brief time, Dragging Canoe and his Chickamaugas both waged war against the British Empire and terrified the

Patriot movement. In an ironic way, Dragging Canoe and his followers may have given the Patriots the necessary righteous indignation to both fight Britain and attempt a separation from the empire. Perhaps it would be more accurate to say that a forged letter by Watauga settler Jesse Benton gave the movement the thrust it needed to succeed.

According to Dragging Canoe's powerful speech at Sycamore Shoals that day, whole Indian nations had melted away like snow in the sun because of white settlement. Surely, then, Dragging Canoe was the snowball, perhaps with a rock inside, whose hard impact left a smarting, stinging blow before it, too, melted away in the sun. His efforts were forgotten by neither his own people nor American soldiers, backcountry residents, or Georgia settlers who had occasion to fight his troops. His actions may well have secured the place of the Cherokees at the top of a list for tribes slated to be removed first during the presidency of Andrew Jackson. Certain Revolutionary leaders certainly voiced that sentiment in the summer of 1776 because of Dragging Canoe.

Notes

1. http://members.iinet.net.au/~royalty/states/America/Cherokee.html.
2. www.aaanativearts.com/cherokee/little-carpenter.htm.
3. www.aaanativearts.com/cherokee/little-carpenter.htm. There is a troubling lack of documentation about Dragging Canoe's early life until he shows up in the records of the British as an adult. He was a rising warrior or raven whose life might have been filled with honorific deeds and obscurity had he not broken with his father's leadership and fought against the Americans during the American Revolution.
4. https://www.geni.com/people/Attakullakulla-Onacona/6000000011727533816.
5. Brent Alan Yanusdi Cox, *Heart of the Eagle: Dragging Canoe and the Emergence of the Chickamauga Confederacy* (Milan, TN: Chenanee Publishers, 1999), 50.
6. Minutes of Congress held at Hard Labour. Oucconnastotah Head Man of Cherokee Speaking, October 15 1768. CO5/74, Fol. 39.
7. Minutes of Congress held at Hard Labour. Oucconnastotah Head Man of Cherokee Speaking, October 15, 1768. CO5/74, Fol. 39.
8. www.aaanativearts.com/cherokee/little-carpenter.htm.
9. E. Raymond Evans, "Notable Persons in Cherokee History: Dragging Canoe," *Journal of Cherokee Studies* II, no. 1 (Winter 1977), 176.
10. James C. Kelly, "Notable Persons in Cherokee History: Attakullakulla," *Journal of Cherokee Studies* III, no. 1 (Winter 1978), 3–4.
11. Kelly, "Notable Persons: Attakullakulla," 4.
12. Evans, "Notable Persons: Dragging Canoe," 176.

CHAPTER 4

13. John P. Brown, *Americans All: The Story of the Chickamaugas*, chapter 3, page 3, unpublished manuscript, Museum of the Cherokee Indian.

14. Paul Kelton, *Cherokee Medicine, Colonial Germs: An Indigenous Nation's Flight against Smallpox, 1518–1824* (Norman: University of Oklahoma Press, 2015), 50–51.

15. Kelton, *Cherokee Medicine*, 87.

16. Kelton, *Cherokee Medicine*, 114.

17. Evans, "Dragging Canoe," 176. There are multiple spellings on Malaquo, Mialaquo. Brown, *Americans All*, chapter 3, 8.

18. Emmet Starr, *History of the Cherokee Indians* (Norman: University of Oklahoma Press, 1984), 466–467.

19. Michael P. Morris, *George Galphin and the Transformation of the Georgia-South Carolina Backcountry* (Lanham, MD: Lexington Press, 2014), 53.

20. Evans, "Notable Persons: Dragging Canoe," 177.

21. David Corkran, *The Creek Frontier 1540–1783* (Norman: University of Oklahoma Press, 1967), 288.

22. Ray, *Cherokees, Empire*, 48.

23. Evans, "Notable Persons: Dragging Canoe," 177.

24. https://dnr.mo.gov/shpo/nps-nr/TrailOfTearsMPS.pdf.

25. Evans, "Notable Persons: Dragging Canoe," 177.

26. Evans, "Notable Persons: Dragging Canoe," 177. Modern towns in this area are Watauga City, Elizabethton, and Johnson City, Tennessee.

27. Evans, "Notable Persons: Dragging Canoe," 177.

28. Evans, "Notable Persons: Dragging Canoe," 177–178.

29. Grace Steele Woodward, *The Cherokees* (Norman: University of Oklahoma Press, 1984), 84.

30. Penelope Allen Johnson, unpublished manuscript of *The History of the Cherokee Indians, Particularly the Chickamauga Group*, Vol. 1, p. 6. Some sources note an alternate name for Dragging Canoe used in the old records as Cheucunsene.

31. Cox, *Heart of the Eagle*, 51.

32. Cox, *Heart of the Eagle*, 38–39.

33. Brown, *Americans All*, chapter 3, 5.

34. Evans, "Notable Persons: Dragging Canoe," 179.

35. Brown, *Americans All*, chapter 3, 8.

36. Brown, *Americans All*, chapter 3, part 1, n.d.

37. James C. Kelly, "Notable Persons in Cherokee History: Attakullakulla," *Journal of Cherokee Studies* III, no. 1 (Winter 1978), 25.

38. Kenneth Coleman, ed., *The Colonial Records of the State of Georgia: Original Papers of Governor John Reynolds 1754–1756*, Vol. 27 (Athens: University of Georgia Press, 1977), 64.

39. Kelly, "Notable Persons: Attakullakulla," 25.

40. Brown, *Americans All*, 3.

41. Cox, *Heart of the Eagle*, 26.

42. Brown, *Americans All*, chapter 3, 3–4.
43. Brown, *Americans All*, chapter 3, 4.
44. Brown, *Americans All*, chapter 3, 4.
45. Brown, *Americans All*, chapter 3, 4.
46. Brown, *Americans All*, chapter 3, 5.
47. Brown, *Americans All*, chapter 3, 5.
48. Brown, *Americans All*, chapter 3, 5–10.
49. Cox, *Heart of the Eagle*, 33.
50. Grace Steele Woodward, *The Cherokees* (Norman: University of Oklahoma Press, 1984), 88–89.
51. Evans, "Notable Persons: Dragging Canoe," 179.
52. John Stuart to William Legge, Earl of Dartmouth, March 28, 1775, *Colonial and State Records of North Carolina*, Vol. 9, 1173.
53. Evans, "Notable Persons: Dragging Canoe," 179.
54. Evans, "Notable Persons: Dragging Canoe," 179–180.
55. J. Russell Snapp, *John Stuart and the Struggle for Empire on the Southern Frontier* (Baton Rouge: Louisiana State University Press, 1996), 159–160.
56. Brown, *Old Frontiers*, 138.
57. Evans, "Notable Persons: Dragging Canoe," 180.
58. Evans, "Notable Persons: Dragging Canoe," 180.
59. William Henry Drayton to Alexander Cameron, September 26, 1775, CO/5: Folio 75.
60. William Henry Drayton to Alexander Cameron, September 26, 1775, CO/5: Folio 75.
61. Alexander Cameron to William Henry Drayton, October 16, 1775, CO/5: Folio 57.
62. John Stuart to Alexander Cameron, December 16, 1775, CO/5: 28–29.
63. John Stuart to Alexander Cameron, December 16, 1775, CO/5: Folio 28–29.
64. John Stuart to William Legge, Earl of Dartmouth, January 8, 1776, *Colonial and State Records of North Carolina*, Vol. 10, 392–393.
65. Evans, "Notable Persons: Dragging Canoe," 180.
66. Evans, "Notable Persons: Dragging Canoe," 180.
67. Johnson, *History of the Cherokee Indians*, Vol. 1, 7.
68. Evans, "Notable Persons: Dragging Canoe," 180.
69. Evans, "Notable Persons: Dragging Canoe," 180.
70. Johnson, *History of the Cherokee Indians*, Vol. 1, 7.
71. Evans, "Notable Persons: Dragging Canoe," 180–181.
72. Allen, *History of the Cherokee Indians*, Vol. 1, 7–8.
73. James Paul Pate, "The Chickamauga: A Forgotten Segment of Indian Resistance on the Southern Frontier" (PhD dissertation, Mississippi State University, 1969), 60–62.

74. Alexander Cameron to John Stuart, Toqueh, July 9, 1776, CO5/77, Folio 167.

75. Letter (translated for Dragging Canoe) from William Thompson to Alexander Cameron, November 14, 1776, CO/5: 94.

76. Henry Stuart to John Stuart, August 25, 1776, *Colonial and State Records of North Carolina*, Vol. 10, 777.

77. Collin Calloway, *The American Revolution in Indian Country: Crisis and Diversity in Native American Communities* (Cambridge: Cambridge University Press, 1995), 195–196.

78. Henry Stuart to John Stuart, August 25, 1776, *Colonial and State Records of North Carolina*, Vol. 10, 779.

79. Brown, *Old Frontiers*, 148.

80. Henry Stuart to John Stuart, August 25, 1776, CO5/77, Folio 169.

81. Allen, *Manuscript of the Cherokee Indians*, 9.

82. Brown, *Old Frontiers*, 148.

83. Allen, *Manuscript of the Cherokee Indians*, 9.

84. Henry Stuart to John Stuart, August 25, 1776, *Colonial and State Records of North Carolina*, Vol. 10, 781.

85. Henry Stuart to John Stuart, August 25, 1776, *Colonial and State Records of North Carolina*, Vol. 10, 783–784.

86. Henry Stuart to John Stuart, August 25, 1776, CO5/77, Folio 169.

87. Henry Stuart to John Stuart, August 25, 1776, *Colonial and State Records of North Carolina*, Vol. 10, 766–767.

88. Henry Stuart to John Stuart, August 25, 1776, CO5/77, Folio 169.

89. Henry Stuart to John Stuart, August 25, 1776, CO5/77, Folio 169.

90. Henry Stuart to John Stuart, August 25, 1776, *Colonial and State Records of North Carolina*, Vol. 10, 773–774.

91. Arrell Morgan Gibson, *The American Indian: Prehistory to the Present* (Lexington, MA: D.C. Heath, 1980), 252.

92. Anthony F. C. Wallace, *Jefferson and the Indians: The Tragic Fate of the First Americans* (Cambridge, MA: Belknap Press, 1999), 55.

93. Wallace, *Jefferson and the Indians*, 55.

94. Evans, "Notable Persons: Dragging Canoe," 181.

95. Evans, "Notable Persons: Dragging Canoe," 181.

96. Evans, "Notable Persons: Dragging Canoe," 181.

97. Morris, *The Bringing of Wonder*, 53.

98. Morris, *The Bringing of Wonder*, 56.

99. Evans, "Notable Persons: Dragging Canoe," 181.

100. Evans, "Notable Persons: Dragging Canoe," 182.

101. Morris, *The Bringing of Wonder*, 56.

102. Morris, *The Bringing of Wonder*, 56.

103. Evans, "Notable Persons: Dragging Canoe," 182.

104. Evans, "Notable Persons: Dragging Canoe," 182.

105. Brown, *Old Frontiers*, 151–152.
106. Brown, *Old Frontiers*, 152–153.
107. Brown, *Old Frontiers*, 153–154.
108. Ben Harris McClary, "Nancy Ward: The Last Beloved Woman of the Cherokees," *Tennessee Historical Quarterly* 21 (December 1962): 357.
109. Brown, *Old Frontiers*, 153.
110. Alexander Cameron to John Stuart, August 31, 1776, CO /5: 78 Folio 22.
111. Alexander Cameron to John Stuart, August 31, 1776, CO /5: 78 Folio 22. Nathaniel Gist had a Cherokee wife, Wurteh Watts, who gave birth to Sequoyah. He lived among the Overhills Cherokees and was employed by Cameron, though he would later change sides in the war.
112. Evans, "Notable Persons: Dragging Canoe," 182.
113. Calloway, *The American Revolution*, 197.
114. Brown, *Old Frontiers*, 156.
115. John McKay Sheftall, "George Galphin and Indian-White Relations in the Georgia Backcountry during the American Revolution" (MA thesis, University of Virginia, 1983), 27–28.
116. Wallace, *Jefferson and the Indians*, 57.
117. Wallace, *Jefferson and the Indians*, 57.
118. Calloway, *The American Revolution*, 197.
119. Evans, "Notable Persons: Dragging Canoe," 182.
120. Allen, *Manuscript of the Cherokee Indians*, 9.
121. Brown, *Old Frontiers*, 158.
122. Brown, *Old Frontiers*, 159.
123. Brown, *Old Frontiers*, 159–161.
124. Evans, "Notable Persons: Dragging Canoe," 183.
125. Letter from William Thompson [Dragging Canoe] to Alexander Cameron, Attowa Hatchee, November 14, 1776, CO5/ 94, Fol. 157.
126. Letter from William Thompson [Dragging Canoe] to Alexander Cameron, Attowa Hatchee, November 14, 1776, CO5/ 94, Fol. 157.
127. Letter from William Thompson [Dragging Canoe] to Alexander Cameron, Attowa Hatchee, November 14, 1776, CO5/ 94, Fol. 157.
128. Letter from William Thompson [Dragging Canoe] to Alexander Cameron, Attowa Hatchee, November 14, 1776, CO5/ 94, Fol. 157.
129. Letter from William Thompson [Dragging Canoe] to Alexander Cameron, Attowa Hatchee, November 14, 1776, CO5/ 94, Fol. 157.
130. Letter from William Thompson [Dragging Canoe] to Alexander Cameron, Attowa Hatchee, November 14, 1776, CO5/ 94, Fol. 157.
131. Letter from William Thompson [Dragging Canoe] to Alexander Cameron, Attowa Hatchee, November 14, 1776, CO5/ 94, Fol. 157.
132. Letter from William Thompson [Dragging Canoe] to Alexander Cameron, Attowa Hatchee, November 14, 1776, CO5/ 94, Fol. 157.

133. Letter from William Thompson [Dragging Canoe] to Alexander Cameron, Attowa Hatchee, November 14, 1776, CO5/ 94, Fol. 157.

134. Letter from William Thompson [Dragging Canoe] to Alexander Cameron, Attowa Hatchee, November 14, 1776, CO5/ 94, Fol. 157.

135. Evans, "Notable Persons: Dragging Canoe," 183.

136. Brown, *Old Frontiers*, 161.

137. Allen, *Manuscript of the Cherokee Indians*, 9.

138. Allen, *Manuscript of the Cherokee Indians*, 9.

139. Brown, *Old Frontiers*, 163–164.

140. Allen, *Manuscript of the Cherokee Indians*, 9.

141. Brown, *Old Frontiers*, 164.

142. John Stuart to General Howe, Pensacola, December 22, 1776, CO5/94, Folio 155.

143. Talk from Gen, McIntosh to the Creeks, December 23, 1776, CO 5/78, Folio 109–110.

144. Talk from Gen, McIntosh to the Creeks, December 23, 1776, CO 5/78, Folio 109–110.

145. John Stuart to General Howe, Pensacola, December 22, 1776, CO 5/94, Folio 155.

146. Talk from William Christian to the Raven, Cherokee Chief, January 19, 1777, CO/5: 78, Fol. 147.

147. Talk from William Christian to the Raven, Cherokee Chief, January 19, 1777, CO/5: 78, Fol. 147.

148. Talk from William Christian to the Raven, Cherokee Chief, January 19, 1777, CO/5: 78, Fol. 147.

149. Talk from William Christian to the Raven, Cherokee Chief, January 19, 1777, CO/5: 78, Fol. 147.

150. Brown, *Old Frontiers*, 165.

151. Brown, *Old Frontiers*, 165–166.

152. Brown, *Old Frontiers*, 165–166.

153. www.tngenweb.org/cession/1770720.html. Treaty with the Cherokee and North Carolina, July 20, 1777.

154. Wallace, *Jefferson and the Indians*, 58.

155. Edgar, *South Carolina*, 229.

156. Allen, *Manuscript of the Cherokee Indians*, 11.

157. Evans, "Notable Persons: Dragging Canoe," 183.

158. Allen, *Manuscript of the Cherokee Indians*, 18. Brainerd Mall occupies this site in modern-day Chattanooga. This same region would be home to the Brainerd Mission, whose missionary work among the nineteenth-century Cherokees is well documented.

159. Evans, "Notable Persons: Dragging Canoe," 183.

160. General Sir William Howe to Governor Chester, New York, July 12, 1777, CO5/94, Folio 273.

161. General Sir William Howe to Governor Chester, New York, July 12, 1777, CO5/94, Folio 273.

162. Allen, *Manuscript of the Cherokee Indians*, 11.

163. Allen, *Manuscript of the Cherokee Indians*, 11.

164. Allen, *Manuscript of the Cherokee Indians*, 13.

165. Allen, *Manuscript of the Cherokee Indians*, 17.

166. Evans, "Notable Persons: Dragging Canoe," 183.

167. Evans, "Notable Persons: Dragging Canoe," 183.

168. Evans, "Notable Persons: Dragging Canoe," 183.

169. Morris, *George Galphin*, 148.

170. Germain to Cameron and Thomas Brown, June 25, 1779, CO 5/ 80: Folio 123.

171. Jim Piecuch, *Three Peoples, One King: Loyalists, Indians, and Slaves in the Revolutionary South, 1775–1782* (Columbia: University of South Carolina Press, 2008), 152.

172. Gibson, *The American Indian*, 255.

173. Evans, "Notable Persons: Dragging Canoe," 183.

174. Calloway, *The American Revolution*, 203.

175. Evans, "Notable Persons: Dragging Canoe," 184.

176. Evans, "Notable Persons: Dragging Canoe," 184.

177. Alexander Cameron to Lord George Germain, Pensacola, December 18, 1779, CO5/81, Folder 37.

178. Allen, *Manuscript of the Cherokee Indians*, 17.

179. Alexander Cameron to Lord George Germain, Pensacola, December 18, 1779, CO5/81, Folder 37.

180. Alexander Cameron to Lord George Germain, Pensacola, December 18, 1779, CO5/81, Folder 37.

181. Alexander Cameron to Lord George Germain, Pensacola, December 18, 1779, CO5/81, Folder 37.

182. Alexander Cameron to Lord George Germain, Pensacola, December 18, 1779, CO5/81, Folder 37.

183. Allen, *Manuscript of the Cherokee Indians*, 18–21.

184. Evans, "Notable Persons: Dragging Canoe," 184.

185. Allen, *Manuscript of the Cherokee Indians*, 18–19.

186. Allen, *Manuscript of the Cherokee Indians*, 18–19.

187. Allen, *Manuscript of the Cherokee Indians*, 21.

188. Allen, *Manuscript of the Cherokee Indians*, 21.

189. Evans, "Notable Persons: Dragging Canoe," 184–185.

190. Allen, *Manuscript of the Cherokee Indians*, 22.

191. Brown, *Americans All: The Chickamaugas*, 33.

192. Allen, *Manuscript of the Cherokee Indians*, 22.

193. Brown, *Americans All*, 33.

194. Allen, *Manuscript of the Cherokee Indians*, 24.

195. Brown, *Americans All*, 35–36.
196. Allen, *Manuscript of the Cherokee Indians*, 24–25.
197. Allen, *Manuscript of the Cherokee Indians*, 25–26.
198. Evans, "Notable Persons: Dragging Canoe," 185.
199. Evans, "Notable Persons: Dragging Canoe," 185.
200. Brown, *Americans All*, 43–44.
201. Evans, "Notable Persons: Dragging Canoe," 185.
202. Allen, *Manuscript of the Cherokee Indians*, 27.
203. Allen, *Manuscript of the Cherokee Indians*, 32.
204. Allen, *Manuscript of the Cherokee Indians*, 55–56.
205. Allen, *Manuscript of the Cherokee Indians*, 33.
206. Brown, *Americans All*, 45–46.
207. Brown, *Americans All*, 45–46.
208. Brown, *Americans All*, 77–78.
209. Allen, *Manuscript of the Cherokee Indians*, 59.

"The Great God of Nature . . . Has Not Created Us to Be Your Slaves" 5

AMERICAN AUDIENCES THINK of only the one declaration statement given by Thomas Jefferson in the turbulent times of the 1770s. Yet Cherokee leader Tsyu-gun-sini, or Dragging Canoe, gave another declaration speech in the fall of 1775, issuing a clarion call of a possible impending doom of the Cherokee people in the face of colonial expansion. Like Jefferson, he issued a declaration calling for the ultimate sacrifice of life in order to reach the goals of freedom and survival for the Cherokees.

Dragging Canoe's father, Attakullakulla, an Overhills settlement chief, had worked consistently to replace Connecorte (Old Hop) as the voice of authority from the Overhills communities. Then he worked to maintain peace between the Cherokees and both the South Carolina government at Charles Town and the Virginia government at Williamsburg. The internal power struggle between Connecorte and Attakullakulla was an ugly contest at the very end, even by modern standards.

Before July 1776, few people outside of Virginia knew much about Thomas Jefferson until he penned a separation document explaining why the American colonies were terminating their relationship with the British government. Even at the time of his famous document, Jefferson had some prior experience with the Cherokees dating back to his childhood. His father Peter, a surveyor by trade, had hosted Cherokee delegates when they came to Williamsburg in Thomas's youth, and the young Jefferson remembered their visits and commented on their oratorical skills. Ultimately, decades later as president, Jefferson would sign peace treaties ending conflicts with the Cherokees started by Dragging Canoe and then ultimately direct an Indian trade management system designed to eliminate their land holdings, as predicted by Dragging Canoe, under the Civilization Program.

However, a series of events occurred between 1775 and the 1800s that linked these two leaders together in Cherokee history as well as U.S. mainstream history. Both men either gave or wrote independence declarations that affected their countries and their people. Dragging Canoe's 1775 speech addressed an impending extinction of the Cherokee people in the face of relentless white settlement. The Cherokees, like other tribal peoples, had hoped that the Appalachian Mountains would halt that settlement, but it did not. Further, the appearance of the Scots-Irish in the backcountry on the western side of the colonies complicated the Indian-Anglo relationship by accelerating the pace of treaty land boundary readjustments due to illegal trespass. Their recent arrival in the region of western South Carolina after the Anglo-Cherokee war may have been the reason for so many readjustments of the Anglo-Cherokee border between 1768 and 1775. Certainly these never-ending adjustments to validate fraudulent occupation caused the next generation of Cherokees to break with the leadership of what I have termed the Cherokee triumvirate leadership of Attakullakulla, Ostenaco, and Oconostota.

Thomas Jefferson's written document highlighted the need of the American people to explain the reasons for their separation from a seemingly oppressive Great Britain. On the face of it, such action was treason, pure and simple, and the Americans needed the people of Europe to understand their reasons for separation so that another nation would not join Britain's cause in extinguishing a rebellion with no good cause. Jefferson's task in his declaration was to explain and expand that cause seeking support for the Patriot side. Thus, Jefferson's task was to paint a great nation, Britain, in a negative light to a global readership.

Dragging Canoe's declaration began by citing the Delawares as a formerly great nation who, in 1775, had been reduced to a mere shadow of their former self. The mountains had been a geographic line in the sand that many tribes naturally thought would stop colonial expansion, as it would put them at too great a distance from their coastal trade with Britain. However, the Cherokees and others saw that the mountains did not stop colonial expansion. Dragging Canoe stated plainly that the Watauga settlers, illegal occupants on Cherokee leased land, now wanted their illegal occupation validated by the Treaty of Sycamore Shoals. Dragging Canoe stated that, after this current land grab, there would be continuing future occupations of Tsalagi land followed by treaty validations of the illegal land grab. Ultimately this process would repeat itself until all Cherokee land would be gone and the Ani Yun Wiya would be a people without a country. Dragging Canoe was thus speaking about the survival of the Cherokee people, a survival based on traditional land for hunting and communal occupation without the kind of land development so valued by Europeans.

Jefferson similarly spoke of a people whose land was in jeopardy unless they took action to break with a destructive government, the British nation, when that movement carried the will of the governed and the government in question threatened the safety of the people it was created to serve. According to Jefferson, a people so threatened could alter or abolish the form of government that threatened their safety and happiness. Jefferson chose to use the phrase "Life, Liberty and pursuit of Happiness" to communicate the natural rights of free people. He replaced John Locke's last phrase, "pursuit of property," with a more uplifting, less materialistic word choice. Thus, Jefferson the Virginian was also talking about the survival of the American colonial population, albeit speaking primarily of a white population, whom he referred to in *Notes on the State of Virginia* as Homo Sapiens Europaeus.[1]

Dragging Canoe's verbal declaration concluded that, without their original land or property, the future of Cherokee people would be that of vagabonds cast adrift in some western wilderness. When this land dispossession had reached its final stage in which there was no land available for retreat, the once great Cherokees would be proclaimed extinct by their white aggressors. Dragging Canoe asked his audience plainly whether all possible consequences should not be risked and all possible actions taken to prevent such a loss of one's country. Dragging Canoe was speaking about the survival of the Cherokee people, lest they become another patch of snow melting in the sun in the face of advancing white settlement.

Similarly, Jefferson asked his readers to consider that the colonies had experienced abuses and usurpations at the hands of the British government, leading inexorably to the establishment of dictatorship. So challenged, it was then the duty and the right of the oppressed people to throw off such oppression and provide new safeguards for the security of their future. Jefferson suggested that the survival of the people was tied to taking action against British rules and forces. Jefferson, keeping in mind a European readership, wanted them to know why the Americans were fighting for independence and proceeded to list a host of grievances levied against King George III.

Dragging Canoe's closing statement in his 1775 declaration speech referenced the Treaty of Sycamore Shoals and stated that such treaties might be all right for men too old to hunt and fight. "As for me," he declared,

"I have my young warriors about me. We will fight to hold our land."[2] Similarly, Jefferson ends his written declaration by stating, "for the support of this declaration . . . we mutually pledge to each other our lives, our fortunes and our sacred honor."[3] Each leader ended his declaration by pledging the lives of the movement supporters in support of the goals of freedom and survival.

The successful passage of the Treaty of Sycamore Shoals caused Dragging Canoe and his followers to branch out on their own military agenda, causing much fear and some destruction in the backcountry among Patriots who already had great fear of British military capabilities. Traditionally, ethnohistorians have interpreted Dragging Canoe's raids as an aberration against traditional Cherokee governments and their policy of appeasement toward first British and later United States expansion. I have argued instead that the Dragging Canoe raids of 1776 were a logical extension of the fight to retain Cherokee sovereignty after the breakdown of the triumvirate of Cherokee leaders by 1775. During the Anglo-Cherokee War, that conflict had no discernible single leader guiding Cherokee actions, while the second conflict, the Cherokee-Patriot War, did. Much of the diplomacy in the first war was managed by Dragging Canoe's father, Attakullakulla, who remained pro-British in his outlook for most of his career. It was also handled by Ostenaco and Oconostota, rotating duties and missions, as each situation demanded, to try to effectively deal with the British. When land accommodations became too frequent in the period of 1768 to 1775, Cherokee leadership failed in the eyes of Dragging Canoe and his followers.

Jefferson became aware of the raids in later summer of 1776, during the time in which he wrote the Declaration of Independence. Thomas Paine's *Common Sense* had galvanized American readers in February of that year, as Paine blamed King George III for "that barbarous and hellish power, which hath stirred up the Indians and the Negroes against us."[4] Jefferson had just written the constitution for the state of Virginia, approved in late June 1776, in which he referred to the tribes as "the merciless Indian savages, whose known rule of warfare is an undistinguished destruction of all ages, sexes, & conditions of existence."[5] Then he was tasked with writing the Declaration right afterward, and he chose to use almost the exact same language about the tribes. In August, he took pen to paper to vent his anger about the Dragging Canoe raids that had hoped to take out Fort Caswell (also known as the Watauga Fort) on the Watauga River, but frontiersmen gave a heavy defense of the fort, killing thirteen Cherokees and wounding Dragging Canoe.[6] Was Jefferson thinking about the Cherokees as he wrote about the merciless Indian savages?

Jefferson had mused once in his *Notes on the State of Virginia* that America's tribal people were comparable to the Vikings of Scandinavia. Over time, the Vikings' warrior culture had become civilized and settled into the quite respectable Northern European countries of Jefferson's era.[7] However, there were no romantic musings in Jefferson's comments about the Cherokees after the Dragging Canoe raids that year. In August 1776, he wrote, "I would never cease pursuing them while any of them remained on this side of the Mississippi. So unprovoked an attack & so treacherous a one should never be forgiven while any of them remains near enough to do us injury."[8] It seems likely that Jefferson had the Cherokee raids in mind when he penned the phrase "the merciless Indian savages" of the American frontier. Do we know that for certain? No, the "American Sphinx" (as Jefferson biographer Joseph Ellis called him) does not give up that secret too easily.

As Jefferson's career progressed, he was afforded multiple opportunities to monitor relations with the Cherokees or to directly interact with them. During the Revolution, Jefferson got to observe militias from Virginia under its first Patriot governor, Patrick Henry, strike back against the Cherokees in conjunction with counterparts from the two Carolinas and Georgia. Those armies laid waste to traditional Cherokee towns, causing the Dragging Canoe followers to relocate to a base near Chattanooga, Tennessee, at Chickamauga Creek. This young Cherokee army was called either the Chickamauga Cherokees or the Secessionist Cherokees. Jefferson enjoyed the success that the Virginia troops had in sending the Cherokees a message they would not soon forget.[9]

Ironically, in writing his autobiography, Jefferson chose to comment on the uncle of Meriwether Lewis, his former secretary and leader of the Lewis and Clark expedition. Nicholas Lewis had commanded troops in a Virginia regiment against the Cherokees in those raids. Jefferson commented that Lewis had commanded a regiment against the Cherokees, who "had committed great havoc on our southern frontier, by murdering and scalping helpless women and children according to their cruel and cowardly principles of warfare."[10] Jefferson later wrote of this time that "the chastisement they [the Cherokees] then received closed the history of their wars, prepared them for receiving the elements of civilization, which, zealously rendered them an industrious, peaceable and happy people."[11]

Jefferson got to see his state make peace with the traditional Cherokees, who were punished for the raids of the secessionists through a treaty in 1777. That treaty transferred a massive amount of land—five million acres—away from the Cherokees and ironically sent new recruits to join

Dragging Canoe's secessionists as an act of protest. The Watauga settlers who had their occupation validated by treaty were some of the first people to break the rules of the new treaty. The Dragging Canoe rebels did not honor the peace treaty either, as they intercepted supply trains meant for the neutral Cherokee towns.[12]

When Thomas Jefferson became governor in July 1779, Virginia was still having problems with the Cherokees, whose society had been polarized by the Dragging Canoe secessionists. Jefferson regarded Utsidsata (Old Tassel) as the legitimate new leader of the Overhills Cherokees, replacing Attakullakulla, who died in either 1780 or 1781.[13] Jefferson also deemed him and the Overhills as deserving of Virginia protection, unaware that continuing manipulation by both the South Carolina government and the Virginia government was as divisive an influence on Cherokee society as were the Chickamauga secessionists. At the time, Jefferson followed a Cherokee policy of friendship and aid toward the peace-loving Cherokees and destruction of the aggressive members.[14]

In summer of 1780, Governor Jefferson sent a military strike against the secessionists with militias from the southwest counties of Virginia. The expedition was to join with troops from the Carolinas in an attack on the Chickamauga towns. The troops did not move out until December of that year, and the Watauga unit refused to go farther than the Hiwassee River, thereby missing the bulk of the new rebel towns near modern Chattanooga. Commanders Joseph Martin and Arthur Campbell of Virginia and John Sevier of the Watauga community proceeded to lay waste to the Overhills towns one more time. In their attack, they routed eleven Cherokee towns and burned some one thousand homes and destroyed some fifty thousand bushels of corn. When Nan-ye-hi (Nancy Ward) tried to mediate this conflict, the Americans took her into protective custody along with her family.[15] Jefferson's term as governor of Virginia ended on June 1, 1781. A few months earlier, in March, he planned a final peace treaty between Virginia and the Cherokees, but General Nathanael Greene received the authority to pursue the treaty. Both the Cherokees and the Shawnees were sending raids into the Holston River and Powell's valley settlements.[16]

The aftermath of the Dragging Canoe raids as well as the aftermath of the American Revolution had regional and local consequences for the Cherokees. On the global stage of the war, the Americans and British signed the Treaty of Paris on November 30, 1782. In the larger scheme of American history, the Americans celebrated the treaty as symbolic of David's victory over Goliath, emboldening America's confidence in its own abilities, especially with tribal peoples. The treaty was less of a symbolic issue for the British and more one of practicality, cutting their losses while they were behind. For the Chickamauga Cherokees, the treaty meant the end of British support to the Loyalist tribes. At that time, the new United States government, confident in its defeat of Great Britain, made new treaties with tribes like the Cherokees and Muskogee Creeks. As their tribal boundaries were redrawn in 1785, the new treaties ripped away thousands of acres of land from both tribes.

The United States government and the mainstream Cherokee leadership continued to meet and sign diplomatic agreements in spite of a continuing Chickamauga insurgency. United States representatives met with the Cherokees on November 18, 1785, at Hopewell on the Keowee River in South Carolina. Nearly one thousand Cherokees attended the meeting, including some of Chickamauga representatives. Treaty negotiations covered ten days, and the resulting Treaty of Hopewell was ready on November 28, 1785. It formally ended hostilities between the mainstream Cherokees and the United States, and thirty-seven chiefs and principal men signed it. Those signatories included some Chickamauga leaders, including Newota, Umatooetha, Wyuka, and Necatee, but Dragging Canoe was not one of them.[17] This latest treaty echoed many of the same talking points of the treaty that ended the Anglo-Cherokee War. Articles 1 and 2 required both the Cherokees and the U.S. government to repatriate their prisoners in the recent conflict. Article 3 put the Cherokees under the protection of the U.S. government. In a sense, the Cherokees had relinquished their sovereignty in order to become civilized under the protection of the United States. Article 4 described the new reduced boundaries of the Cherokee lands. Article 5 stated that if U.S. citizens settled on treaty-reserved Cherokee lands and did not vacate after six months of notification, the Cherokees could do with them as they pleased, with the exception of the Watauga settlers.[18]

The Hopewell Treaty went further to state that tribes who harbored people who committed criminal acts against the United States or its people would have to surrender them, according to article 6. Article 10 acknowledged the rights of Indian traders and stated that any of them might trade with the Cherokees and were to enjoy kind treatment by the tribes. Article 12 authorized the Cherokees to send a tribal representative to Congress when they so desired so that the tribe would have confidence in the new national government. This concession probably gave Cherokee optimists a hope that the sovereignty they had given up was bringing them into the American political system, with the end result of a lasting peace. Finally, article 13 stated that "the hatchet shall be forever buried and the peace given by the United States, and friendship re-established between the said states on the one part, and all the Cherokees on the other, shall be universal."[19] Some Cherokee people felt that the new treaty, despite massive land concessions, would create a better future for the Cherokees under federal protection, not quite a sovereign people anymore but ideally better off than dealing with multiple governors. The Cherokees assumed the new Articles of Confederation government that had made the treaty with them was superior to the will of the many states with which they had previous conflict. Sadly, they would learn over time that it was not the final voice in Indian affairs.[20]

The latest treaty did not heal old wounds. Some frontier settlers reported that the Overhills settlements, while claiming to be friendly, actually were harboring the Chickamauga Cherokees. In 1788, a group of settlers traveling under a white flag murdered Old Tassel and other chiefs there. The murder sent more Cherokees to join the Secessionists near Lookout Mountain. When North Carolina ceded the land of Franklin to the federal government, President George Washington at first tried, through Secretary of War Henry Knox, to get the Franklin settlers to give up their lands. When that effort failed, Washington reached out to the Cherokees for yet another settlement of land. Washington's government was plain spoken with the Cherokees—they asked for yet another treaty cession that would validate the illegal occupation of the Franklin settlers because the federal government could not compel those settlers to evacuate Cherokee lands. The Washington government pledged, however, that it would keep future white squatters from the remainder of their lands.[21]

The events leading up to the next diplomatic agreement, the Treaty of Holston, were, in many ways, a repeat of the earlier Watauga leased land debacle. Secretary of War Knox, who was invested with authority over tribal peoples, tried to get backcountry settlers to vacate Cherokee lands, but these settlers claimed the land was part of the new frontier state of Franklin. Those settlers, led by John Sevier, were determined to drive Indians from the region. Not only did the settlers not abandon their lands, but they also waged guerilla war against the Cherokees, often targeting the Overhills communities, now labeled as a hideout for the Chickamauga Cherokees.[22] Their actions in turn led Dragging Canoe and his followers to continue their strikes against backcountry settlers, often Scots-Irish who had settled on the borders of Kentucky, Tennessee, and Georgia.[23] To settle this latest trouble, in June 1791 Colonel James Robertson met with traditional Cherokee leaders, who signed the Treaty of Holston giving up the land, creating the future state of Tennessee.

Tennessee governor William Blount presided over negotiations, which ended on July 2, 1791. Washington let Blount handle the diplomacy, and the Tennessee governor was anxious to obtain as much land from the Cherokees for western settlers as possible. His investments in land claims of the contested territory also stood to yield him a good profit as a result of the treaty cession. The result was the new Treaty of Holston, which redrew boundary lines for the Cherokees again in return for an annuity of $1,000 and certain trade goods. Blount ran the boundary lines when no Cherokees were present and had it surveyed to his own advantage.[24] The treaty granted backcountry settlers right of passage on the Tennessee River, and the Cherokees placed themselves under the protection of the United States government and pledged to return all U.S. prisoners held by them. This time, even traditional Cherokee chiefs objected to the treaty, but Blount threatened them, saying it was the only answer to border violence. The U.S. Senate ratified the treaty in November 1791. Supporters credited Governor Blount with achieving a final peace to end hostilities with the Cherokees.[25] Not surprisingly, frontier whites still settled on the new, revised Cherokee borders. When Chickamauga Cherokee leader Bloody Fellow visited Washington to seek redress for this, Washington increased the yearly payment to $1,500 as compensation for the injury.[26]

Some Overhills Cherokees felt the many protective features built into the Holston Treaty were again signs of a desire on the part of the United States government to gradually accept the Cherokees into the Union. Such features included the right to expel U.S. citizens in their lands illegally and the requirement that whites visiting their territory must carry a passport. The Cherokees allowed the federal government to continue the Cumberland Road through their territory connecting Philadelphia with both Knoxville and Nashville.[27]

This Cherokee odyssey ended for Tsyu-gun-sini in March 1792, when he died at Running Water on the Tennessee River. In the face of continuing illegal land occupations followed by treaties like the Treaties of Hopewell and Holston, it is not surprising that new leaders took over the Chickamauga insurrection because the original reason for the rebellion was still an ongoing problem—boundary problems caused by illegal settlement, only settled when the Cherokees gave up the land. The new leaders included John Watts, Bloody Fellow, and Doublehead.[28]

This new leadership of the Chickamauga Cherokees was finally defeated in November 1794 by the U.S. government. By that time, Chickamauga leaders had made an alliance with the Spanish and were being funded by them, much as British Indian superintendent Thomas Brown had once suggested. Since the Lower Town settlements were driving this movement, Colonel James Ore of Tennessee led a series of destructive raids on the Lower Towns. Although the Shawnees had been frequent allies in the past, General Anthony Wayne's attacks on the Northwestern Indian Confederacy deprived the Lower Town Cherokees of Shawnee support. In the wake of the final surrender of the Chickamauga Cherokees, the United States required the secessionist leaders of the Lower Towns to confirm their acceptance of the recent 1791 Treaty of Holston.[29]

Several months after Dragging Canoe's death in 1792, Black Fox, a participant in the annual summer council of the nation at Eustanaula in summer 1793, memorialized him. After 1802, Black Fox became the leader of the Cherokees, but that summer of 1793 he stated, "the Dragging Canoe has left the world. He was a man of consequence in his country. He was a friend to both his own and to the white people."[30] His eulogizer was absolutely correct on several points—Dragging Canoe was a man of consequence in Cherokee society. He was an absolute patriot to Cherokee society based on events occurring at the time. The repeated settler land frauds followed by concession on the part of the Cherokees with yet another land cession treaty to keep the peace were the reasons for his rebellion. To this Cherokee man and his followers, these settler transgressions were no different from Jefferson's written grievances against King George III. This was the Cherokee moment of crisis, and Dragging Canoe's rebellion was the Cherokee Patriot movement that rose to the challenge.

Dragging Canoe's commitment to the British Indian authority and its vision for the Cherokee people was based on John Stuart's authority and wisdom. Stuart's death probably finished any limited chances the Chickamauga rebellion ever had for success. Dragging Canoe's prediction seventeen years earlier of a future of incessant illegal land occupations followed by cession treaties validating the land theft had come true several times by his death. Although it had virtually no chance of success, it was a movement that vented the frustrations a younger generation of Cherokees felt at the continuing appeasement policies of their leaders. The rebellion also expressed a genuine desire by these young people for true sovereignty instead of a continued shadow sovereignty based on the whims of state governments like Virginia and South Carolina. Although Dragging Canoe was now gone, the other declaration author, Jefferson, was still alive and witness to all that had happened to the Cherokees.

Jefferson's political career continued his connections to the Cherokees, and he witnessed new leaders arise among them. The new Cherokee leaders were not always pleased with policy developments between themselves and the United States. Old Tassel, even before his death, found himself disenchanted with the new Civilization Program of the American government. In response to the great land cessions and the enthusiasm of the Civilization Program's plan to detribalize Indians, he wrote, "the great God of nature has placed us in different situations. It is true that he has endowed you with many superior advantages; but he has not created us to be your slaves. We are a separate people!"[31]

Later, as the third president of the country, Jefferson was placed in his most powerful position of all—to decide the fate of tribes like the Cherokees as director of the Civilization Program first begun by George Washington. In his first annual message to Congress, he spoke broadly about the tribes, telling the members of that body, "I am happy to inform you that the continued efforts to introduce among them the implements and the practice of husbandry, and of the household arts, have not been without success; that they are becoming more and more sensible of the superiority of this dependence for clothing and subsistence over the precarious resources of hunting and fishing."[32] In reality, Jefferson subscribed to an Indian Policy with a more defined path or goal. He instructed Indian agents to maintain the peace as their primary goal, followed by a secondary goal of obtaining Indian lands whenever possible.

In truth, the existence of the Cherokees at the dawn of Jefferson's presidency was precarious at best. Return J. Meigs, federal Indian agent to the Cherokees, in 1801 found them prey to vulnerable attacks by frontier whites who neither wanted to share the borderlands with them nor wanted them brought into the Union.[33] Ironically, many Cherokees knew that these white neighbors who pushed into their lands were not the best examples of U.S. citizens; rather, they thought them to be some degenerate offshoot stock who did not enjoy the Creator's preference for the Ani Yun Wiya.[34]

At the national level, Jefferson continued to address both chambers of Congress and the nation about the fate of the nation's Indian people—residents but not citizens. In his second inaugural address, he wrote of Native people that they were "endowed with the faculties and the rights of men, breathing an ardent love of liberty and independence, and occupying a country which left them no desire but to be undisturbed, the stream of overflowing population from other regions directed itself on these shores."[35] Originally unable to stop the advance of European colonists and now unable to stop the westward expansion of U.S. citizens, the American Indian in 1805 now found himself "reduced within limits too narrow for, the hunter's state, [thus] humanity enjoins us to teach them agriculture and the domestic arts; to encourage them to that industry which alone can enable them to maintain their place in existence, and to prepare them in time for that state of society, which to bodily comforts adds the improvement of the mind and morals."[36]

Though Jefferson seemed to indicate an eventual admission of the Cherokees to the Union, he also included a fairly serious disclaimer for his listeners. He warned them that Indians had a strong desire to preserve their traditional lifeways to the point of claiming reason as a false guide, or, as Jefferson noted, "their duty is to remain as their Creator made them."[37]

Life for the Cherokees after the Dragging Canoe insurrection was hard indeed and far removed from elegant speeches made about them in the frontier village capital of Washington City. White settlers continued to squat on treaty-reserved land, and some Cherokees stole the horses of their new neighbors in retaliation and converted them to money. Some traditional Cherokees, wishing to remain a hunting-based people, emigrated out to Spanish territory that would later become Arkansas with the blessing of the Spanish governor. Others withdrew to the Smoky Mountains area of their territory, generally not desired by whites, where they could live traditional lives and forget about the white world that had intruded into different parts of their domain for so long now.[38]

As the Cherokees struggled to adapt, they experienced famines in 1804, 1807, and 1811, punctuated by the return of smallpox yet again in 1806, 1817, and 1824. Their transformation to agriculturists was slow and uneven while intermarriage with whites also began to reshape Cherokee society, bringing its own inevitable transition from matrilineal kinship to patrilineal kinship, with surname identity replacing clan identity. Many traditionalists would have considered this a form of a cultural melting away. Even Cherokee agent Return J. Meigs referred to the full-bloods as "the real Indians" as a new generation of mixed-bloods appeared.[39]

Thomas Jefferson departed the presidency and public life in March 1809 as his successor and protégé, James Madison, replaced him. From his home at Monticello he once more became a commentator on Indian life rather than an active participant in it. As Jefferson entered his final year in office, he received a delegation from the Overhills Cherokees, who complained about the behavior of the Lower Towns. The Overhills Cherokees proposed to separate themselves from the Lower Towns by becoming citizens of the United States. Jefferson responded that a mutually agreeable boundary line between the two communities might be hard to achieve and suggested that the "disappointed minority" might wish to relocate west of the Mississippi River. He forwarded the Cherokee application for citizenship to Congress, which did not act on it.[40] Jefferson followed his own strategy of always asking for more land from the Cherokees no matter what issue brought them to his door. Ultimately, for Jefferson, the Cherokees and all native peoples were like his political antagonists the Federalists—if they could not convert to simple European-style farmers of the Democratic-Republican philosophy, there was little place for them in the Early Republic. Like the Federalists, if they could not assimilate, they were a doomed species consigned to oblivion.[41]

The Cherokees navigated a treacherous journey from the time of the Articles of Friendship in 1730 down to the Treaty of Holston in 1791. Various leaders arose during the odyssey from the time of Old Hop down to era of Old Tassel. For much of this journey, their leaders struggled to find balance, known as duyvktv in Cherokee, in their trade and diplomatic relationship with the Euroamerican colonies and later worked to achieve a diplomatic balance in turbulent political times. When the traditional leadership failed to stem the tide of settler trespass, a remarkable patriot named Dragging Canoe arose to fight for Cherokee justice. He was first and foremost a warrior but also a messenger and a prophet. He was the inevitable expression of Cherokee sovereignty and one of loudest voices in the Cherokee journey from sovereignty to participation in the Civilization Program of the federal government. Ultimately, survival meant abandoning sovereignty and becoming one of the South's Five Civilized Tribes.

Notes

1. Thomas Jefferson, *Writings: Autobiography, A Summary View of the Rights of British America, Notes on the State of Virginia, Public Papers, Addresses, Messages, and Replies, Miscellany, Letters* (New York: Viking Press, 1984), 187.

2. Chief Dragging Canoe Speech 1775, http://thejamesscrolls.blogspot.com/2009/04/speech-given-by-dragging-canoe.html.

3. Thomas Jefferson, Declaration of Independence, https://www.monticello.org/site/jefferson/transcript-declaration-independence-final.

4. Wallace, *Jefferson and the Indians*, 55.

5. Wallace, *Jefferson and the Indians*, 337.

6. Wallace, *Jefferson and the Indians*, 57.

7. Jefferson, *Writings*, 189.

8. Wallace, *Jefferson and the Indians*, 57.

9. Wallace, *Jefferson and the Indians*, 57.
10. Wallace, *Jefferson and the Indians*, 58.
11. Jefferson, *The Writings, Autobiography, Correspondence, Reports, Messages, Addresses, and Other Writings Official and Private*, Vol. VIII (Philadelphia: J.B. Lippincott & Co., 1871), 479.
12. Wallace, *Jefferson and the Indians*, 58.
13. James C. Kelly, "Notable Persons in Cherokee History: Attakullakulla," *Journal of Cherokee History* III, no. 1 (Winter 1978).
14. Wallace, *Jefferson and the Indians*, 59.
15. Wallace, *Jefferson and the Indians*, 59–60.
16. Wallace, *Jefferson and the Indians*, 59.
17. Allen, *Manuscript of the Cherokee Indians*, 32.
18. http://webtest2.cherokee.org/About-The-Nation/History/Facts/Treaty-of-Hopewell-1785.
19. http://webtest2.cherokee.org/About-The-Nation/History/Facts/Treaty-of-Hopewell-1785.
20. McLoughlin, *Cherokee Renascence*, 22–22.
21. McLoughlin, *Cherokee Renascence*, 23.
22. McLoughlin, *Cherokee Renascence*, 23.
23. McLoughlin, *Cherokee Renascence*, 22–23.
24. McLoughlin, *Cherokee Renascence*, 23–24.
25. Brown, *Americans All*, 77–78.
26. McLoughlin, *Cherokee Renascence*, 24.
27. McLoughlin, *Cherokee Renascence*, 25.
28. McLoughlin, *Cherokee Renascence*, 24.
29. McLoughlin, *Cherokee Renascence*, 25.
30. Allen, *Manuscript of the Cherokee Indians*, 59.
31. Wallace, *Jefferson and the Indians*, 303.
32. Jefferson, *Writings*, 501.
33. McLoughlin, *Cherokee Renascence*, 47–48.
34. McLoughlin, *Cherokee Renascence*, 47–48.
35. Jefferson, *Writings*, 520.
36. Jefferson, *Writings*, 520.
37. Jefferson, *Writings*, 520.
38. McLoughlin, *Cherokee Renascence*, 56–57.
39. McLoughlin, *Cherokee Renascence*, 56–57.
40. Jefferson, *Writings*, 302.
41. Joseph Ellis, *American Sphinx: The Character of Thomas Jefferson* (New York: Vintage Books, 1998), 239.

Selected Bibliography

I. Primary Sources

http://webtest2.cherokee.org/About-The-Nation/History/Facts/Treaty-of-Hopewell-1785.

Adair, James. *Adair's History of the American Indians*. Edited by Samuel Cole Williams. Johnson City, TN: Watauga Press, 1930.

Articles of Friendship. Lords Commissioners for Trade and Plantations, Colonial Office Series number 5, 4, Nos. 46.

Chief Dragging Canoe Speech 1775. http://thejamesscrolls.blogspot.com/2009/04/speech-given-by-dragging-canoe.html.

Coleman, Kenneth, ed. *The Colonial Records of the State of Georgia: Original Papers of Governor John Reynolds 1754–1756*. Athens: University of Georgia Press, 1977.

Grant, Ludovic. "Historical Relation of Facts etc." *South Carolina Historical and Genealogical Magazine* (10): 54–68.

Great Britain. Public Records Office, Kew. *Colonial Office, Series Five Material* (Volumes 7–459, but primarily volumes 67–79).

Jefferson, Thomas. *Writings: Autobiography, A Summary View of the Rights of British America, Notes on the State of Virginia, Public Papers, Addresses, Messages, and Replies, Miscellany, Letters*. New York: Viking Press, 1984.

———. *The Writings, Autobiography, Correspondence, Reports, Messages, Addresses, and Other Writings Official and Private*. Vol. VIII. Philadelphia: J.B. Lippincott & Co., 1871.

Journal of the Council, June 9, 1762, South Carolina Department of Archives and History. Columbia, South Carolina.

Journal of the Commons House of Assembly, July 20, 1761, South Carolina Department of Archives and History. Columbia, South Carolina.

Journal of the Commons House of Assembly, August 29, 1761. South Carolina Department of Archives and History. Columbia, South Carolina.

Lawson, John. *A New Voyage to Carolina*. Edited by Hugh Talmadge Lefler. Chapel Hill: University of North Carolina Press, 1967.
Letterbooks of William Henry Lyttelton. www.accessgenealogy.com/dataset/letterbooks-of-william-henry-lyttleton.
McDowell, William L., Jr., ed. *The Colonial Records of South Carolina: Documents Relating to Indian Affairs: May 21, 1750–August 7, 1754*. Columbia: South Carolina Archives Department, 1958.
———. *The Colonial Records of South Carolina: Documents Relating to Indian Affairs 1754–1765*. Columbia: South Carolina Department of Archives and History, 1970.
Mooney, James. *Myths of the Cherokee*. New York: Dover, 1995.
Moore, Alexander, ed. *Nairne's Muskhogean Journals: The 1708 Expedition to the Mississippi River*. Jackson: University Press of Mississippi, 1988.
The South Carolina Gazette (Columbia, January 5–8, 1760).
Timberlake, Henry. *Lieutenant Henry Timberlake's Memories 1756–1765*. Edited by Samuel Cole Williams. Marietta, GA: Continental Book Company, 1948.

II. Secondary Sources

https://www.geni.com/people/Attakullakulla-Onacona/6000000011727533816.
https://dnr.mo.gov/shpo/nps-nr/TrailOfTearsMPS.pdf.
members.iinet.net.au/~royalty/states/America/Cherokee.html.
www.aaanativearts.com/cherokee/little-carpenter.htm.
Alderman, Pat. *Nancy Ward: Cherokee Chieftainess*. Johnson City, TN: Overmountain Press, 1978.
Anderson, Fred. *Crucible of War: The Seven Years' War and the Fate of Empire in British North America, 1754–1766*. New York: Alfred A. Kopf, 2000.
Axtell, James. *After Columbus: Essays in the Ethnohistory of Colonial North America*. New York: Oxford University Press, 1988.
———. *The Invasion Within: The Contest of Cultures in Colonial North America*. New York: Oxford University Press, 1985.
Blethen, H. Tyler, and Curtis W. Wood Jr. *From Ulster to Carolina: The Migration of the Scotch-Irish to Southwestern North Carolina*. Raleigh: North Carolina Department of Cultural Resources Division of Archives and History, 1998.
Boulware, Tyler. *Deconstructing the Cherokee Nation: Town, Region and Nation among Eighteenth-Century Cherokees*. Gainesville: University Press of Florida, 2011.
Brown, John P. *Americans All: The Story of the Chickamaugas*. Unpublished manuscript, Museum of the Cherokee Indian.
———. *Old Frontiers: The Story of the Cherokees Indians from Earliest Times to the Date of Their Removal to the West, 1838*. Kingsport, TN: Southern Publishers, 1938.

Brown, Philip M. "Early Indian Trade in the Development of South Carolina Politics, Economics, and Social Mobility during the Proprietary Period, 1670–1719." *South Carolina Historical Magazine* 76 (July 1975): 118–128.

Carter, Clarence. "Observations of Superintendent John Stuart and Governor James Grant of East Florida on the Proposed Plan of 1764 for the Future Management of Indian Affairs." *American Historical Review* 20 (October 1914–July 1915): 37–56.

Calloway, Collin. *The American Revolution in Indian Country: Crisis and Diversity in Native American Communities*. Cambridge: Cambridge University Press, 1995.

———. *The Scratch of a Pen: 1763 and the Transformation of North America*. Oxford: University Press, 2006.

Cashin, Edward J. *Lachlan McGillivray, Indian Trader: The Shaping of the Southern Colonial Frontier*. Athens: University of Georgia Press, 1992.

Conley, Robert J. *The Cherokee Nation: A History*. Albuquerque: University of New Mexico Press, 2005.

Corkran, David C. *The Carolina Indian Frontier*. Columbia: University of South Carolina Press, 1970.

———. *The Cherokee Frontier: Conflict and Survival, 1740–62*. Norman: University of Oklahoma Press, 1962.

Cox, Brent Alan Yanusdi. *Heart of the Eagle: Dragging Canoe and the Emergence of the Chickamauga Confederacy*. Milan, TN: Chenanee Publishers, 1999.

Crane, Verner W. *The Southern Frontier: 1670–1732*. Ann Arbor: University of Michigan Press, 1964.

Dean, Nadia. *A Demand of Blood: The Cherokee War of 1776*. Cherokee, NC: Valley River Press, 2012.

Dickens, Roy S., Jr. "The Origins and Development of Cherokee Culture." In *The Cherokee Indian Nation: A Troubled History*, edited by Duane King. Knoxville: University of Tennessee Press, 1979.

Dowd, Gregory Evans. *A Spirited Resistance: The North American Indian Struggle for Unity, 1745–1815*. Baltimore: Johns Hopkins University Press, 1992.

Edgar, Walter. *South Carolina: A History*. Columbia: University of South Carolina Press, 1998.

Ellis, Joseph. *American Sphinx: The Character of Thomas Jefferson*. New York: Vintage Books, 1998.

Evans, E. Raymond. "Notable Persons in Cherokee History: Dragging Canoe," *Journal of Cherokee Studies* II, no. 1 (Winter 1977): 176–189.

———. "Notable Persons in Cherokee History: Ostenaco." *Journal of Cherokee Studies* I, no. 1 (Summer 1976): 41–54.

Fischer, David Hackett. *Albion's Seed: Four British Folkways in America*. New York: Oxford University Press, 1989.

Fogelson, Raymond D. "Cherokees in the East." In *Handbook of North American Indians*, edited by William C. Sturtevant. Washington, DC: Smithsonian Institution, 2004.

Furstenberg, Francois. "The Significance of the Trans-Appalachian Frontier." *American Historical Review* 113, no. 3 (June 2008): 647–677.

Gallay, Allan, ed. *Voices from the Old South: Eyewitness Accounts 1528–1861.* Athens: University of Georgia Press, 1994.

Gibson, Arrell Morgan. *The American Indian: Prehistory to the Present.* Lexington, MA: D. C. Heath, 1980.

Goodwin, Gary C. *Cherokees in Transition: A Study of Changing Culture and Environment Prior to 1775.* Chicago: University of Chicago, 1977.

Gragson, Ted, and Paul V. Bolstad. "A Local Analysis of Early Eighteenth Century Cherokee Settlement." *Social Science History* (September 2007): 435–468.

Grant, Ludovic. "Historical Relation of the Facts." *Journal of Cherokee Studies* XXVI (2008).

Green, E. R. R. "Queensborough Townships: Scotch-Irish Emigration and the Expansion of Georgia, 1763–1776." *William and Mary Quarterly* 17 (1960): 183–199.

Gridley, Marion E. *American Indian Women.* New York: Hawthorn Books, 1974.

Hatley, Tom. *The Dividing Paths: Cherokees and South Carolinians through the Revolutionary Era.* New York: Oxford University Press, 1995.

Herman, Arthur. *How the Scots Invented the Modern World: The True Story of How Western Europe's Poorest Nation Created Our World & Everything in It.* New York: Three Rivers Press, 2001.

Higgins, W. Robert, ed. *The Revolutionary War in the South: Power, Conflict, and Leadership.* Durham, NC: Duke University Press, 1979.

Hoffer, Charles P., ed. *Indians and Europeans: Selected Articles on Indian-White Relations in Colonial North America.* New York: Garland, 1988.

Hudson, Charles B. *The Southeastern Indians.* Knoxville: University of Tennessee Press, 1984.

Jennings, Francis. *Empire of Fortune: Crowns, Colonies, and Tribes in the Seven Years War in America.* New York: W. W. Norton, 1988.

———. *The Invasion of America: Indians, Colonialism, and the Cant of Conquest.* W. W. Norton, 1976.

Johnson, Penelope Allen. *The History of the Cherokee Indians, Particularly the Chickamauga Group*, Vol. 1 (unpublished Mmanuscript).

Kelly, James C. "Notable Persons in Cherokee History: Attakullakulla." *Journal of Cherokee Studies* III, no. 1 (Winter 1978): 2–34.

Kelton, Paul. *Cherokee Medicine, Colonial Germs: An Indigenous Nation's Fight against Smallpox, 1518–1824.* Norman: University of Oklahoma Press, 2015.

———. "Shattered and Infected: Epidemics and the Origins of the Yamasee War, 1696–1715." In *Mapping the Mississippian Shatter Zone: The Colonial Indian Slave Trade and Regional Instability in the American South*, edited by Robbie Ethridge and Sheri M. Shuck-Hill. Lincoln: University of Nebraska Press, 2009.

King, Duane H. *The Cherokee Indian Nation: A Troubled History.* Knoxville: University of Tennessee Press, 1979.

———. *The Memoirs of Lt. Henry Timberlake: The Story of a Soldier, Adventurer, and Emissary to the Cherokees, 1756–1765*. Cherokee, NC: Museum of the Cherokee Indian Press, 2007.

Kovalcik, Charles F., and John J. Winberry. *South Carolina: A Geography*. Boulder, CO: West View Press, 1987.

LeMaster, Michelle. *Brothers Born of One Mother: British-Native American Relations in the Colonia Southeast*. Charlottesville: University of Virginia Press, 2012.

Leyburn, James G. *The Scotch-Irish: A Social History*. Chapel Hill: University of North Carolina Press, 1962.

Mails, Thomas E. *The Cherokee People: The Story of the Cherokees from Earliest Origins to Contemporary Times*. New York: Marlowe & Company, 1996.

McClary, Ben Harris. "Nancy Ward: The Last Beloved Woman of the Cherokees." *Tennessee Historical Quarterly* 21 (December 1962): 352–364.

McLoughlin, William L. *Cherokee Renascence in the New Republic*. Princeton, NJ: Princeton University Press, 1986.

Mereness, Newton G. *Travels in the American Colonies*. New York: Antiquarian Press, 1961.

Meriwether, Robert Lee. *The Expansion of South Carolina, 1729–1765*. Kingsport, TN: Southern Publishers, 1940.

Meyers, Maureen. "From Refugees to Slave Traders: The Transformation of the Westo Indians." In *Mapping the Mississippian Shatter Zone: The Colonial Indian Slave Trade and Regional Instability in the American South*, edited by Robbie Ethridge and Sheri M. Shuck-Hill. Lincoln: University of Nebraska Press, 2009.

Morris, Michael P. *The Bringing of Wonder: Trade and the Indians of the Southeast, 1700–1783*. Bridgeport, CT: Greenwood, Press, 1999.

———. *George Galphin and the Transformation of the Georgia–South Carolina Backcountry*. Lanham, MD: Lexington Books, 2014.

Murphy, Michael. *The Appalachian Dulcimer Book*. St. Clairsville, OH: Folksay Press, 1987.

O'Donnell, James H., III. *Southern Indians in the American Revolution*. Knoxville: University of Tennessee Press, 1973.

O'Meara, Walter. *Daughters of the Country: The Women of the Fur Traders and Mountain Men*. New York: Harcourt, Brace & World, 1968.

Pate, James Paul. "The Chickamauga: A Forgotten Segment of Indian Resistance on the Southern Frontier." PhD Dissertation, Mississippi State University, 1969.

Perdue, Theda. *Cherokee Women: Gender and Culture Change, 1700–1835*. Lincoln: University of Nebraska Press, 1998.

———. *Slavery and The Evolution of Cherokee Society 1540–1866*. Knoxville: University of Tennessee Press, 1979.

Piecuch, Jim. *Three Peoples, One King: Loyalists, Indians, and Slaves in the Revolutionary South, 1775–1782*. Columbia: University of South Carolina Press, 2008.

Pressly, Paul M. *On the Rim of the Caribbean: Colonial Georgia and the British Atlantic World.* Athens: University of Georgia, 2013.

Ramsey, William. *The Yamasee War: A Study of Culture, Conflict and Economy in the Colonial South.* Lincoln: University of Nebraska Press, 2008.

Randolph, Randolph F. *British Travelers among the Southern Indians, 1660–1763.* Norman: University of Oklahoma Press, 1973.

Ray, Kristofer. *Before the Volunteer State.* Knoxville: University of Tennessee Press, 2015.

———. "Cherokees and Franco-British Confrontation in the Tennessee Corridor, 1730–1760." *Native South* 7 (2014): 33–67.

Rothrock, Mary U. "Carolina Traders among the Overhills Cherokees, 1690–1760." *East Tennessee Historical Society's Publications* 1 (1929): 3–18.

Sheftall, John McKay. *George Galphin and Indian-White Relations in the Georgia Backcountry during the American Revolution.* MA thesis, University of Virginia, 1983.

Silver, Timothy. *A New Face on the Countryside: Indians, Colonists, and Slaves in South Atlantic Forests, 1500–1800.* Cambridge: Cambridge University Press, 1990.

Smith, Betty Anderson. "Distribution of Eighteenth-Century Cherokee Settlements." In *The Cherokee Indian Nation: A Troubled History*, edited by Duane H. King. Knoxville: University of Tennessee Press, 1979.

Snapp, John Russell. *John Stuart and the Struggle for Empire on the Southern Frontier.* Baton Rouge: Louisiana State University Press, 1996.

Starr, Emmet. *History of the Cherokee Indians.* Norman: University of Oklahoma Press, 1984.

———. *History of the Cherokee Indians and Their Legends and Folklore.* New York: Kraus Reprint Company, 1969.

Stewart, George R. *Names on the Land: A Historical Account of Place-Naming in the United States.* Boston: Houghton Mifflin, 1967.

Swanton, John Reed. *The Indians of the Southeastern United States.* Grosse Pointe, MI: Scholarly Press, 1969.

Tortora, Daniel J. *Carolina in Crisis: Cherokees, Colonists, and Slaves in the American Southeast, 1756–1763.* Chapel Hill: University of North Carolina Press, 2015.

Wallace, Anthony F. C. *Jefferson and the Indians: The Tragic Fate of the First Americans.* Cambridge, MA: Belknap Press, 1999.

Washburn, Wilcomb E. *The Indian in America.* New York: Harper & Row, 1975.

Williams, Samuel Cole, ed. *Early Travels in the Tennessee Country 1540–1800: With Introductions, Annotations, and Index.* Johnson City, TN: Watauga Press, 1928.

Woodward, Grace Steele. *The Cherokees.* Norman: University of Oklahoma Press, 1984.

Index

Adair, James, 7, 27, 83
Alejoy, 98
American Revolution, 13, 126–27, 129, 172
Amherst, Jeffrey, 42, 65–66, 69, 73–75, 82, 84, 86–87, 94–96, 101, 105–6
Ammonscossittee, 38, 46, 56n62
Anglo-Cherokee Peace Treaty. *See specific entries*
Anglo-Cherokee War (1760–1761), 12, 13, 21–22, 124, 136, 154, 168, 170, 173; 1757 battlefield, 42–44; alienating Cherokees, 35–42; assessing French threat, 28–32; Britain-France-Spain relationship, 22–25; calling for aid, 32–34; cementing loyalties, 25–26; Cherokee participation, 46–54
Ani-yun-wiya, 21, 43, 123, 158, 169, 177. *See also* Cherokees
Appalachian Mountains, 23, 51, 114, 168
Appalachian Summit, 3
Arthur, Gabriel, 8
Articles of Friendship, 12, 17, 38, 67, 144, 158, 179; cementing loyalties, 25–26; Cherokees and, 23–26, 29, 31; decline of spirit of, 72–73; thirty-one years after, 99; violating, 129–30
Atkin, Edmond, 47, 100
Attakullakulla, 11–12, 14, 17; in Anglo-Indian War, 32–33, 35–36, 46, 49–51, 53; diplomacy after Easton, 61–64, 66–73, 75–80, 82, 84, 86; diplomacy after Fort Loudoun, 93, 95, 97–109, 111, 116–17; and Dragging Canoe, 123–27, 129–31, 133, 139, 142, 145, 147, 149–50; responses to pressure, 21–22, 25, 32–33, 35–36, 46, 49–51, 53
Augusta, Georgia, 27–28
Ayoree, 98

The Badger, 124, 157
Bartram, William, 3
Benton, Jesse, 129
Black Fox, 158, 176
Bloody Fellow, 158, 175
Blount, William, 99, 158, 175
Bolstad, Paul, 8–9
Boone, Daniel, 128–29
Boone, Israel, 128
Boone, Thomas, 108, 111

187

188   INDEX

Boulware, Tyler, 14
Brainerd, Tennessee, 148, 164n158
Brant, Molly, 115
Britain. *See* Great Britain
British Indian, 2, 16, 37, 70, 125, 133, 136, 144, 147, 151–53, 156, 158, 163, 176
Brown, Jacob, 129
Brown, Rea, and Company, 115
Browne, Thomas, 151, 156
Bull, William, 94
Bunning, Robert, 16
Burning Town, 98
Byrd, William, II, 47
Byrd, William, III, 95

Calloway, Collin, 114
Cameron, Alexander, 116–18, 123–30, 132–33, 135–39, 141–47, 150–53, 158
Campbell, Arthur, 154, 172
Campbell, Robert, 154
Canuga, 98
Catawbas (Ye Iswa), 8, 15, 26, 30, 71, 96, 98, 103, 131–32
Cayugas, 61
Charles Town, South Carolina, 8, 12, 25, 27, 29, 36, 39, 41, 47, 62–63, 65–69, 71–72, 77, 80–81, 83, 93, 96, 99, 102, 104–11, 115–17, 132, 136, 146
Chattanooga, Tennessee, 1, 128, 171–72
Cherokee-Haudenosaunee alliance, 115–17
Cherokee-Patriot War, 170
Cherokees, 1; alienating, 35–42; Anglo-Indian War, 21–54; Cherokee-British alliance, 22–26, 44–46; Cherokee-French alliance, 44–46; Chickamauga, 124, 141–42, 145–46, 148, 150–51, 154, 156, 171, 173–76; coming into contact with English, 8; defining towns, 8–9; Dragging Canoe rebellion, 21–22, 75, 134–56; and Jefferson, 167–72, 176–79; Overhills, 9, 23, 56n70, 64, 78, 108–9, 137, 142, 150, 172, 178; post-Easton diplomacy, 61–87; relationship with English, 9–17; river importance to, 1–7; settlements, 13–14; seven clans of, 3, 14; traditional land usage, 13; Western Band, 16. *See also* Dragging Canoe
Chickasawas, 156
Choctaws, 28, 30, 34–35, 38, 94–95, 134, 151, 156
Chota, 12–13, 16–17, 33–34, 37, 40, 44, 46, 49, 52, 61–66, 70, 77, 85, 100, 107, 125, 132, 145
Christian, William, 142
Civilization Program, 177
Clogittah, 11
Collanah, 11
Commons House of Assembly, 115
Congarees, 8, 96
Coosa River, 97
Cowhee, 98
Cowitchie, 98
Coytmore, Richard, 62, 65, 71, 74–77, 79–81
creation stories, 4–5
Croghan, George, 43
Cumberland River, 13, 156
Cuming, Alexander, 9–11, 17
Cunneshote, 14, 47, 63, 78, 82, 85, 95, 100–101, 109–10, 110

Declaration of Independence, 170
Delawares, 30–33, 43–44, 51, 61, 135, 168
Demeré, Paul, 63–65, 67, 70, 77–78, 84–86
Demeré, Raymond, 36–38, 40–45
Denny, William, 51

de Soto, Hernando, 7–8
Dinwiddie, Robert, 30–31, 43, 52
diplomacy, post-Loudoun: British war plans, 95–97; Etchoe raid, 97–100; news of French intrigue, 93–94; post-Etchoe negotiations, 100–108; regulating Cherokee trade, 108–18; visiting Fort Prince George, 93–95
disease, 21–22, 26–27, 30, 71–72, 74, 106, 126. *See also* smallpox, outbreak of
Donaldson, John, 127
Dragging Canoe, 2, 21–22, 123–24; aftermath of death of, 175–79; death of, 175, 158–59; early life of, 124–26; and Holston Treaty, 157–58; and Hopewell Treaty, 156–57; independence declaration written by, 167–70; during January 1777, 147–50; and Jefferson, 167–69; leading attacks, 155–57; and Patriot-Chickamaugas saga, 151–55; and Proclamation Line, 126–29; rebellion of, 134–56; report of, 141–44; setback of, 150–51; as sidebar, 145–44; and Transylvania Purchase, 128–31; and Treaty of Sycamore Shoals, 130–35
Drayton, William Henry, 132, 142

Earl of Dunmore, 130
Eastern Band Cherokee Nation (EBCI), 1
Easton, Pennsylvania. *See* Treaty of Easton, diplomacy following
Edgar, Walter, 108
Edisto River, 10
Elliott, John, 41–42
Ellis, Henry, 86, 95, 114
Emissaries of Peace, 110–11
English: Anglo-Indian War, 21–54; Dragging Canoe rebellion, 21–22, 134, 136–56; records, 4, 8–9; in South Carolina, 9–17. *See also* Great Britain
Etchoe, 84; negotiations after, 100–108; raid on, 97–100
Ethridge, Robbie, 9

Fauquier, Francis, 62, 95, 100, 109
Florida, 132–34, 137–38, 151–52, 155
Forbes, John, 47–51, 62, 108
Fort Duquesne, 31, 43, 45, 50, 73
Fort Loudoun, 40, 63, 126; diplomacy after, 93–118; siege of, 81–82, 84, 86–87
Fort Patrick Henry, 147–48
Fort Prince George, 12, 34, 72, 93, 98, 112; hostage situation at, 75–87
Fox (man-of-war), 11
France: alienating Cherokees, 35–42; Articles of Friendship, 23–25; backcountry efforts, 28–30
French and Indian War, 17, 30–31, 33, 36, 39, 61, 63, 71, 77–78, 96, 112
fur traders, 8–11, 16–17, 25, 27–28, 32, 35, 75, 103, 123, 126, 128, 136, 154
Furstenberg, Francois, 42

Galphin, George, 115
George II, 10–11, 24, 47, 67, 73, 102, 125
George III, 109–11, 113–14, 138, 144, 169
Germain, George, 151, 152
Gist, Nathaniel, 33, 43, 48, 141, 142
Glen, James, 28–30, 34, 39, 41
Go-ohsohly, 116
Gragson, Ted, 8–9
Grant, James, 94–96
Grant, Ludovic, 10
Great Britain (Britain), 11, 28, 101, 125, 130, 133, 146, 150, 156, 168, 173; alienating Cherokees, 35–42;

Articles of Friendship, 23–25. *See also* Proclamation Line
Great Tellico, 36
Great War for Empire, 30, 71, 113–15
Great Warrior of Virginia, 144
Green Corn Ceremony, 46, 48, 50, 53
Guaquili, 7

Halkett, Francis, 52
Hall, Johnson, 116
Hamilton, Henry, 153–54
Harlin, Ellis, 129
Hatley, Tom, 12
Haudenosaunee, 25, 31, 43–44, 46–47, 51, 96, 116, 135
Henderson, Richard, 129–31
Hickory Nut Gorge, 13
Hiwassee River, 16, 154–55, 172
HMS Revenge, 110
Holston River, 2, 13, 100, 108, 118, 127, 136, 139, 147, 151–52, 172
Hopewell. *See* Treaty of Hopewell
Horrocks, James, 109
Howe, William, 146, 148

Indian superintendents, 2, 51, 70, 100, 114–15, 124, 126, 133, 151–53, 176
Iroquois. *See also* Haudenosaunee
Iwassie, 10, 37

James River, 8
Jefferson, Thomas: on Cherokee admission, 178; and Declaration of Independence, 167–70; departing presidency, 178–79; in *Notes on the State of Virginia*, 171; progressing career of, 171–72
Johnson, Robert, 11
Johnson, William, 43, 114–15, 116

Kanawha River, 157
Kelton, Paul, 27, 31, 51, 61

Keowee River, 7, 12–13, 80, 157, 173
Keowee, Lower Town, 2, 13, 34, 44–47, 66–71, 74, 81, 105, 107, 111, 126
Kittagusta, 11–12, 72, 133
Kituwah, 98
Knox, Henry, 174

Lamboll, Thomas, 113
Lamore, Charles, 65
Lantagnac, Antoine Adhemar de, 93
Lantagnac, Louis, 62–63
Lassee, 98
law of blood, 14, 54
Lee, Charles, 141
Lewis, Andrew, 35, 39
linguisters, 16, 71
Little Tennessee River, 2, 12, 97, 146, 147
Locke, John, 169
Long, Alexander, 9
Long Man (Yunwi Gunahita), 3, 17
Lower Towns, 7–8, 9–10, 13–16, 26, 45–46, 51, 53, 64–65, 71, 79, 83, 85–86, 107, 111, 116, 136, 153; Cherokees, 33, 77, 138, 176; settlements, 3, 7, 12–13, 176
Loyalist, 132, 134, 137, 147, 151, 156, 173
Lyttelton, William Henry, 38, 44, 63, 69

Manigault, Gabriel, 113
Mankiller of Tellico, 38–40
Martin, Alexander, 155
Martin, Joseph, 172
McCunningham, Charles, 67
McDonald, John, 128, 145–46, 148, 150–54, 156
McGillivray, Lachlan, 35
McIntosh, Lachlan, 72, 95, 111
McKee, Alexander, 157

Middle Towns, 2, 10, 16, 71–72, 77, 79–80, 83, 86, 94, 97, 101, 141
Mingos, 30–32, 51, 61
Mohawks, 61, 96, 135
Mooney, James, 3, 4, 8
Moytoy of Settico, 46, 48–49, 63
Moytoy of Tellico, 10, 12, 23–24, 38, 46, 67, 99
Murray, John, 130
Muskogee Creeks, 17, 30, 54, 63, 77, 87, 101, 127, 146, 151, 153, 156, 173

Necatee, 157, 173
Neowee, 98
New River, 2
Newcassee, 98
Newota, 157, 173
Nicholson, Francis, 10
Nikwasi (Franklin, North Carolina), 10
Ninety-Six, South Carolina, 40, 75, 80, 82
North American Empire, 127
Noyohee, 10

Oconaluftee River, 1
Oconostota: in Anglo-Cherokee War, 21–22, 30, 32, 35; and Dragging Canoe, 124, 129–31, 136, 142, 147, 170; following Easton diplomacy, 64, 66–69, 71–73, 77–86; Fort Loudoun diplomacy, 94–95, 97–98, 101–2, 108, 116–18
Oglethorpe, James Edward, 27
Ohio River Valley, 23, 26, 28, 30–32, 36, 43, 51, 65, 96
Old Hop (Connecorte), 12, 32, 36, 40, 42, 63, 67–70, 75, 78, 82, 102, 167, 179
Oneidas, 61
Onondagas, 61
Ookoooneka, 129

Ore, James, 176
Ostenaco: and Anglo-Cherokee War, 21–22, 33, 35, 38–39, 46, 110; diplomacy after Easton, 65–66, 68, 75, 77–78, 82, 85–86; and Dragging Canoe, 129, 145, 150, 168, 170; Fort Loudoun diplomacy, 95, 99–101, 109–11, 116–17
Otassite, 72
Oukah-Ulah, 11
Oukanekah. *See* Attakullakulla
Ounakannowie, 11
Overhills Cherokees, 9, 12–14, 23, 56n70, 64, 78, 108–9, 137, 142, 150, 172, 178

Paine, Thomas, 170
Patriots, 123, 127, 132, 134–35, 137–39, 141–44, 146–51, 154, 159, 170
Pearis, Richard, 129
Pepper, Daniel, 45
Perdue, Theda, 6, 14
Petty, William, 114
Physic Dance, 6
Post, Christian Frederick, 51, 61
Powhatans, 8
Price, Thomas, 129
Proclamation Line of 1763, 13, 51, 114–15, 126–28, 131, 137

Qualla Boundary, 1, 4, 16

Ramsey, William, 62
Rea, John, 115
Reconciliation Ceremony, 6
Reid, John Phillip, 14
rivers: and ceremonies, 6–7; creation stories involving, 4–5; and new mothers, 5–6; significance in Cherokee history/culture, 1–7; during war time, 7
Robertson, Charles, 129

Robertson, James, 150, 157, 174–75
Running Water, 157

Saluda River, 10
Santee River, 10
Savage, John, 113
Savannah River, 3
Scots-Irish, 9, 14, 17, 21, 52, 115–16, 123, 126, 128, 168, 174
secessionists, 171, 174
Seed of Settico (Overhills town), 97
Senecas, 61, 116
Seroweh, 76, 93–97, 100
settlements: Cherokee, 12–16, 74; Lower Town, 3, 7, 12–13, 176; Middle Town, 2, 16, 83; Overhills, 10, 13, 16, 71, 78–79, 167, 174; river, 1–7; Valley, 13, 16
Sevier, John, 129, 154, 155
Shawanos, 8
Shawnees, 30–34, 39, 43, 45, 47, 51, 53, 61, 111, 125, 128, 131, 135, 152–53, 157, 172, 176
Shelby, Evan, 151
Shelby, Isaac, 129
Shorey, William, 99
Shubrick, Thomas, 113
smallpox, outbreak of, 26–27, 39, 70–73, 76–77, 79–81, 83, 86–87, 99, 101, 105, 108, 126, 178
Smith, Thomas, 113
South Carolina, 132; Cherokee-English relationships in, 9–17; Oconee County, 13; Pickens County, 34, 126, 141, 148
South Carolina Assembly, 65, 87, 108, 111, 115
Spain, 22–23, 28, 113, 155
St. Lawrence River, 31
Stecoe, 16, 75, 79, 98
Stuart, Henry, 132–39
Stuart, John, 17, 176; and Dragging Canoe, 2, 124–28, 131–35, 137, 139, 141, 143–44, 146, 148, 150–51, 158; Easton diplomacy, 69–70, 79, 85–86, 99–100, 102, 113, 115–18
Sumter, Tom, 100, 109
Sycamore Shoals, 2, 13, 126, 129, 131–33, 157, 159, 168–70. *See also* Treaty of Sycamore Shoals

Tallapoosa River, 97
Tapelchee, 10
Tathtiowie, 11
Tellico, 10
Tennessee Warrior, 129
Terron, Samuel, 86
Tessantee, 98
Thompson, William, 143
Tiftowe of Keowee, 68
Timberlake, Henry, 100, 109–11
Timberlake, Richard, 111
Tortora, Daniel, 11
towns: Lower, 3, 7, 12–13, 33–34, 44, 66, 70, 74–75, 77, 83, 112, 126, 137–38, 176; Middle, 2, 16, 71–72, 77, 79–80, 83, 86, 94; Overhills, 12, 33–36, 46, 52, 62, 66, 73, 93, 97, 107–8, 125, 132, 146. *See also* settlements
Toxaway River, 13
Transylvania Land Company, 144
Transylvania Purchase, 128–31
Treaty of Charles Town: components of, 72–73; responses to, 73–76
Treaty of Easton, diplomacy following, 51–52, 61–62; Angle-Cherokee relation strain, 65–67; Charles Town events, 67–70; cultural stress following, 62–63; declaring war on Cherokees, 65–66; Fort Prince George hostage situation, 75–87; frontier violence, 62–65; smallpox outbreak, 70–72; trade issues, 64–65; Treaty of Charles Town, 72–76

Treaty of Hard Labor Creek, 115–17
Treaty of Holston, 158, 174–76, 179
Treaty of Hopewell, 156–57; articles of, 173–74
Treaty of Long Island, 149
Treaty of Paris, 156, 172
Treaty of Sycamore Shoals, 126, 130–35, 157, 168; response to, 169–70
Tsyu-gun-sini. *See* Dragging Canoe
Tuckabatchee, 156
Tuckoritchee, 98
Tuscaroras, 61

Umatooetha, 157, 173
United States, government of, 156–58, 173
Ussanah, 98
Utsidsata, 172

Vann, John, 129

Vann, Joseph, 131

Wall, Robert, 41
War of Austrian Succession, 28
War of Jenkins' Ear, 27
Washington, George, 31, 34, 43, 174
Watauga River, 13, 129, 170
Wattoquiu, 98
Watts, John, 158
Wauhatchee, 42
Whitewater River, 123
Wiggan, Eleazar, 8–11
Wilkinson, Edward, 113
Willanawaugh, 129
Woyi, 10
Wyuka, 157, 173

Yamassee War, 111
yi (town). *See* settlements; towns
Young Tassel, 145
Young Warrior. *See* Seroweh

About the Author

Michael P. Morris holds the doctorate in history from Auburn University in early America and Native American studies. For the past twenty years, he has researched and written about life in the Southern backcountry from both a native and colonial perspective. One of his mentors, the late Dr. Edward J. Cashin, believed that understanding the backcountry was key to understanding the full history of a place. He is especially fascinated by the cultural interactions between Scots-Irish fur traders and their Native American wives. Their biracial children were very important in the interaction of native and colonial societies. He has worked at various colleges across the South, including one regional university and several small colleges.

www.ingramcontent.com/pod-product-compliance
Lightning Source LLC
Chambersburg PA
CBHW061447300426
44114CB00014B/1866